CAMBRIDGE
UNIVERSITY PRESS

Cambridge IGCSE™
English
(as an Additional Language)

COURSEBOOK

Graham Newman & Jane Boylan

CAMBRIDGE
UNIVERSITY PRESS

University Printing House, Cambridge CB2 8BS, United Kingdom

One Liberty Plaza, 20th Floor, New York, NY 10006, USA

477 Williamstown Road, Port Melbourne, VIC 3207, Australia

314–321, 3rd Floor, Plot 3, Splendor Forum, Jasola District Centre, New Delhi – 110025, India

103 Penang Road, #05–06/07, Visioncrest Commercial, Singapore 238467

Cambridge University Press is part of the University of Cambridge.

It furthers the University's mission by disseminating knowledge in the pursuit of
education, learning and research at the highest international levels of excellence.

www.cambridge.org
Information on this title: www.cambridge.org/9781009150057

First published 2022

20 19 18 17 16 15 14 13 12 11 10 9 8 7 6 5 4 3 2 1

Printed in Poland by Opolgraf

A catalogue record for this publication is available from the British Library

ISBN 978-1-009-15005-7 Paperback with Digital Access (2 Years)
ISBN 978-1-009-15003-3 Digital Coursebook (2 Years)
ISBN 978-1-009-15004-0 Coursebook - eBook

Additional resources for this publication at www.cambridge.org/go

Cambridge University Press has no responsibility for the persistence or accuracy
of URLs for external or third-party internet websites referred to in this publication,
and does not guarantee that any content on such websites is, or will remain,
accurate or appropriate. Information regarding prices, travel timetables, and other
factual information given in this work is correct at the time of first printing but
Cambridge University Press does not guarantee the accuracy of such information
thereafter.

....

....

Exam-style questions have been written by the authors. In examinations, the way marks are
awarded may be different. References to assessment and/or assessment preparation are the
publisher's interpretation of the syllabus requirements and may not fully reflect the approach of
Cambridge Assessment International Education.

Cambridge International copyright material in this publication is reproduced under licence and
remains the intellectual property of Cambridge Assessment International Education.

› Contents

5 The world of work	Nouns: compound nouns Noun forming affixes Adjectives: compound adjectives Compound adverbs Pronouns: demonstrative Modals: *can* (ability, possibility, permission), *could* (ability) Causative *have /get*	Synonyms Suffixes Planning written work Identifying the main point of a paragraph Reading longer text	101
6 Getting around	Numbers Time Adverbs: time; frequency; sequence Present continuous for future plans Present simple with future meaning Verbs + dependent preposition	Talking about advantages and disadvantages to make answers longer Listening for key information with time expressions	128
7 People and places	Reported speech: statements / commands / questions Adverbs: degree Conditionals: zero; first; second Prepositions: direction Gerunds used as nouns + gerunds after verbs and prepositions	Building conversation skills by learning about world topics Phrases relating to themes The importance of reflection and setting goals	152
8 The natural world	Adjectives: quantitative Adverbs: manner Pronouns: quantitative Comparative and superlative adverbs Adverbs: place (*here / there*)	Using the adverbs here and there to talk about places Identifying different question types in role play tasks Building knowledge of the world to make tasks easier Identifying expressions of quantity	176
9 Buildings and technology	Prepositions: place Tenses: present perfect simple; past perfect simple Infinitives; use of verb + object + infinitive + (in) direct object; use of *about to* + infinitive Adverbs: direction	Close reading skills Learning irregular verbs Measurements to describe distances and objects Working with a partner	201
10 Cultures and celebrations	Future forms: going to Simple phrasal verbs Pronouns: relative and relative clauses Passives Prepositions: method Modal passive	Irregular verbs and phrasal verbs Reflecting on progress	227
The English-speaking world			248
Glossary			251
Syllabus vocabulary list			253
Classroom language			264
Acknowledgements			265

⟩ Introduction

This book will help you develop your English language skills. It supports the Cambridge IGCSE™ English (as an Additional Language) course for examination from 2023.

The book contains ten units. They cover the topic areas you will study in your course. You will develop your knowledge of topics such as home and family life. You will also study topics such as education, work and travel. In each unit, there are activities that will help you to practise reading, writing, speaking and listening.

Each unit contains grammar guidance with activities. These activities will help you to practise using grammar accurately. At the end of each unit there are some assessment tasks. Use these tasks to help you see how much progress you are making. We hope you enjoy the project tasks at the end of each unit. They will help you to develop your knowledge in an enjoyable way.

Learning with other students is a key part of education. As you work through this book you will be able to discuss and share ideas with others. Be open to feedback and be prepared to redraft your work. You should also speak and listen to English with your friends as often as you can. The more practice you have, the better you will become.

Good luck on the next stage of your learning journey.

Graham Newman and Jane Boylan

> How to use this series

All the components in the series are designed to work together.

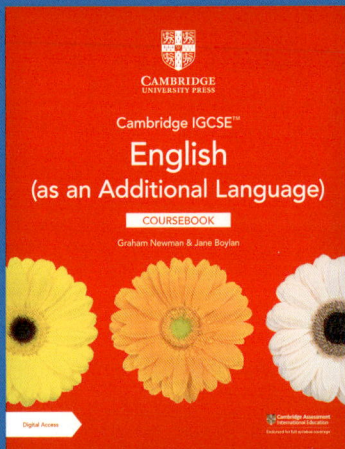

The Coursebook is designed for students to use in class with guidance from the teacher. It offers complete coverage of the IGCSE™ English (as an Additional Language) syllabus (0472/0772). Ten topic-based units engage students and help them to develop the necessary reading, writing, speaking and listening skills, as well as encouraging everyday communication in English. Each unit provides opportunities to check progress, with self-assessment features and exam-style questions and ends with a Grammar Practice.

A digital version of the Coursebook is included with the print version and available separately. It includes the audio as well as simple tools for students to use in class or for self-study.

The Digital Teacher's Resource provides everything teachers need to deliver the course. It is packed full of useful teaching notes and lesson ideas, with suggestions for differentiation to support and challenge students, ideas for formative assessment and homework.

The Digital Teacher's Resource contains downloadable word lists, Coursebook answers and audioscripts of the listening activities, as well as differentiated worksheets for additional grammar practice and more!

> How to use this book

There are lots of different features that will help your learning in this book.

This is what you will learn in the unit. →

IN THIS UNIT YOU WILL:

- learn vocabulary about clothes and accessories
- talk about clothes using the present simple and present continuous
- describe hobbies using the past simple and past continuous
- talk about sports events
- learn vocabulary about sport and hobbies

Each unit has activities for vocabulary, reading, writing, speaking, listening or pronunciation. You can do these on your own, with a partner or as a group. →

Activity ABC XYZ 📖 📝 💬 🎧 🗣️

This helps you learn about grammar. You will then try the grammar in activities. →

GRAMMAR FOCUS

We can also use the prepositions 'like' and 'as' to compare things. Look at these sentences from Katie and Alex's descriptions:

- …we don't really look **like** each other… (we don't look similar to each other)
- …my hair is not **as** curly **as** Mimi's… (Mimi's hair is curlier than my hair)

Remember: 'like' is also used as a verb:

- We **like** doing the same things, mainly sport.

These tell you about important grammar words. →

KEY TERM

subordinating conjunction: a word that joins a main clause and a subordinate clause, such as 'although', 'because', 'if'

These give you quick tips about reading, writing, speaking or listening. →

SPEAKING TIP

When you meet someone, saying 'hello' or 'hi' is usual. You should also use words and phrases such as 'please' and 'thank you', to be polite. Practise using these in your role play.

These boxes tell you about the skills that you need for your course. They give advice on how you can get better at using these skills. →

STUDY SKILLS

When talking about an uncountable noun, you have to use extra words to talk about the amount of something:

- I need two **pieces of** equipment.
- There is a **pile of** work on his desk.
- There is a **lot of** information on that laptop.

Here you will find words for everyday English. These help to develop your knowledge of the English language. →

active   annoying   good-looking   handsome
pleasant   quiet   rude   sad   unpleasant   worried

Here you learn facts about the English language, or English-speaking countries and cultures.

ENGLISH AROUND THE WORLD

It is no surprise that many English words are often used in other languages, especially in European countries. Some examples include 'le selfie' (in French), 'call' (a business call in Italian) and 'footing' (means 'jogging' in Spanish). Words such as 'OK' and 'cool' are used in many European languages by people of all ages. These words are known as 'loan words'. English, of course, has many loan words too, especially to talk about food (pizza, ketchup, chocolate).

Here you will find groups of English phrases. These also help to develop your knowledge of the English language.

USEFUL EXPRESSIONS

To be born: I was born in Kolkata.

To be pregnant: My auntie is pregnant.

To call/be called: I am called Marius.

To die: My grandfather died last year.

To grow/grow up: I want to be a teacher when I grow up.

To live: I live in Sri Lanka.

To spell (your name): I spell my name with a K.

childhood: I spent my childhood in France.

These boxes help you learn how to pronounce different words and sounds. They also show you how pronunciation works with different types of sentences and questions.

PRONOUNCING ENGLISH

Short and long 'i' sound

Some words with the vowel 'i' have a short sound, for example: *in, amazing*.

There are also words with 'i' that have a long sound, for example: *like, flight*.

These let you work with other students, using what you have learned. You might do some research or make something.

PROJECT

As a class you are going to produce a spoken book about different cultures around the world for the younger students in your school.

Each class member should select a different country or nationality. Find out unusual information about the country you select, such as interesting customs, foods or history. When you have found your information, write some notes and practise speaking about the country for 2 minutes.

When you have practised, each person in the class should record their talk. You can use a phone to record your talk. You could even add some music or sound effects. Have fun listening to them. Which country sounded the most interesting to you?

These questions help you to try exam tasks.

EXAM-STYLE QUESTIONS

Writing practice

Use this activity to practise your writing skills. Try to write 80-90 words.

Describe a member of your family. Write about:

- their name and appearance
- what you like about them

Here you will find some questions. These help you to think about what you have learned in the unit.

CHECK YOUR PROGRESS

How confident do you feel about what you have learned and practised in this unit? How many of the things below could you do?

1 Write two sentences explaining what job you would like when you are older.
2 Give three examples of compound nouns.
3 Write a sentence containing a demonstrative.
4 Identify the main point of a text.
5 Give two tips for reading longer texts.

Each unit ends with a grammar section. You will learn more grammar and then try grammar activities.

> ## Grammar practice

> Unit 1
Family and home

> 1.1 About us

Use these activities to describe people's character and appearance.

1 Reading 📖 ABC XYZ

Work in pairs. Copy the table into your notebooks. Can you put the words below into the group?

Feelings and qualities	Appearance
happy	slim

> stupid   excited   angry   bored   old   curious   fat   exhausted
> hard-working   slim   polite   ugly   sensible   worried   greedy   happy
> good/bad mood   intelligent   young   poor   friendly
> silly   lazy   sociable   beautiful   short   old-fashioned

2 Speaking 💬

Work with a partner. What is happening in the picture? Which feelings and qualities from Activity 1 can you see?

3 Reading 📖 ABC XYZ

Match sentences a–e to photos i–v.
Can you find another word from Activity 1 to describe each person?

a In some countries, it is polite to shake hands.

b Jenny is an intelligent girl. She enjoys solving difficult maths problems.

c It is Dad's birthday. He is very excited.

d Mahfuz is friendly. He always chats with people when he's shopping.

e Hinata works hard every day. He is exhausted.

4 Listening (track 1.1) 🎧

Listen to Jack's description of himself. Which photo describes him the best? Then decide if sentences b–f are true or false.

a

long dark hair, blue eyes

short or long blonde / fair hair and blue eyes

short, dark hair, brown eyes

b Jack likes everything about school.

c All of Jack's family think that he works hard.

d Jack sometimes feels unhappy when he thinks about problems.

e Jack enjoys spending time with other people.

f He never enjoys being alone.

LISTENING TIP

Most listening activities ask you to listen for key information such as numbers, times or key words. Read the questions carefully before you listen. Make sure you know which information you need to hear.

5 Speaking 💬 ᴬᴮᶜ

Can you describe yourself using words from Activity 1? Can you think of any more words? Work in pairs. Describe yourself to your partner. Ask each other:

a What is your name?

b What is your age?

c What are the colour of your hair and eyes?

d How can you describe your personality?

STUDY SKILLS

Regular conversation practice is the best way to learn a language. When you work in pairs, talk to each other in English. Help each other to learn new words.

GRAMMAR FOCUS

Look at the sentences Jack used to describe himself. The words in **bold** are called **coordinating conjunctions**:

*   I have dark brown hair **and** blue eyes.

    └── Similar point

Both clauses describe Jack's appearance. They are similar points so we use 'and' to connect them.

Here Jack has used a coordinating conjunction to connect two clauses.

*   I enjoy going to school, **but** I get bored easily.

    └── Contrasting point

The first clause describes a positive feeling about school. The second clause describes a negative feeling. They are in contrast so we use 'but'.

KEY TERMS

coordinating conjunction: a connecting word, such as 'and', 'but' and 'or', that joins two main clauses

clause: a group of words containing a **verb**

verb: the 'doing' word of a phrase or sentence such as 'to do', 'to be'

6 Writing 📝

Work in pairs. Write two sentences describing yourself using coordinating conjunctions. Make one sentence false. Use the word box to help with your descriptions. Now show your partner. Can they guess which sentence is false?

active annoying good-looking handsome
pleasant quiet rude sad unpleasant worried

GRAMMAR FOCUS

Jack also uses **subordinating conjunctions** to join two points. Look at the different meanings:

1 I try to work hard, **although** my sister thinks I'm lazy!
   └── Point 1   └── Contrasting point 2

2 I think I'm a friendly person **because** I like meeting new people.
   └── Point 1   └── Reason

Look at the two clauses in Example 1. Notice that one clause makes sense on its own:

* I try to work hard ✓

…but the second clause can't exist without the first clause.

* **although** my sister thinks I'm lazy! ✗

The second clause is a subordinate clause. Notice that it adds extra information to the main clause:

* I try to work hard, **although** my sister thinks I'm lazy! ✓

KEY TERM

subordinating conjunction: a word that joins a main clause and a subordinate clause, such as 'although', 'because', 'if'

7 Writing 📝

a Read the Grammar focus. Choose the correct conjunction to complete the sentences. Then tick [✓] the ones that are true about you.

although   because

i   Sometimes I get angry <u>although</u> most people think I'm a quiet person.
ii I look like my sister _____ we both have dark hair and blue eyes.
iii I know my brother is quite sociable _____ he is sometimes shy.
iv My best friend is an intelligent boy _____ he can often be lazy.
v   My friends and I are all excited _____ the holidays start soon.
vi I'm worried about one class next week _____ we have an important test.

b Which sentences were not true about you? Change the sentences to make them true. You can write about yourself, your family or a friend.

Sometimes my best friend gets worried although most people think she's a calm person.

STUDY SKILLS

Learning vocabulary improves language skills. If you don't understand a word, try to work out the meaning from the sentence. Then use a dictionary or glossary if the meaning still isn't clear. Keep a list of new words and their meanings.

> 1.2 Family

In this session you will name and describe family members and write about a family occasion.

1 Speaking 💬 ABC XYZ

In pairs, look at the photo.
Which words in the word box could be used to describe each person?

I think she is this girl's aunt. What do you think?

adult   aunt   boy
child   daughter
father   girl
granddaughter
grandmother
grandparent
grandson   husband
nephew   niece
brother   single
sister   parent
relative   son   uncle

2 Reading 📖 ABC XYZ

Read Priya's description of her aunt's wedding. Talk about the family members.

Aunt Binita's Wedding

Last summer, I went to my aunt's wedding. It was a big family occasion and took place in a beautiful town in England. My grandparents managed to travel from India. They thought the flight was uncomfortable and too long, but my elderly grandmother said she was delighted to be there. She told my brother and I about our parents' wedding. It was lovely to hear that story. She even showed us photos!

Aunt Binita's new husband is called Alan. He is a pleasant, kind man, and my twin brother and I are so pleased that he is our new uncle. I'm very happy that they got married. It was an amazing day for everyone. That is why family occasions are so important – they bring everyone together.

3 Reading 📖

Read Priya's description of Aunt Binita's wedding again. Answer the questions.

a Who didn't enjoy the flight from India?

b Who was very pleased to be at the wedding?

c How does Priya describe Binita's new husband?

d What relation is Priya to Binita?

GRAMMAR FOCUS

When we write, we use a **subject pronoun** to avoid repeating the name of the person.

• My **grandparents** travelled from India. **They** didn't enjoy the flight.
    └─ Subject   └─ Subject pronoun

Object pronouns work in a similar way:
                    ┌─ Object
• She told **my brother and I** about our parents' wedding.
   She even showed **us** photos!
              └── Object pronoun

Possessive pronouns show possession – who the object belongs to.

• ...**my twin brother and I** are so pleased to have him as **our** new uncle.

KEY TERMS

subject pronoun: words such as 'he', 'she' and 'they' that talk about who or what is doing the action in a sentence

object pronoun: words such as 'him, 'her' and 'them' that talk about *who* or *what* has the action done to them

possessive pronoun: words that show who the object belongs to, such as 'his', 'her', 'their'

4 Reading 📖

Look at the sentences about Aunt Binita's wedding. Choose the correct pronoun. Then decide which pronouns are subject, object or possessive in each sentence.

| it | He | Their | her | him | they |

a Aunt Binita's new husband is very kind. I really like _____.

b Alan has two brothers. _____ invited both of them to the wedding.

c My grandmother wanted to show me _____ photos.

d My grandparents flew from India to the UK. _____ flight took 10 hours.

e Aunt Binita and Alan are really excited because _____ go on honeymoon next week.

f Aunt Binita wore a beautiful sari. I really liked _____.

STUDY SKILLS

Grammar terms are useful ways to talk about language. Try to learn and use grammar terms as you do this course.

GRAMMAR FOCUS

The word 'it' is an **impersonal pronoun** that makes **noun phrases** shorter and avoids repeating words. 'It' can be used as a subject or object pronoun. Compare the following two examples:

- I'm very happy that they got married. **The wedding** was an amazing day for everyone.
- I'm very happy that they got married. **It** was an amazing day for everyone.

Demonstrative pronouns (this, these, that, those) talk about a person or thing that has already been mentioned. Here is an example.

- It was an amazing day for everyone. **That** is why family occasions are so important.

KEY TERMS

impersonal pronoun: words such as 'it' and 'there' that are used for non-human things

noun phrase: a group of words that go together as a noun, for example, 'the wedding day'

demonstrative pronoun: used to talk about things near or further away (for example, this, these, that, those)

5 Reading 📖

In pairs, read Priya's messages with her friend, Anna. Complete the conversation with the missing sentences. Find one impersonal pronoun and two demonstrative pronouns.

a I'd like to meet them. Are they still here?

b That is great news! Was it a big wedding?

c That is enormous!

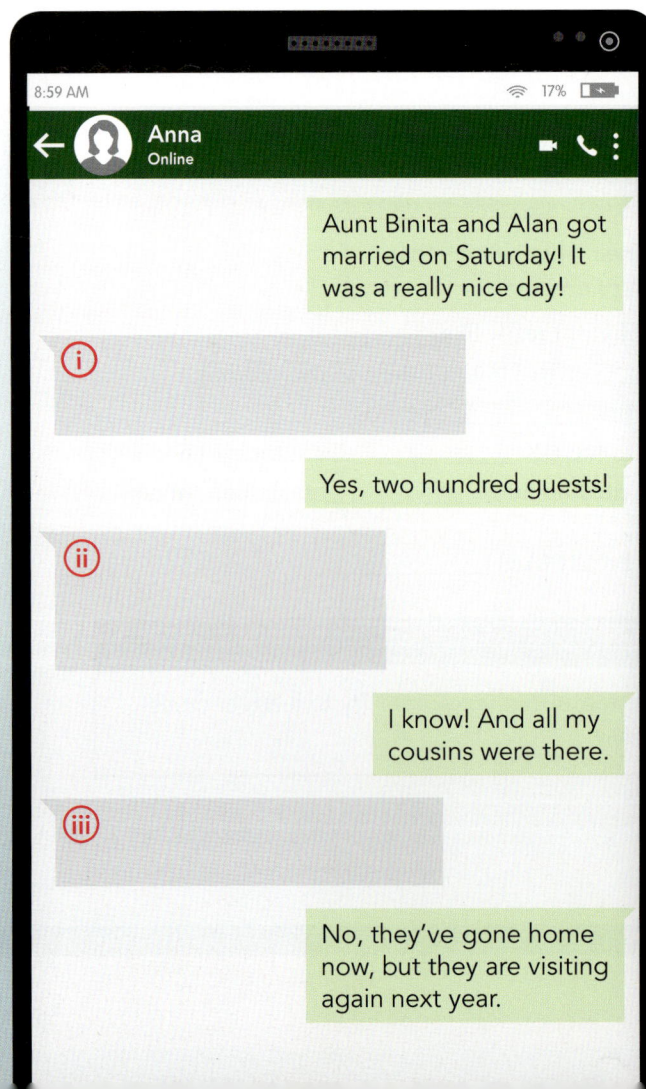

Conversation with Anna (Online), 8:59 AM, 17% battery:

- Aunt Binita and Alan got married on Saturday! It was a really nice day!
- **(i)** _____
- Yes, two hundred guests!
- **(ii)** _____
- I know! And all my cousins were there.
- **(iii)** _____
- No, they've gone home now, but they are visiting again next year.

6 Writing

Write four sentences about a family occasion. It could be a special dinner, a birthday or a day out. Use different types of pronouns to avoid repeating names or family members. Start your first sentence with a time phrase:

USEFUL EXPRESSIONS

To be born: I was born in Kolkata.

To be pregnant: My auntie is pregnant.

To call/be called: I am called Marius.

To die: My grandfather died last year.

To grow/grow up: I want to be a teacher when I grow up.

To live: I live in Sri Lanka.

To spell (your name): I spell my name with a K.

childhood: I spent my childhood in France.

7 Speaking

With a partner, read your four sentences from Activity 6 aloud. Check that you have both used pronouns correctly. Use the Key term boxes on pronouns to help you.

WRITING TIP

Make sure the first sentence of your writing clearly shows the main noun or noun phrase. This helps your reader understand what any later pronouns are describing.

STUDY SKILLS

Practising writing and speaking about your family is an important part of your studies. Learn different ways to give details about family members and events. You could learn the words and phrases in the Useful expressions box.

> 1.3 Friends

In this session you will listen, speak, read and write about friends and friendship.

1 Listening (track 1.2) 🎧

Listen to the two speakers describe their friends and say what they like about them. Answer the following questions.

a How long has Katie known Mimi?
b What does Mimi's hair look like?
c What does Katie like most about Mimi?
d Where did Alex first meet Andros?
e What do Alex and Andros like doing together?
f What does Alex like most about Andros?

2 Speaking 💬 🗣

a Say these words again from Activity 1. Can you add one more word to each group?

Silent w	Silent h	Silent k
who write	what	know

b In pairs, read the words below aloud. Which letter is silent? Can you think of one more word with the same silent letter?

climb   walk   watch

3 Speaking 💬

In pairs, take turns to talk about a friend. Use these prompts:

• What is your friend's name and how long have you known him/her?
• When did you first meet him/her?
• What do you like about him/her?
• What do you do together?

For example, you could say:

• My friend is called Abdul. I have known him for ten years.
• I first met him at school.
• I really like him because he is funny and kind.
• We play football together.

LISTENING TIP

Before you listen to a recording, make sure you read the listening activity questions first. Then you know what information to listen for.

PRONOUNCING ENGLISH

Silent letters

Many words in English have a silent letter – a letter that is not pronounced.

STUDY SKILLS

Remember that it takes time and practice to become confident in a language. In pair work, support each other by choosing to speak in English rather than your own language. Ask each other questions, giving each other time to speak, and help each other with unknown words.

4 Writing ✎

Imagine you are going to introduce your friend to someone who has not met them. Write three interesting things to tell them about your friend. Here are some sentence starters to help you.

Maya has an interesting hobby – she likes…	Last year, Marcus won a…	Joe's best quality is _____ He always…

GRAMMAR FOCUS

In English, we often use **comparative adjectives** to compare things.

Regular comparative adjectives

Look at the sentences from Katie and Alex's descriptions. They use a comparative adjective + 'than' to compare one thing with another. Notice how the regular adjectives change in a comparative sentence:

- short   ➔ She is **shorter** than me.
- funny   ➔ No one is **funnier** than Mimi!
- sociable   ➔ He is **more sociable** than me.

Note: with longer adjectives, we use 'more', but the adjective does not change.

Katie also uses the form '(not) as + adjective as', to compare something that is not equal:

- …my hair is not **as curly as** Mimi's.

Irregular comparative adjectives

Look at the sentences from the descriptions. Notice how the irregular verbs change form in the comparative sentences.

- good   ➔ She usually gets **better** grades **than** me at school.
- bad   ➔ …there is nothing **worse than** losing a good friend.

KEY TERM

comparative adjectives: a type of adjective that compares something for example, 'happier' or 'taller'

5 Reading 📖

Read the sentences about friends. Change the adjectives in brackets to the correct comparative form. Which adjective *doesn't* change? Which sentences are true for you?

a   My best friend is _____ (tall) than me.

b   I am _____ (happy) with just one or two friends than in a large group.

c   One of my friends gets _____ (good) grades than all the others.

d   There is no one who is _____ (kind) than my best friend.

e   One of my friends is not as _____ (confident) as the others.

f   Some of my friends are _____ (generous) than others.

6 Reading 📖

Read Beth's description of her friend, Sasha. Write down five adjectives Beth uses to talk about Sasha. Which adjectives describe Sasha's character? Which describe Beth's relationship with her?

MY FRIEND SASHA

Sasha is my best friend. We first met at school, and of all my friends, she is the one I have known for the longest time. I have lots of good friends, such as Jess and Mel, but I am the closest to Sasha. Sasha is the most generous person I know. She is also the funniest. She can make me really laugh! I love spending time with her. I am happiest when I am with her.

Last year her family nearly moved to another city, but they changed their minds. I was so relieved! It is the worst thing in the world when your best friend moves away!

GRAMMAR FOCUS

We can also use the prepositions 'like' and 'as' to compare things. Look at these sentences from Katie and Alex's descriptions:

- …we don't really look **like** each other… (we don't look similar to each other)

- …my hair is not **as** curly **as** Mimi's… (Mimi's hair is curlier than my hair)

Remember: 'like' is also used as a verb:

- We **like** doing the same things, mainly sport.

GRAMMAR FOCUS

Superlative adjectives are used to describe something as having more of a quality than anything else.

Regular superlative adjectives

Look at the sentences from Sasha's description. Notice how the regular adjectives change in a superlative sentence:

- long → She is the friend I have known for **the long<u>est</u>** time.
- happy → I am <u>happ**iest**</u> when I am with her.
- generous → Sasha is **the <u>most generous</u>** person I know.

Note: with longer adjectives, we use 'most', but the adjective does not change.

Irregular superlative adjectives

Look at the sentences from the description. Notice how the irregular verbs change form in the superlative sentences.

- good → Sasha is my **<u>best</u>** friend.
- bad → It is **the <u>worst</u>** thing in the world when your best friend moves away!

KEY TERM

superlative: a type of adjective that shows that the thing or person has more of something than any others that are similar (for example, 'funniest' or 'smallest')

7 Reading 📖

Here are some more sentences about good friends. Choose the correct adjective for each sentence and change it to the superlative form. Then choose the sentences that could describe any of your friends.

> confident   kind   good   funny   **bad**   close

a Lena is the _____ person I know – she always helps people.

b No one makes me laugh like Jake – he is the _____ of all my friends.

c It is the _____ thing to have an argument with your best friend – it is awful.

d Karim is the _____ person I know – he can talk to anyone!

e Josh is my _____ friend – I can tell him anything.

f We had the _____ day out for Mia's birthday – we all had so much fun.

8 Reading 📖

Rohan and his mum are making a plan for a day out for his birthday. He is deciding which friends to invite. Read the conversation, then write the correct adjective form in your notebook to complete it.

> **Mum:** You should invite Ali, Rohan. He is your oldest friend – you've known him ᵃ**longer / longest** than any of your other friends. You used to play with him when you were a baby!
>
> **Rohan:** But he doesn't know my other friends, Mum.
>
> **Mum:** Yes, but he's a very ᵇ**confident / most confident** boy. He'll soon make friends with the others!
>
> **Rohan:** Yes, you're right. He's also my ᶜ**funny / funniest** friend. The others will like him.
>
> **Mum:** How about Danny? I like him. He's the ᵈ**politer / politest** boy I've ever met!
>
> **Rohan:** Yes, all the mums say that! He's great. He's probably my ᵉ**closer / closest** friend at the moment.
>
> **Mum:** I thought Alex was your ᶠ**good / best** friend.
>
> **Rohan:** I think I've got ᵍ**many / more** lessons at school with Danny than I do with Alex. We see each other a lot.
>
> **Mum:** Yes, but make sure you stay friends with Alex – he's a nice boy. There's nothing ʰ**worst / worse** than losing a friend. Are you going to invite him?

9 Writing 📝

Imagine that you are making a plan for a day out for a special occasion.
Who would you invite? Choose four friends and write why you would invite them.
Use comparative and superlative adjectives.

I'd like to invite Mina because I've known her for the longest time.
I'll invite Jack because he's more sociable than some of my other friends.

10 Writing 📝 ABC XYZ

Social expressions are words and phrases you use to greet people and talk to them in a polite, sociable way. Match the phrases and replies from the Useful expressions box on the next page.

a Hi, how's it going?

b Good morning everyone. Welcome to the class.

c Why don't we go for a coffee?

d Hello! My name's Sam.

e Sorry, but I have to go.

i Sorry, but I can't now. Let's do it another day.

ii Nice to meet you. I'm George.

iii What a shame! Shall we arrange another time?

iv Great! How about you?

v Thank you.

USEFUL EXPRESSIONS

Good morning/good afternoon/good evening	See you later/tomorrow
Goodbye	Sorry/excuse me
Hello/hi	Thank you
How are you?	Thank you, but I can't
I'm well/I'm not well	Welcome!
How's it going?	Why don't we…?/Shall we…?
I have to go	How annoying!
Let's do it another day	How interesting!
Nice to meet you	How nice!
Pardon?	What a shame/what a pity!

11 Reading 📖 🔤

Now match the correct pairs of expressions from Activity 10 to these social situations.

a   A teacher greets a new class for the first time.

b   Two good friends greet each other. They are the same age.

c   Two people introduce themselves to each other for the first time.

d   One person makes an excuse; the other feels disappointed.

e   One person makes a suggestion; the other makes an excuse but suggests meeting another time.

12 Writing and Speaking 📝 💬

Work in pairs. Choose two of the following situations and write a short conversation. Then perform the conversations for another pair. Can they work out which situation (a–d) it is?

a   Introduce yourself to a friend of the family who doesn't know you. Tell them a bit about yourself.

b   Greet a good friend in the street. Suggest meeting another day.

c   Welcome a group of students from another country to your school. Suggest an activity to do together.

d   A friend suggests going out. You have another arrangement – make an excuse.

> 1.4 At home

These activities will help you to practise describing your house and the things you do at home.

1 Writing

Draw a rough plan of your home as if you were looking from above. Name each room. Choose one room and make a quick drawing. Name at least five items of furniture. Use the word box to help you.

> bathroom   bath   shower   duvet   blanket   sheet   microwave   toilet
> bedroom   washing machine   bed   closet   cupboard   pillow   lamp   plug
> dining room   garage   table   tap   living room   desk   lounge   sofa   rug
> chair   armchair   chest of drawers   iron   kitchen   sink   study   garden
> cooker   dishwasher   freezer   speaker   shelves   wardrobe   carpet

2 Reading and Speaking 📖 💬 ABC XYZ

In pairs, read the following descriptions of houses and apartments for sale. Find words from Activity 1 in the descriptions. Check new words in a dictionary. Which home do you like best? Which one would be most suitable for your family and you?

Places to live

How it works   Explore more   For sale   For rent   Contact us   Login

🔺 33 South Close

This cosy one bedroom flat with low ceilings is next to a large park. It has a bath but no shower. There is a new fridge and dishwasher in the kitchen. Next to the bedroom, there is a small study with space for a desk and computer.

🔻 6 West Road

This house has three bedrooms. It is a lovely house but needs some repairs. The new owner will need to repair the windows, and replace the kitchen and bathroom furniture. A new heating system is needed too.

🔺 25 North Avenue

This is a large family home with four bedrooms. It has a double garage, a study, a balcony and air conditioning. The house has a new washing machine, new cooker and new carpets. A shower room was installed last year. The neighbours are friendly and helpful.

3 Reading and Speaking 📖 💬

Adam, Mick, Zara and Sisi are looking for a new place to live.
In pairs, decide if any of the places described in Activity 2 would be good for them.

Adam

I would like a place with two or three bedrooms. I can fix things very well, so I would be satisfied with a house that needs some repairs.

Mick

I am looking for a flat. If possible, I would like to be near a garden or park. The flat must have a shower and some furniture.

Zara

I have a large family, so we need a place with at least three bedrooms. I am very busy, so I need somewhere which does not need repairs.

Sisi

I would like a flat for myself. I would be happy with a one bedroom place, but it must have a study.

GRAMMAR FOCUS

We use the **gerund** (verb + ing) after verbs describing likes and dislikes. For example, like, love, enjoy, don't mind, hate.

Look at the sentences from the conversation between Aaron and his friend on the next page:

- I **like** <u>cutting</u> the grass…
- I **don't mind** <u>doing</u> most jobs…
- I **don't enjoy** <u>cleaning</u> the bathroom…
- I **hate** <u>ironing</u> clothes!

KEY TERM

gerund: a verb that ends in -ing that works as a noun

4 Reading 📖

Look at the verbs describing likes and dislikes in the conversation.

Friend:	Hey Aaron! Are you free on Saturday?
Aaron:	I'll be free from about 12 o'clock. I have to help at home on Saturday mornings.
Friend:	Oh no! What do you have to do?
Aaron:	It depends… I don't mind actually. I like doing anything outside… you know… cutting the grass or sweeping the drive.
Friend:	I hate cleaning the house. It's the worst job! Luckily, I don't have to do it very often as it doesn't get too dirty.
Aaron:	I don't mind doing most jobs, but I don't enjoy cleaning the bathroom or washing the windows. It takes too long. But I love ironing clothes! I know it's strange but for me, it's relaxing. And I enjoy tidying my room – it feels much better when it's clean.

Look at the verbs in the word box below. Put the verbs in order, according to their meaning. Which verb has the same meaning as 'like'?

> don't mind   enjoy   hate   don't enjoy   like   love

5 Speaking 💬

Work in pairs. Make a list of all the things that need doing that Aaron and his friend mention. Which of these jobs do you do at home? Which other jobs do you do? Describe how you feel about doing jobs around the house.

For example, you could say:

I like watering the plants.

I don't enjoy loading the dishwasher.

> **SPEAKING TIP**
>
> Giving reasons for your views is important. Use the linking word 'because' before you give a reason. For example:
> - 'I don't like cleaning the bathroom because it takes a long time.'

6 Listening (track 1.3) 🎧

Listen to Sam describe what he does before bed. Answer the questions below.

a Which routine does Sam like best – having a bath or a shower? Why?
b What does he do afterwards?
c What mistake did Sam make tonight?
d What doesn't Sam do at the end of the day? Why not?

Check your answers with a partner. Which of Sam's actions are similar to your bedtime routine? What other things do you do before going to bed?

7 Reading 📖 ABC XYZ

Read about what Eva does to get ready for school. Match the pictures to the underlined words and phrases.

My alarm clock rings at 7 a.m. I try to get out of bed straight away. I like to have a shower before school. I wash my hair every day and dry it with a towel rather than a hairdryer. Once I'm dressed, I usually have breakfast with my brother. After that, I go back to the bathroom, brush my teeth with my toothbrush, wash my face and use my hairbrush. Then I leave for school.

8 Writing 📝

a   Now write your own description of what you do in the morning or evening. Use Sam and Eva's descriptions to help you. Start by writing a list of things you do. Try to write 75 words.

Every morning, I ....

b   Check your work and then read it to a partner. Which of your routines are similar? What different things do you do?

WRITING TIP

Asking a partner to read your work can help you find mistakes. You could also use a spelling and grammar checker on your computer.

> 1.5 Garden and kitchen

In this final session for Unit 1, you will practise answering questions on a longer text.

1 Reading 📖 ABC XYZ

Look at the word box. Work in pairs. Copy the table into your notebook. Divide the words into two groups: natural and not natural. How many of these things can you find in the picture? Which words did you already know? Which are new?

> bird   branch   flower   garden   gate   grass
> leaves   path   plant   tree   wall   workshop

Natural	Not natural

2 Listening (track 1.4) 🎧 ABC XYZ

Listen to Ben talk about his grandad's garden. Which words from Activity 1 does he mention? Then answer these questions:

a   Why did Ben do some gardening recently?
b   How did Ben feel about doing the gardening?
c   Name three things Ben did in the garden.
d   What does Ben plan to do soon?
e   What is Ben's grandad going to give him?

GRAMMAR FOCUS

We use the **prepositions** to talk about where things happen or where they are.

Look at Ben's sentences from the recording:

- My grandad loves spending time **in** his garden.
- Next weekend I might fix the lock **on** the gate.
- There's a spare piece of ground **behind** his shed, **next to** the tree.

KEY TERM

preposition: words that show where things are

3 Speaking 💬

Work with a partner. Take turns to describe what you see in the picture. Ask your partner:

a   What activity is the boy doing?

b   What can you see behind him?

c   What is next to him?

> **SPEAKING TIP**
>
> When you are describing things in a picture, use prepositions such as 'on', 'in', 'next' and 'behind' to help you explain where things are in the picture.

4 Speaking 💬

Work with a partner. What activities can you do in a garden? Which activity can you see in the photo below?

5 Reading 📖

Read Part 1 below. Which activity does Vanessa describe? Answer questions a-e. To help you with some of the vocabulary: a barbecue is a meal cooked outdoors over an open fire; chopping is another word for cutting; boiled is when something is cooked in hot water; to grill is to cook using fire.

> ### The barbecue, part 1
>
> Last Saturday, my grandparents, aunts, uncles and cousins came to our house for a **barbecue**. It was a special day. My brother, Alexei, was going to live in New Zealand, so we were meeting to say goodbye to him.
>
> I told my mum that I would do the cooking. Our kitchen is quite small, so whenever we get lunch or dinner ready, only one of us can be in the kitchen. I started by washing the vegetables in the kitchen sink and then **chopping** them. I **boiled** and roasted some potatoes too. Finally, I fried some rice and got the meat ready for my dad to **grill** later.

| barbecue   chopping |
| boiled   grill |

a   The barbecue was a family celebration.

b   Everyone wanted to celebrate Alexei's birthday.

c   Everyone helped Vanessa to prepare the barbecue.

d   First, Vanessa prepared some vegetables.

e   Then she cooked some meat.

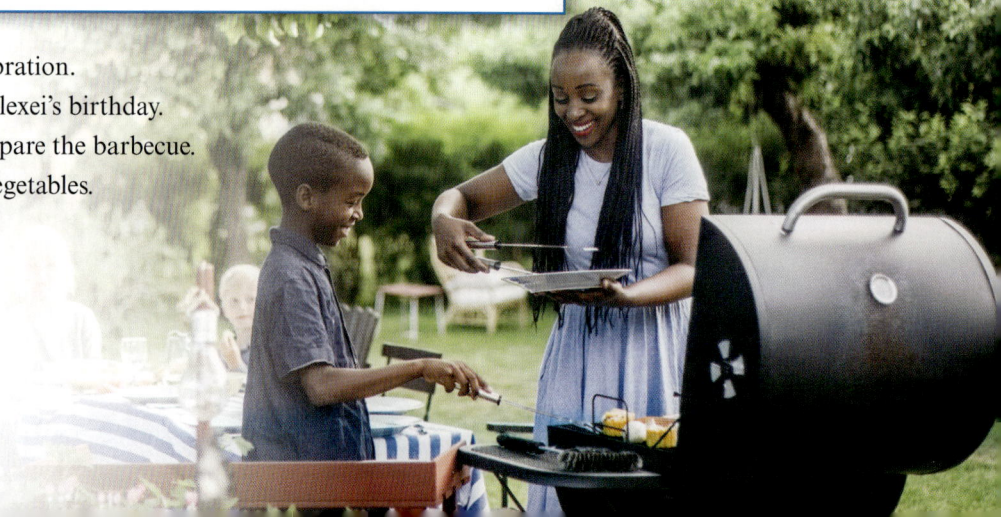

6 Reading 📖

Now read Part 2 and then answer questions a-d.

The barbecue, part 2

Alexei had been awake early, so he was feeling sleepy and wanted to rest. That is why he went to bed again at 10 a.m. My family arrived just before midday. It was a very hot day. I got them some bottles of water and cans of soft drinks from the icebox in the fridge. My grandmother was shocked to hear that Alexei was in bed!

Alexei got up at 1 p.m. and was given some presents by the family. Then it was time for the barbecue. My dad loves cooking. I think he enjoys the fire a bit too much but the meat was cooked perfectly! It was a lovely celebration. The only bad thing was tidying up afterwards. There was lots of food left over, so I froze it.

---

a   What did Alexei do in the morning?
b   How did Vanessa look after her guests?
c   Why does Vanessa think her dad likes to barbecue so much?
d   What didn't Vanessa like doing at the end?

> awake
> **feeling sleepy**
> midday   fridge
> fire

7 Writing 📝

Which jobs around the house does Vanessa mention in 'The barbecue'?
Who does the jobs around the house in your home? Write six sentences to explain.

For example, you could write:

At home, my father usually does the washing up.

Use some of the phrases in the word box and pictures to help you.

> bakes   cleans   does the laundry   does the washing up   does the ironing
> **sets the table**   clears the table   tidies up   **takes the rubbish out**

STUDY SKILLS

Take your time when answering reading questions. Read the question carefully and use the question to look for the information you need in the text. Use the reading activities in this book to practise these skills. Remember that the more you practise, the more you will improve.

WRITING TIP

Using **adverbs of frequency**, (such as 'often', 'usually', 'never' and 'sometimes') can add more detail. For example:
- My brother **usually** tidies up after dinner.
- I **never** take the rubbish out.

KEY TERM

adverbs of frequency: adverbs are words that describe a verb. Adverbs of frequency describe how often an action happens

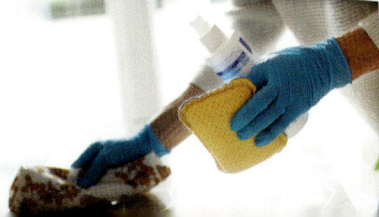

PROJECT

You are going to design a new house. In groups, discuss some things you are going to have in your new house. Ask each other:

- How many rooms do you have in the house?
- What things do you have in each room?
- What does your bedroom look like?
- Where in the world is your new house?

You could use phrases such as:

- 'My house has...'
- 'In the kitchen, I have a...'

Make a plan and drawings of your new house. Add notes and write some sentences explaining your ideas. Finally, present your ideas to the class.

EXAM-STYLE QUESTIONS

Writing practice

Use this activity to practise your writing skills. Try to write 80-90 words.

Describe a member of your family. Write about:

- their name and appearance
- what you like about them
- what you do together
- why they are important to you. [12]

CHECK YOUR PROGRESS

How confident do you feel about what you have learned and practised in this unit? How many of these things could you do?

1 Describe the appearance and personality of a friend.
2 Find and use different types of pronouns.
3 Use comparatives and superlatives correctly.
4 Describe the rooms in your house.
5 Give a description of doing jobs around the house.

Rate yourself from 1 (not confident) to 5 (very confident).

Which things would you like to learn more about?
Which things would you like to practise again?

Share your thoughts with a partner.

› Grammar practice

Articles: definite and indefinite

GRAMMAR FOCUS

We use **indefinite articles**, **a** or **an**, when we talk about something for the first time:

- This cosy one bedroom flat is next to **a** large park.
- It has **a** bath but no shower.

We use **a** before a word beginning with a *consonant*, and **an** before a *vowel*.

- There is **a b**ig comfortable living room with **a l**arge sofa and **an a**rmchair.

We also use **a/an** to show that the person or thing is part of a group.

- It is **a one bedroom flat** in **Park View Court**.

We do not use **a/an** with plural nouns or uncountable nouns.

- It is a lovely house but needs **repairs**. (plural noun)
- It has a double garage, a study, a balcony and **air conditioning**. (uncountable noun)

KEY TERM

indefinite article: the words, **a** or **an**, that are used before singular noun phrases to talk about something for the first time

1 Reading 📖

Copy and complete the sentences with *a* or *an*.

a Anya lives in _____ house near to her school.
b They have bought _____ armchair for their living room.
c Granddad's garage has _____ orange door.
d Our family would like a new house with _____ garden.
e My aunt lives in _____ expensive flat near the beach.
f There is _____ wall next to the shed that needs some repairs.

2 Reading 📖

Copy and complete the description with *a*, *an* or - (no article).
The first one has been done for you.

Park View Court is ᵃ _a_ block of flats, next to ᵇ ___ park in the north of the city. It is ᶜ ___ popular place to live because it is in ᵈ ___ attractive neighbourhood. There are ᵉ ___ flats which overlook the park on the east side and other flats which face ᶠ ___ quiet road on the west side. All the flats have ᵍ ___central heating and ʰ ___ 24-hour security.

GRAMMAR FOCUS

We use the **definite article**, **the**, when the listener knows what we are talking about, because:

1 it was mentioned before:

- This is a large family home with four bedrooms. **The** house has a new washing machine…

2 there is only one:

- The house is in the centre of **the village**, next to **the church**. (There is only one village and one church here).
- The house faces south, so **the sun** shines on the garden in the morning. (There is only one sun).

We also use **the** with superlative adjectives:

- Sasha is **the most generous** *person* I know. She is also **the funniest**.

KEY TERM

definite article: the word, **the**, that is used before noun phrases to talk about things that are already familiar

3 Reading 📖

Copy and complete the paragraph with the correct article.
The first one has been done for you.

This is a perfect house for [a] **a / the** growing family. It is [b] **a / the** largest house in [c] **a / the** centre of the village and has four bedrooms. There are also two bathrooms and [d] **a / the** garage for two cars. [e] **A / The** back garden has [f] **a / the** barbecue area and views of [g] **a / the** countryside.

Pronouns: indefinite and reflexive

GRAMMAR FOCUS

Indefinite pronouns are used to talk about people or things without saying exactly who or what they are, or exactly how many.

- That is why family occasions are so important – they bring **everyone** together.
- There's **nothing** worse than losing a friend.

Pronouns ending in -**body/one** = **people**

Pronouns ending in -**thing** = **things**

Pronouns ending in -**where** = **places**

KEY TERM

indefinite pronoun: we use these to talk about people, things or places without being exact

CONTINUED

We always use a singular verb after an indefinite pronoun, even if it has a plural meaning.

- **Everybody enjoys** a family wedding.
- Samira's wedding was wonderful. **Everyone was dressed** in their best clothes. **Everything was** planned very well. There were decorations in the reception room. **Everywhere** was so beautiful.

When we start a sentence with an indefinite pronoun with **no-**, we follow it by a verb in the affirmative:

- **Nobody knew** that it was Alex's birthday.
  ~~**Nobody didn't know**~~ that it was Alex's birthday.

However, if we start a sentence with a negative clause, we use an indefinite pronoun with **any-**.

- Alex **didn't want anyone** to know that it was his birthday.

1 Reading 📖

Copy and choose the correct pronoun.

a   There were lots of flowers at Aunt Binita's wedding. **Everywhere / Everyone** was so colourful.
b   **Anybody / Nobody** expected my grandparents to travel from India for the wedding.
c   **Everybody / Everywhere** was so pleased to see my grandparents at the wedding.
d   **Somebody / Something** posted a lovely photograph of the wedding on social media – do you know who it was?
e   There wasn't **anywhere / anyone** who didn't enjoy the wedding.
f   Everybody loved the food at the wedding – at the end there was **anything / nothing** left.

2 Reading 📖

Copy and complete the sentences with the correct indefinite pronoun.

> somewhere   anywhere   everything   nothing   eveyone   anyone

a   _____ in Tariq's bedroom is blue because it's his favourite colour.
b   Nobody knew Petra's exam results because she didn't tell _____.
c   Why can't you open the door? I'm sure there is a key _____.
d   There's _____ in the room – it's empty.
e   _____ was really happy about Jana's wedding – all her family and friends.
f   We didn't go _____ yesterday. We stayed at home.

GRAMMAR FOCUS

We use **reflexive pronouns** to draw attention to the person or people we are talking about. Reflexive pronouns always agree with the main pronoun.

- **We** prepare **our** breakfast **ourselves**.
- **He** always wants to cook everything on the barbecue **himself**.

If we do not want to emphasise the person or people who do the action, we can omit the reflexive pronoun.

- **We** prepare **our** breakfast.

We can use reflexive pronouns with a <u>preposition</u> when it is the same as the subject of the verb:

- **I** would like a flat <u>**for**</u> **myself**.

KEY TERM

reflexive pronoun: these are used to draw attention to the person or people in the sentence

3 Reading 📖

Choose a reflexive pronoun to complete the sentences.

| myself | yourself | himself | herself | ourselves | yourselves | themselves | itself |

a I always tidy my bedroom _____ – I don't expect anyone else to do it.
b Karina worked hard and bought her flat _____.
c We are going to repair the house _____, to save money.
d Ben wanted a part of the garden for _____.
e Ben and Granddad have designed the garden _____
   – it's all their own work.
f The food looks lovely – have you prepared
   it all _____?

> **Unit 2**
Clothes and leisure

IN THIS UNIT YOU WILL:

- learn vocabulary about clothes and accessories
- talk about clothes using the present simple and present continuous
- describe hobbies using the past simple and past continuous
- talk about sports events
- learn vocabulary about sport and hobbies
- practise finding information in texts.

> 2.1 What we wear

In this session you will learn vocabulary about clothes and accessories.
Accessories are small items such as belts and glasses.

1 Reading and Speaking 📖 💬 ABC XYZ

Work in pairs. Copy the table in your notebook. Put the words below into three groups:
clothes, shoes and accessories. Then look at photos a–d below. What kinds of activities
are happening? Which types of clothes or items can you see?

Clothes	Shoes	Accessories

backpack bag belt boots cap coat dress earrings glasses
gloves hat jacket jeans jewellery jumper necklace purse
raincoat sandals scarf shirt shoes shorts skirt socks suit
sunglasses tie tights T-shirt trainers trousers umbrella watch

2 Listening (track 2.1) 🎧

Listen to Alice describe the clothes she wears.
Match her description with two of the photos in Activity 1.

Answer the following questions:

a What does Alice wear to go to school?
b Why does Alice like her school uniform?
c What does Alice wear when she meets her friends?
d What type of shoes does Alice wear a lot? Why?

3 Speaking 💬 🗣️

Say these words with a partner. Can you find six minimal pairs?
Which pair of words did you hear in Activity 2?

| skirt | mouth | sheep | fan | thing | mouse | shirt | hard | thin | heart | van | ship |

4 Speaking 💬

In pairs, take turns explaining what you wear at school. Ask your partner:

• What does your uniform look like?
• What do you like about it? Why?
• What do you dislike about it? Why?

You could use these sentence starters: 'When I am at school, I wear…'
'One of the things I like about my uniform is…'

LISTENING TIP

When people give opinions, they usually follow it with a reason. Listen carefully for the key words that explain *why* they have that opinion. These words are often **adjectives**.

PRONOUNCING ENGLISH

Minimal pairs

A minimal pair is two words that sound very similar because they only have one sound that is different (for example, *mat* and *cat*)

KEY TERM

adjective: a word that describes a noun (for example, red or beautiful)

5 Reading 📖

Here are three people explaining what clothes they like to wear and why.
Read what they say. Then answer the questions.

Sophie

> I like to wear jeans.
> I feel relaxed in jeans. I don't waste time
> thinking about what to wear each day. I'm not
> very interested in fashion.

Hassan

> I play a lot of sports, so I feel most
> comfortable in shorts and trainers. I have lots
> of these type of clothes.

Chen

> I love wearing formal clothes
> like smart dresses. They make me more
> confident and feel good about myself. I don't
> really have many casual clothes.

---

waste time   feel good about myself

formal clothes   casual clothes   fitted

Which person (Sophie, Hassan or Chen) says:

a They enjoy wearing clothes that are tidy and fitted?

b They like choosing clothes quickly when they get dressed?

c They wear clothes that show something that they often do?

d Their clothes make them feel strong and positive?

e They have a large amount of clothes that are the same style?

f They don't feel so relaxed in smart clothes?

6 Writing 📝

Which of the comments in Activity 5 are closest to your attitude
to clothes? Write two comments explaining the clothes you like to
wear. Explain why you like to wear them.

For example: I like wearing jeans because they are comfortable.

› 2.2 Colours, size and shape

In this session you will practise describing clothes in different ways.

1 Speaking 💬 ABC XYZ

Look at the words for things you wear. Which colours do you think of? Compare your ideas with a partner. Do you both agree?

jewellery	a sports kit	a school uniform	casual clothes	clothes for a special occasion

black **brown** gold **green** grey orange pink
purple red silver white yellow

2 Reading 📖 ABC XYZ

a   What clothes do you prefer to wear? What clothes do you wear for different activities? Match the comments to the activities in the word box. Which are similar to your habits?

doing an outdoor activity   going shopping   **going to football practice**
going out with friends   going to a special occasion

i
I always try on clothes before I buy them. Then I don't have to send them back if they don't fit.

ii
On weekdays, I always carry my kit in a backpack and get changed at the sports club.

iii
It's important to be comfortable, so I wear loose clothes, a light raincoat and strong boots.

iv
I have a suit and a smart shirt that I always wear, and some nice black shoes.

v
I usually wear trainers, my favourite jacket, and some casual trousers – jogging bottoms or jeans. My best friend wears similar clothes to me.

b Which words and phrases from Activity 2 can you find in the Useful expressions box?

USEFUL EXPRESSIONS

it fits/it doesn't fit	it is too loose/tight	to get dressed/undressed	to try on
it is casual	the trousers are comfortable	to put on	to wear
it is smart		to take off	what size?

GRAMMAR FOCUS

We use the present simple tense to talk about facts, habits and routines (things that we do regularly and rarely change).

Look at these two examples of **affirmative** sentences from Activity 2. Notice that the verb is in the basic form.

- I **have** a suit and a smart shirt that I always **wear**…

In the third person, add **-s** to the verb:

- My best friend **wears** similar clothes to me.

Notice what happens in a **negative** sentence:

- This shirt **isn't** the right size. (using the verb, **be**)
- I always try on clothes before I buy them. Then I **don't have** to send them back if they **don't fit**.

Notice what happens when you make a question (**interrogative**) with or without question words:

- How much **is** that jacket? (using the verb, **be**)
- Which clothes **do** you **like**?
- Where **do** you **buy** your clothes?
- **Does** Bao always **buy** his clothes online? (Answer: Yes, he **does.**/No, he **doesn't.**)

Present simple tense sentences usually have time expressions or adverbs of frequency. For example:

- I *usually* **wear** trainers…
- On weekdays, I *always* **carry** my kit in a backpack…

STUDY SKILLS

Build your vocabulary with different verbs and expressions. This will help you to write and speak at a higher level. Use the Useful expressions boxes in this book to help you. Use these phrases in role plays and conversations.

KEY TERMS

affirmative: an affirmative sentence says a fact or something that is true or correct

negative: a negative sentence says that something is not correct or not true

interrogative: an interrogative sentence asks a question and has a question mark (?) at the end

3 Writing and Speaking 📝 💬

Write three sentences in your notebook describing what clothes you prefer. Then compare with a partner. Which preferences are similar? Which are different? How? Here are some sentence starters to help you:

At school, I…   When I meet friends, I…
At the weekend, I…   I usually…
When I play sport, I…   On weekdays, I…

4 Reading 📖 ᴬᴮᶜ

Luis and his mum are shopping for holiday clothes. During the trip, his dad calls his phone. Read their conversation and then answer the questions.

Dad:	Hi! Where are you?
Luis:	We're still shopping, Dad. We're looking for holiday clothes for the trip to Canada.
Dad:	Good idea. Have you seen anything yet?
Luis:	Yes, I'm trying on some walking boots now.
Dad:	What are they like? Make sure they fit you well.
Luis:	I've tried lots of pairs but these are the best. They are strong but comfortable.
Dad:	Great. Is Mum there? What's she doing?

Luis: She's looking for a raincoat for me. I tried one on in the last shop, but it was far too big.

Dad: Ok. Remember you need a hat too.

Luis: Yes, I've got one – a lovely green sun hat to keep me cool!

Dad: Good. Have fun. I'll see you both later.

Luis: Ok Dad, we'll be a while. I still need to find some trousers and a belt.

a Why is Luis shopping?
b How does Luis describe the boots he is trying on?
c What was wrong with the raincoat in the last shop?
d What three adjectives does Luis use to describe the hat?
e What does Luis still need to buy?

holiday   clothes   walking boots
tried on   raincoat

GRAMMAR FOCUS

We use the present continuous tense to show something that is happening at the moment of speaking. For example:

Notice: we use the verb, 'to **be**' (am/is/are) + **verb + ing**.

- I **am** try**ing** on some walking boots now.
- She **is** look**ing** for a raincoat.
- We **are** look**ing** for holiday clothes.

Notice: when we speak, we contract the verbs:

- I**'m** trying on…
- She**'s** looking…
- We**'re** looking…

Notice what happens in a negative sentence:

- I**'m not** buying that jacket. (I am not…)
- He **isn't** shopping at the moment. (He is not…)
- They **aren't** looking for holiday clothes in this shop (They are not…)

Notice what happens when you make a question:

- What **is** she **doing**? Or What**'s** she **doing**?
- **Is** she **trying** the boots on? (Answer: Yes, she **is**. No, she **isn't**)

5 Writing 📝 ABC XYZ

Look at the photos. You are going to write sentences about each one, using the present continuous tense and multiple adjectives.

a Read the Writing tip below and copy the table. Put the adjectives in the word box into the correct part of the table. Can you add two more adjectives to each description?

b Now write sentences for each photo. Choose interesting adjectives to describe what the people are wearing.

lovely	big	square
tiny	cotton	long
tall	horrible	short
English	thin	
rough	round	
~~old~~	modern	red
large	blue	
~~Indian~~	plastic	

WRITING TIP

When you use more than one adjective in a sentence, they need to be in the right order. Here is the order of adjectives:

	Opinion	Size	Physical quality	Shape	Age	Colour	Origin	Material	
She's wearing a	beautiful		soft				Indian	silk	shirt
He's wearing	funny				old			nylon	trousers

6 Reading and Speaking 📖 💬

a In pairs, give each other your sentences. Can your partner match your sentences to the correct photos? Then check your sentences together. Look for accurate descriptions, correct tense use and adjective order. Read the Speaking tip and make corrections if necessary.

b Now imagine why the people in the photos are wearing these clothes. What are they doing? Where are they going?

I think the man in Photo i is going to a...
Maybe the girl in Photo ii is...

SPEAKING TIP

When pointing out mistakes in a partner's work, remember to be polite. For example, use a question: 'Can you see a small mistake in this sentence?'

〉 2.3 Hobbies

In this session you will describe hobbies. Hobbies are things that people do for fun in their spare time.

1   Reading 📖

In pairs, match these four descriptions of people's hobbies to photos i–iv.

a   Majid loves climbing. He usually does it outside.

b   Adriana is a musician. Her favourite instrument is the drums.

c   Calum gets a great sense of achievement from his artwork.

d   Agata often sits outside to write her stories and poems.

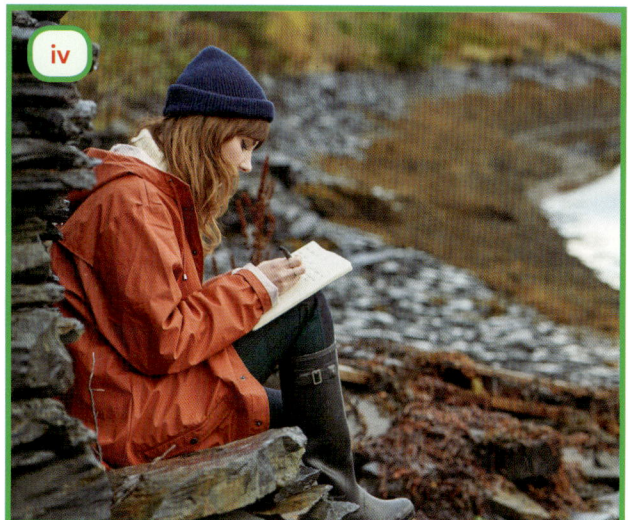

2 Listening (track 2.2) 🎧

Listen to Majid, Adriana and Calum talk about their hobbies. If something is physically demanding, it requires a lot of energy and strength.
Are these questions true or false?

a At the moment, Majid enjoys places where he can climb inside.

b For Majid, the best thing about climbing is feeling strong and fit.

c Adriana started playing the drums when she was a teenager.

d Adriana likes doing an activity that some people think is quite unusual.

e There is one part of the body that Calum finds difficult to draw.

f Calum likes winning prizes for his pictures the best.

3 Speaking 💬

In pairs, discuss your own hobbies. Ask your partner:

- What is your hobby?
- What does your hobby involve – what do you do?
- Why do you like your hobby?

4 Listening (track 2.3) 🎧

Now listen to Agata talk about her hobby. Answer the questions.

a How does Agata feel when she writes poems?

b What part of writing does she think is difficult?

c Where does she enjoy writing?

d Which member of her family has a talent for writing?

e What would she like to write in the future?

5 Reading 📖

Read the text. What is Dev's hobby? Does he describe present or past events?

> I started playing guitar when I was a little boy. When I was very young I was amazed by a musician who came to our school to do a concert. He played guitar. It was so beautiful that I ran home and asked my mum for guitar lessons. She agreed: I think she knew that I had a talent for music. She bought me my first guitar when I was six years old.
>
> Today I play in a local band with my two best friends, Ravi and Zac. I met them two years ago when I was playing in another local group. Afterwards, while we were packing away our instruments, Zac invited me to join his group with Ravi. We've been good friends ever since!

LISTENING TIP

Some listening activities require you to listen to a whole speech and find the correct answers. One way to do these activities is to listen out for sentences that are definitely *not* correct. When you listen again, there should be, a smaller number of possible correct sentences to concentrate on.

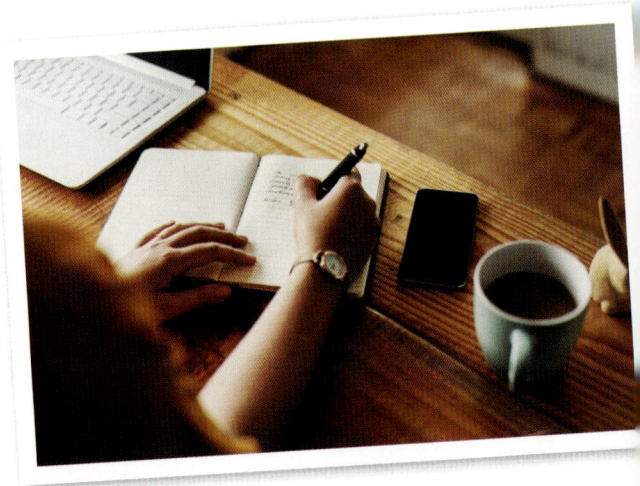

GRAMMAR FOCUS

We use the past simple tense to talk about actions and events in the past that happened at one time (and are now finished).

Look at the examples from Activity 5. Notice how the verb changes with regular and irregular verbs.

Regular verbs

* I start**ed** playing guitar when I was a little boy.

As the pronoun changes, there is <u>no</u> change to the verb:

* He play**ed** guitar.

Irregular verbs

* She **knew** that I **had** a talent for music.

Past simple sentences often have time expressions. This tells us the time of the action and that it has finished. For example:

* She **bought** me my first guitar when I was six years old.
* I **met** them two years ago…

Notice what happens in a negative sentence:

* There **weren't** (were not) many opportunities to learn a musical instrument. (using the verb, **be: was/were**)
* He **didn't** (did not) **start** playing the guitar until he was six.

Notice what happens when you make a question:

* How long **was** the concert? (using the verb, **be: was/were**)
* Which instrument **did** you **play** when you were a child?
* Where **did** Dev **learn** to **play** the guitar?
* **Did** you **know** that there are singing parts in the school play? (Answer: Yes, I **did.**/ No, I **didn't.**)

KEY TERMS

regular verb: a verb that -ed is added to when writing in past tense

irregular verb: a verb where the ending changes in past tense (for example, 'buy' becomes 'bought')

6 Reading 📖

Anisa and Beth are talking about hobbies. Copy the conversation, changing the verbs in brackets () to complete it. Which verbs are regular and irregular?

Write down the time expressions in each sentence.

Beth:	Do you still play the piano?
Anisa:	No, I ^a_____ (stop) when I was ten. I ^b_____ (like) it but it ^c_____ (be) quite difficult. I ^d_____ (want) to try something new. Soon after, I ^e_____ (begin) singing lessons. My parents ^f_____ (buy) me singing lessons for my birthday and I'm learning with a really good teacher.
Beth:	Great. Did you know that there are singing parts in the school play this year?
Anisa:	Yes, of course. I ^g_____ (do) a singing test last week and I ^h_____ (get) a part!

GRAMMAR FOCUS

We use the past continuous tense to show a continuous action that was interrupted by another action in the past. For example:

Notice: we use **was / were** (past of 'be') + **verb + ing.**

- I met them two years ago, when I **was playing** in another local group.
  (the action, met, interrupts the action, **was playing**)

- …while we **were packing** away our instruments,
  Zac invited me to join his group.
  (the action, invited, interrupts the action, **were packing**)

Notice what happens when you make a question:

- What instrument **was** he **playing** in the concert?

---

7 Writing

Copy and complete the sentences with the correct verb in the past continuous.

> practise ~~play~~ sing climb walk draw

a Adriana _was playing_ her drums when her phone rang.
b Agata suddenly had an idea for a poem, when she _____ her dog.
c As Calum _____, his pencil broke.
d Majid _____ when he hurt his leg.
e While Dev, Ravi and Zac _____, Dev's guitar broke.
f As Anisa _____ her part, the thunder started outside.

8 Writing

Write a short presentation about your hobby. Answer these questions, using past tenses:

- When did you start?
- What was the reason? Who or what made you want to do it?
- What happened next?

Include interesting information to make your audience want to hear more.
Your presentation should last 2–4 minutes.

9 Speaking

Present your description of your hobby to your class or a small group.
When you are listening to each other's presentations, listen for facts in common.

Saif and I both started playing football when we were seven years old.

❯ 2.4 Sports

These activities will help you learn vocabulary about sport.

1 Reading and Speaking 📖 💬 ABC XYZ

Look at the word box of sports and activities. Work in pairs. Copy the table. Then put the activities into the groups. Which activities are in both? How many of the activities can you see in the pictures?

athletics badminton **baseball** basketball cricket **cycling** fishing
football golf gymnastics hockey jogging rugby running
sailing skateboarding skating **skiing** **snowboarding** surfing
table tennis tennis volleyball **walking** yoga

Team activities	Individual activities

2 Speaking 💬 ABC XYZ

Tick the sports or activities in Activity 1 that you have tried. Compare with your partner. Ask each other:

- Which activities did you enjoy? Why?
- Which other sports and activities do you do? How do you feel about them?

I love playing football. I enjoy it because my team often win.

I really like swimming. It makes my body feel strong and full of energy.

I don't mind doing yoga. I find it relaxing and it's good for you.

I enjoy playing golf. The golf course is so green and beautiful.

I don't enjoy playing hockey. I find it difficult to control the ball.

STUDY SKILLS

Many speaking activities ask you to give opinions about how you feel about things. Develop different phrases to talk about these types of opinions. Doing this will give your speech some detail and variety.

SPEAKING TIP

Look back at Session 1.4 for verbs to describe likes and dislikes.

3 Reading 📖

People often enjoying watching sport. Read Harry's description of a game of football. Then answer the questions.

The final minute

It was the last game of the season for our football team. We needed to win this game. Then we would win the competition and be champions. My dad has been a supporter of this football club for thirty years. I have supported them since I was seven. This was the best season ever. As we sat down to watch, I was feeling nervous.

There was ten minutes before the end of the game and still no score. Then, in the last minute, our brilliant player, Johnson, scored a goal. All of the fans were so happy! We jumped up and down laughing and singing. We stayed at the end and were allowed on the football pitch to take photos. It was great to see the team and the coach finally win a medal.

a How long has Harry been a fan of the team?

   i for seven years   **ii** since he was a child   **iii** for 30 years

b At the start of the game, Harry felt:

   i happy   **ii** excited   **iii** worried

c Johnson scored his goal:

   i ten minutes before the end   **ii** after the other team scored   **iii** when the game was almost finished

d What did the supporters do after the end of the game?

   i They took photos.   **ii** They gave the team a medal.   **iii** They laughed and sang.

READING TIP

Some words have the same spelling but different meanings. For example, 'season' can mean **1** a time of the year, such as summer; **2** the series of games played in a year in sport. When you check words in a dictionary, always make sure you choose the right meaning of that word.

4 Listening (track 2.4) 🎧

Do you discuss sports games with your friends? Listen to Ezra and Nathan discussing a basketball match. Answer the questions.

a What time did the basketball game begin?

b How did Ezra watch the game?

c What did his family eat during the game?

d What did he enjoy most about the game?

e In Ezra's opinion, how has Jay Diaz made a difference to the team?

5 Speaking 💬

In pairs, create a role play to discuss a sports match or event. Use Ezra and Nathan's conversation and the questions to help you.

- Start by deciding who will ask questions and who will answer.
- The partner who answers should use the role play to practise explaining things in detail.

Use questions a–e on the card for the role play.

Role play: sports game

Setting: you are friends who are discussing a sports game.

a What time did the sports game start?

b Did you watch it on television or did you go the live game?

c What did you eat and drink during the game?

d What did you enjoy about the game?

e Was there anything you didn't enjoy?

> **SPEAKING TIP**
>
> A role play is when you act a situation with a partner, asking and answering questions. This develops your conversation skills.
>
> When you ask questions in a role play, help your partner out. If they find a question hard, try to ask it again in a different way.

6 Speaking 💬

Now change roles and do the role play again. You could discuss another sports game or event. Use the activity to give feedback to each other. Tell each other what you did well and discuss what you would like to improve.

ENGLISH AROUND THE WORLD

When international football matches are played, referees often speak good English. If a referee doesn't speak the language of the teams who are playing each other, then they will talk to players in English. If you train to be an international referee, you will also need to understand Spanish, French and German.

> 2.5 Things to do

This session will help you learn about things that people like to do in their spare time, when they aren't studying or working.

1 Reading and Speaking 📖 💬 ABC XYZ

Work in pairs. Copy the table. Then put the free-time activities into the different parts of the table. Which do you do in your spare time?

Media entertainment	Cultural activities	Creative activities

> listen to music on headphones   watch TV and online videos
> write short stories   play an instrument   go to the theatre
> go to concerts or music festivals

SPEAKING TIP

When you talk about any type of activity, look for ways that you can make your answer longer. For example, you could talk about how long it takes, where you do it, who you do it with, what you wear and what equipment you need.

2 Speaking 💬

a   Work in pairs. Talk about activities you do in your spare time. Ask each other questions to make your answers longer. Use the question starters below to help you.

> What activities do you do in your spare time?

> When did you start...?

> How often do...?

> What equipment do...?

> Who do...?

> Where...?

> What do ... wear?

b   Look at the musical instruments below. Which ones do you know or play? Which do you like best? Why? What other musical instruments do you know?

> flute   guitar   piano   trumpet   violin   clarinet

3 Reading and Speaking 📖 💬 ABC XYZ

How much TV do you watch? Or do you prefer watching programmes online? Here are four people describing the types of programmes they like to watch. First, discuss the meaning of the underlined words and phrases with a partner.

romantic   comedies
thrillers   musician

Sara: I like watching romantic films. Sometimes these films make me cry, but they usually have a <u>happy ending</u>.

Kai: After a day at school, I love watching comedies. I like them because they <u>make me laugh</u> and make me feel happier.

Olivia: I'm a <u>musician</u>, so I love watching music concerts on TV. I learn useful tips from watching other musicians. I enjoy watching how they play and perform.

Anton: I really think that thrillers are the best type of TV programme. I love it when they are so scary that I am <u>on the edge of my seat</u>!

4 Reading and Speaking 📖 💬 ABC XYZ

Here is a page from a magazine listing TV programmes. Which programmes would Sara, Kai, Olivia and Anton like? Share your answers with a partner.

series   mysterious
dramatic   detective
bands

TONIGHT'S TV

6 PM — FAST AND FUNNY
This is another programme from the funny Smith Brothers series.

7 PM — FAMILY TIES
An hour of love and sadness in the exciting lives of the Bass family.

8 PM — JOHN COOPER SMITH
A brilliant new series about a detective whose own life is a mystery, just like the criminals he tries to catch.

9 PM — FESTIVAL LIVE!
Tonight's programme has lots of exciting new bands from around the world.

10 PM — WHO'S THERE?
New series. A dangerous and very exciting story about lives on the edge.

5 Speaking 💬

In pairs, talk about a TV programme or film you have watched.
Ask your partner:

- What is the name of the programme or film?
- When did you watch it?
- What was it about?
- Why did you like it?

Last night, I watched a programme called... It was about a guy who... I love it because it is...

6 Reading 📖 ABC XYZ

Your school has decided to offer some new creative after-school clubs.
Read the list and choose one of the clubs that you would like to attend.

Monday

Creative writing session with Mr Ruiz. Do you have a novel or idea for a film? Mr Ruiz will teach you how to bring your ideas to life on the page.

Tuesday

Games club with Miss Khan. Play all your favourite board games with your friends. You can learn new ones too. Mr Pike is also running a chess workshop at the Games club. A great opportunity to learn this ancient game.

Wednesday

School band with Mrs Novak. Our aim is to enter the city School Bands Competition next year, so we need to start practising now! We need some new guitar players especially.

Thursday

Film club with Mr Ross. If you like to watch and talk about movies, this is the club for you. Watch the best films of the moment and share your opinions in the lively online discussion on the school website.

workshop
board games
chess   opportunity
ancient

Here is a form for the school clubs. Copy and complete your own form.

SCHOOL CLUB FORM

First name	Cami
Last name	Ramirez
Age	15
Club you would like to join	School band
Name of teacher	Mrs Novak
Why do you want to join this club?	I want to have more opportunities to play my guitar.

WRITING TIP

Some answers in a form only require one or two words. Some answers require you to write in sentences. Make sure you understand what is required in each part of a form.

PROJECT

What activities would you like to try in the future? They could be sports, hobbies or other things you might do in your spare time. In groups, talk about these activities. Choose one activity each and make your own notes on:

- the type of activity – what is it?
- what equipment or other things you might need to do it
- why you would like to try the activity.

Next, present your activity to the group. Use your notes to help you. Listen carefully to everybody's ideas and then decide which activity would be the most interesting to try.

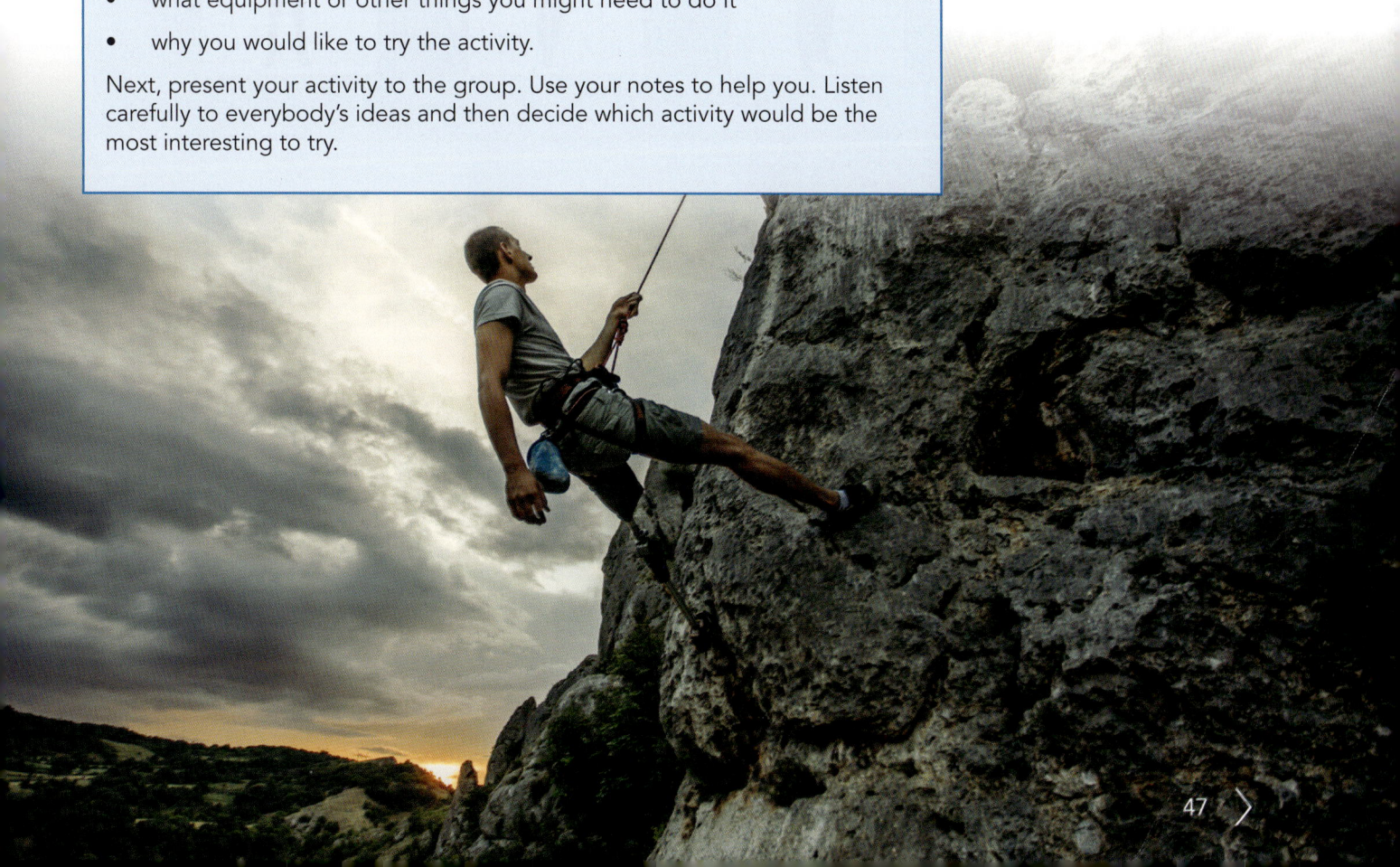

EXAM-STYLE QUESTIONS:

Listening practice (track 2.5)

Listen to Sam talk about a sport he would like to try. Answer the questions below. Choose the correct answers.

a What sport would Sam like to try?

i  ii  iii  iv    [1]

b Where did Sam see people play this sport?

i  ii  iii  iv    [1]

c Which piece of equipment does Sam not need?

i  ii  iii  iv    [1]

d Who thinks the sport is dangerous?

i 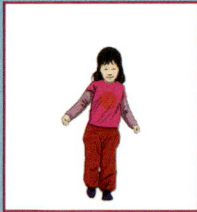 ii 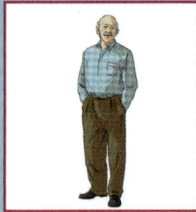 iii  iv    [1]

[Total: 4]

CHECK YOUR PROGRESS

How confident do you feel about what you have learned and practised in this unit?
How many of the things below could you do?

1 Name ten items of clothes.
2 Give an example of present simple tense and present continuous tense.
3 Give two examples of irregular verbs.
4 Name ten types of sport.
5 Think of a TV programme you enjoy. Give four details about it.

Rate yourself from 1 (not confident) to 5 (very confident).

Which things would you like to learn more about?
Which things would you like to practise again?

Share your thoughts with a partner.

〉 Grammar practice

Regular past tense verbs

> **GRAMMAR FOCUS**
>
> We form the **past simple** tense, with the base of the verb + **-ed**. Look at these examples from Unit 2:
>
> - Recently, I **started** to write poems and I really love it.
> - He **played** acoustic guitar.
> - We **jumped** up and down cheering and singing.
>
> When we say the **-ed** endings of past tense verbs, we pronounce them in three different ways. For example:
>
> | /t/ | /d/ | /id/ |
> | --- | --- | --- |
> | jumped | played | started |

1 Reading and Speaking 📖 💬 ABC XYZ

Work in pairs. Look at the past simple forms in the word box.
Which verbs do they come from? Which verbs do you know?

> achieved   approached   arranged   asked for   borrowed   chatted
> climbed   completed   contacted   continued   copied   covered   delayed
> dreamed   dried   dropped   encouraged   ended   filled   finished
> followed   hugged   hurried   increased   invited   jumped   kicked
> kissed   laughed   lied   loaned   looked   missed   mixed   needed
> pulled   pushed   reminded   rented   screamed   shouted   smiled
> smoked   thanked   turned   worried

2 Listening (track 2.6) 🎧

Listen to the pronunciation of each past simple form. Which sound do you hear at the end? Copy the table and write the verb forms in the correct part of the table.

/t/	/d/	/id/
jumped	played	started

3 Speaking 💬

Now ask and answer these questions with your partner. Remember to use the correct pronunciation when you use a regular past simple verb. Use the sentence starters to help you.

a Last term, what was the best grade that you achieved?

Last term I achieved an 'A' in Maths...

b Which projects did you do?

We did a History project on...

c Who encouraged you the most with your studies?

My older brother really helped me a lot last term. He...

d Which topics did you cover in English?

Last term, we covered...

Prepositions before nouns

GRAMMAR FOCUS

A preposition is a word which shows a <u>link</u> between a noun and other parts of the sentence; this often indicates information such as location or time. Look at these examples from Unit 2. The examples show how common prepositions, **at**, **in** and **on**, can be used before nouns within specific topics:

Location

Preposition + noun phrases that describe places and where things are, often use the preposition **at**:

- I like climbing. I started when I was five, **at** an indoor climbing centre.
- I was **at** football practice.

Time

Preposition + noun phrases that describe when things happen, also often use the preposition **at**:

- I missed the basketball game because it started **at** two o'clock.

Clothes

When we describe how someone is dressed, we can use the preposition **in**:

- I feel relaxed **in** jeans.
- ...so I feel most comfortable **in** shorts and trainers.

Communication

The preposition **on** is used in phrases connected with the media and ways to communicate:

- Did you see the basketball **on** TV yesterday?
- ...share your opinions in the lively online discussion **on** the school website.

In examples such as these, the noun is the object of the preposition.

Remember: when you are learning how prepositions link to nouns, it is helpful to learn examples within specific themes like this. Noticing these patterns can help you learn how to use prepositions before nouns correctly.

---

4 Reading 📖

Billy and Jamal are chatting about a football match.
Copy and complete the conversation with the correct prepositions below.

> in   at   on

Billy: Did you go to the football match ª_____ the new stadium last weekend?

Jamal: Yes, it was great! Did you watch it ᵇ_____ TV?

Billy: No, but I listened to it ᶜ_____ the radio with my dad. We were in the car, going to see my cousins ᵈ_____ their new house. It was raining a lot during the game, wasn't it?

Jamal: Yes, I was only dressed ᵉ_____ shorts and a T-shirt, so I got a bit wet! My older brother was ᶠ_____ a big raincoat, so he was fine. He kept laughing at me!

Billy: And that new player, Kovic, scored the winning goal ᵍ_____ 2.57 - just before the end of the game!

Jamal: Yes, he's great. After the game, there were lots of comments ʰ_____ social media about him. Everybody loves him!

Prepositions after nouns

GRAMMAR FOCUS

Some nouns are followed by a **preposition**, which connects the noun to other ideas in the sentence. These are called **dependent prepositions**. Here are some examples from Unit 2:

- Calum gets a great sense of achievement **from** his art work.
- My dad has been a supporter **of** this football club for thirty years.
- Last year, I was very surprised when I won a prize **for** one of my paintings.
- I think she knew that I had a talent **for** music.
- He's made a huge difference **to** the team.

Sometimes nouns have more than one dependent preposition:

- What is the difference **between** football and rugby?

Remember: when you are recording vocabulary, record any dependent prepositions too and learn the words together. Look in a good dictionary to find out which nouns have dependent prepositions.

KEY TERM

dependent preposition: a preposition that is used next to a noun, verb or adjective

5 Reading 📖

Here are some common noun and dependent prepositions. Copy the words and choose the correct preposition to match the noun. The first one has been done for you.

a equipment for/~~about~~

b information of/about

c example on/of

6 Writing and Speaking 📝 💬

Now copy and complete these questions about school. Add the correct preposition from Activity 5. Then choose three questions to ask a partner.

a Where can someone find information _____ your school?

b Can you give an example _____ a subject you like at school?

c What do you think is the best equipment _____ studying?

d What are the similarities _____ your school and other schools in your area?

Unit 3
Food and health

IN THIS UNIT YOU WILL:

- learn vocabulary about food
- write about different meals using the different persons of a verb
- practise reading texts about food
- use modal verbs to talk about food and health
- describe people
- listen to people talk about food and health.

> 3.1 Food and drinks

Use these activities to learn vocabulary about drinks and snacks.

1 Reading and Speaking 📖 💬 ABC XYZ

a   Work in pairs. Copy the table into your notebook. Then write the words in the box in the correct group.

Types of drinks	Things you use to eat or drink	Types of food

> biscuit   bowl   burger   cereal   chips   chocolate   chopsticks   cola
> coffee   crisps   cup   fork   glass   honey   ice cream   jelly   juice
> knife   milk   mug   pan   pasta   pizza   plate   pot   sandwich   saucer
> seafood   snacks   spoon   sweets   tea   toast   water   yoghurt

b   In your pairs, talk about photos i–v. Which things from the word box can you see?

2 Speaking 💬

Look at the pictures in Activity 1 again. In pairs, discuss with your partner:

• When would you eat these types of food? Which meal or occasion?
• Which foods do you like? Which do you eat regularly?
• Are there any foods that you don't like, or never eat? Why not?
• Are there any foods that are typical of your country or region?

3 Reading 📖 ABC XYZ

The Patak family are talking about food. Which meals do they mention?

Work in pairs. What do the underlined phrases mean?

Mum:	I'm going to prepare some lunch. Is anyone hungry?
Mia:	Yes, I am! I'm thirsty too.
Mum:	Well, have a drink now. Then I'll get lunch ready.
Martha:	I don't want any lunch yet. I'm still full. I had a big breakfast.
Mia:	I thought you were on a diet?
Martha:	No, I'm not on a diet. I don't want to lose weight, just eat more healthily. Less sugar and more fruit and vegetables.
Mum:	Good idea. For lunch, I'm serving soup as a starter and then chicken with a nice big salad as a main course. Martha, are you sure you don't want any?

4 Speaking 💬 ABC XYZ

Work in pairs. Ask each other these questions. Use the phrases in the Useful expressions box to help you. How similar or different are your answers?

a What do you usually have for breakfast?
b What do you often have for lunch at school?
c What does your family usually serve for dinner?
d When do you get very hungry or thirsty?
e Do you know anyone who is on a diet? What kind of diet is it?
f Who prepares the food and gets meals ready in your family?

USEFUL EXPRESSIONS

To be full: I am full. I have had too many chips.

To be hungry: I am hungry. I would like some chicken.

To be thirsty: I'd like something to drink. I will have a lemonade.

To have a drink: I will have a drink with my burger.

CONTINUED

To get lunch/dinner ready: I need to get lunch ready for midday.

To go on a diet: I want to eat less sugar, so I will go on a diet.

To have breakfast/lunch/dinner: It's time to have lunch.

To prepare food: I'm going to prepare some vegetables for dinner.

To serve: I will serve ice cream for dessert.

5 Speaking and Writing 💬 📝 ABC XYZ

a What adjectives can you use to describe food? Work in pairs.

- Which of the adjectives in the word box describe someone's opinion about food?

- Which ones describe the taste?

| huge   sweet   amazing   sour   horrible   bitter |

b Some adjectives are made by adding a **-y** to a noun. Copy and complete this table.

Noun	Adjective
taste	
	oily
salt	
	spicy

6 Listening (track 3.1) 🎧

a Listen to these students giving opinions about food. Write the sentences in your notebook. Then number them in the order that you hear them. Underline the adverbs.

i I don't like cakes. They are too sweet.

ii …that coffee was so bitter.

iii My favourite food is my mum's home-made ice cream. It is very tasty.

b Copy the sentences in your notebook. Then listen again and write down the missing words.

i Anika likes _____. She says it is _____ _____ .

ii Tom does not like _____ . He says it is _____ _____ .

iii Rose did not like her _____. It was _____ _____ .

iv Ahmed enjoyed his _____ . It was _____ _____.

WRITING TIP

When you change a noun ending in -e, to an adjective ending in **-y**, you usually delete the -e.

- *spice = spicy*

SPEAKING TIP

If you want to describe the size or taste of something, you can put these adverbs in front of an adjective: *very, too, so, really*.

7 Speaking 💬

Work in pairs. Can you think of a food example for each adjective in Activity 5?
Then use the adjectives to give your opinions about types of food.

I made a cheese sauce last week, but it was too salty.

8 Reading 📖

Clare recently visited a new café. Read her review of her visit.
Are the sentences true or false? Can you correct the false sentences?

a   Clare has now been to the café twice.

b   Clare thought the café served delicious food and drink.

c   Ayesha doesn't eat food with meat.

d   Ayesha wasn't happy with the food in the café.

e   Both girls ordered dishes that were made with eggs.

f   Clare liked everything about her experience at the café.

9 Writing 📝

Write a short review for a café. Use the review in Activity 8 to help you. Use food words, adverbs and adjectives from the activities in this session. Use these questions to organise your review:

* What is the name of the café? How many times have you visited?
* Who did you go with?
* What did you eat and drink?
* Did you enjoy the food? Why? Why not?

Green Café

◉◉◉◉◉ 1372 reviews | #5 of 2350 Cafe | 🖥 Website ↗

◉◉◉◉◉ Reviewed by: Clare T   📱 via mobile

Date of visit: 1st February

A friend and I had lunch at the Green Café yesterday. It was my second visit. The food was very tasty, but, unfortunately, the coffee wasn't so good. We both thought it was too bitter.

My friend, Ayesha, is a vegetarian and she thought that the café offered some good vegetarian dishes. She had vegetable soup and then an egg salad. I had soup too, and then a tomato and cheese omelette.

In general, we enjoyed our visit, but they need to improve the coffee!

ENGLISH AROUND THE WORLD

It is no surprise that many English words are often used in other languages, especially in European countries. Some examples include 'le selfie' (in French), 'call' (a business call in Italian) and 'footing' (means 'jogging' in Spanish). Words such as 'OK' and 'cool' are used in many European languages by people of all ages. These words are known as 'loan words'. English, of course, has many loan words too, especially to talk about food (pizza, ketchup, chocolate).

> 3.2 Meals

In this session you will read and write about different meals.

1 Reading and Speaking 📖 💬 ABC XYZ

These words are all types of food.

> apple apricot banana beans cabbage carrot
> chicken coconut cucumber garlic grape lamb
> lemon lettuce mango melon mushroom onion orange
> peach pear pepper pineapple plum potato raspberry
> sausage steak strawberry tomato watermelon

a Copy and complete this table, putting the foods in the correct group.
Add two more words to each section.

Fruit	Vegetables	Meat
apple	cabbage	steak

b Then work in pairs and ask each other:

- Which foods do you eat regularly?
- Which foods do you sometimes eat?
- Which ones do you never eat? Why not?

2 Speaking 💬

Read the Speaking tip. In pairs, use the following prepositional phrases and if clauses in bold to talk about your eating habits. Compare your habits. Which are similar and which are different?

- **In the morning,** I usually eat…
- **At lunch time,** I often have…
- **For dinner,** I…

- **If it's the weekend**, my family…
- **If I eat with my friends**, we…
- **If**…

3 Reading 📖

Read Beth's description of her family's attitude to food. Which sentences are true for your family too?

My family loves food! We have our best times around the dinner table – chatting, laughing or spending time with our family or friends. If you come to our house, there will always be something wonderful to eat! Both my mum and dad love cooking. They share the cooking at home and I am learning to cook too. I really like trying different dishes and food from other countries. My sister, Millie, is not so brave. She prefers food that she knows she likes. If Millie tries something new, everyone is very surprised. My dad is teaching her to cook as well. He thinks that it will encourage her to try different types of food.

GRAMMAR FOCUS

All persons of verbs – singular and plural

There are six different persons that are used with verbs in English: first person singular and plural; second person singular and plural; third person singular and plural.

'Person' = the subject of the sentence; noun or pronoun

There is little difference in verb endings according to the 'person' of the verb, except for the verb, 'be', which is irregular.

Look at these examples from Beth's description in Activity 3:

First person = 'I' (singular pronoun) or 'we' (plural pronoun)

- **I** am learning to cook too. (I = subject)
- **We** have our best times around the dinner table. (We = subject)

Second person = 'you' (singular and plural)

- If **you** come to our house… (you = subject)

Third person = 'he', she', 'it' (singular); 'they' (plural) or nouns.

Notice: the regular verb ending adds 's' in third person singular, but not in third person plural.

- **My sister, Millie,** is not so brave. (My sister, Millie, (noun) = subject)
- **She** prefers food that she knows she likes. (She = subject)
- **He** thinks that it will encourage her… (He = subject)
- **My family** loves food! (My family = noun)
- **They** share the cooking at home. (They = subject)

4 Writing 📝

Can you describe your family's attitude to food? Write a paragraph, with a sentence for each family member, including yourself. Write in the present tense and remember to use the correct pronoun. Then compare with a partner and check each other's use of nouns and pronouns.

WRITING TIP

When writing about others, remember there are different ways to name them. For example, by their name ('Millie'), a pronoun ('she') or their relationship to you ('my sister'). Try to use these in different ways to make your writing more interesting.

5 Listening (track 3.2) 🎧 ABC XYZ

What is your favourite café? What kind of food does it serve? Listen to Rosa's conversation with a waiter in a cafe. She orders some food for herself and her younger brother. How similar or different is it to your favourite café?

Listen and choose the correct answer:

a   What drink does Rosa order for herself?

   i   sparkling water

   ii lemonade

   iii orange juice

b   What drink does Rosa order for her brother?

   i   sparkling water

   ii lemonade

   iii orange juice

c   What food does Rosa want?

   i   A pizza

   ii A burger

   iii A salad

d   What food does Rosa order for her brother?

   i   A pizza

   ii A burger

   iii A salad

GRAMMAR FOCUS

Modal verbs, **would** and **will.**

We can use **would** to make polite requests and offers.

- **Would** you like to order some drinks?
- I'**d** (would) like some water…
- **Would** you like some food too? Yes, we would.
- What **would** he like?

Notice: when we speak, we often contract **would** to '**d**:

- I'**d** like some water…

We can use **will** to talk about a decision that is spontaneous (at the moment of speaking).

- My brother will have lemonade.

Notice: when we speak, we often contract **will** to '**ll**:

- Shall I have a salad? No! I'**ll** have the four cheese pizza, please!

6 Reading 📖

Put the lines of the conversation into the correct order. Which lines are for the waiter? Which are the customer's?

a I'd like the noodle salad, please, and some cola.

b Ok. Would you like the chicken in your salad, or on the side?

c Hello. What would you like to order?

d Would you like ice in the cola?

e Great! Thank you.

f Er… I'll have it in my salad, please.

g Yes, please. Oh… and I'll have some chicken, please.

PRONOUNCING ENGLISH

Intonation in questions

When we ask a wh- question, our voice usually rises and then falls at the end. When we ask a yes/no question, our voice usually rises at the end.

---

7 Speaking 💬 🗣

Listen and write the questions from Activity 6. Can you mark the intonation? Listen again and repeat with a partner.

Would you like to order some drinks?

8 Writing 📝

Imagine you are at your favourite café. What would the waiter say? What would you order? Write a short conversation. Use **would** and **will**, and the examples in Activities 5 and 6 to help you.

9 Speaking 💬

Work in pairs. Act out each other's conversations in a role play. Student A is the waiter; Student B is the customer. Then change roles. Afterwards, think about which parts of your role play went well and which need more practice. Give each other some feedback.

SPEAKING TIP

When you meet someone, saying 'hello' or 'hi' is usual. You should also use words and phrases such as 'please' and 'thank you', to be polite. Practise using these in your role play.

› 3.3 Food shopping

In this session you will talk about food shopping and future events.

1 Reading 📖 ABC XYZ

Ben is going shopping for food. His shopping list got wet, so he cannot read it. Can you read what each word says? Compare your answers in pairs.

Shopping list
Cau••f•ower
M••go
Pe•ch
Pe••er
B•tte•
Ch••se
•gg•
Chi••en
R•ce

2 Listening (track 3.3) 🎧

Listen to Ben and Claudia talk about food shopping. Which items from Ben's list in Activity 1 do they mention? Then listen again and answer the questions:

a   Why does Claudia say that they need cakes?
b   What kind of strawberries does Claudia ask Ben to get?
c   Which supermarket does she tell him to go to?
d   Name two vegetables Ben says he will buy.
e   Name two things Claudia reminds Ben to take shopping.

LISTENING TIP

When people talk about food, they often use words to describe amounts. For example:

We need some bread – we've only got a **quarter** of a loaf left…

…we can have **half** a pizza each when we eat tonight…

STUDY SKILLS

Develop your listening skills by hearing as many natural conversations as you can. Listen to the way real conversations sound.

Real conversations are usually more relaxed than writing. Listen to the way people ask and answer questions in conversation with words such as 'ok' and 'right'. These words confirm that the speakers understand each other's comments.

GRAMMAR FOCUS

Modal verbs, can, could, need, need not (needn't).

We can use **can** and **could** to make direct requests. We follow **can** and **could** with the verb (without 'to'):

- **Can** you get some rice, chicken, coconut milk and red chillies?
- **Can** you buy flour, jam, sugar and butter too?

We can use **could** to make more polite requests, or if the request is more difficult.

- I'd like some strawberries. **Could** you get some of those big ones? They are a bit more expensive.

We can use **need** to talk about something that is necessary.

- …what do we **need** at the shops?

Notice: when **need** is followed by a verb, we add '<u>to</u>'.

- We also **need** to make some cakes…

We can use **don't need**, **need not** or **needn't** to talk about something that is **not** necessary.

- You **don't need** to go to that big one – go to the small supermarket.

Notice: can, could and **need** stay the same with all pronouns (<u>I, you, he, she, it, we, they</u>). **Remember:** with **need**, use **don't** or **doesn't** according to the subject of the sentence.

- <u>Ben</u> **doesn't need** to take cash to the supermarket – <u>he</u> can use his card to pay.
- <u>I</u> **don't need** to buy a new plastic shopping bag – <u>I</u> can reuse one.

3 Writing 📝

Copy the sentences, choosing the correct modal verb to complete them. Remember to change the verb form if necessary.

> can   could   need   not need

a   Claudia <u>doesn't need</u> to visit the supermarket – Ben will go.

b   _____ you get some milk? There isn't any in the fridge.

c   Do we _____ any pasta? No, there is a big packet in the cupboard.

d   _____ you buy some of those expensive chocolates?

e   We _____ to buy any more apples – there are already plenty on the table.

f   _____ you get some shopping for Grandma? She's not feeling very well.

4 Speaking 💬 ABC XYZ

Look again at some items on Ben and Claudia's shopping list. Which items do you and your family eat regularly? Which items are new to you? Compare with a partner.

> cauliflower   peppers   coconut milk   **butter**   cheese
> **eggs**   chicken   rice   red chillies

5 Reading 📖

Read the comments about the shopping list. Which comments do you agree with? Which do you think are most possible?

> I think Claudia and Ben **might** make a chicken curry.

> They **may** cook a chicken pasta dish.

> They **could** prepare different kinds of omelettes with those ingredients.

> They **might** just prepare chicken and vegetables. They **might not** have time to prepare anything else.

GRAMMAR FOCUS

Modal verbs, might, may, could

We can use **might, may** and **could** to talk about something that we think is possible.

- I think Claudia and Ben **might** make a chicken curry.
- They **may** cook a chicken pasta dish.
- They **could** prepare different kinds of omelettes with those ingredients.

All of these sentences are saying 'It is a possibility, in my opinion.'

We can use **might** and **may** in the negative form: **might not/may not.**

- They **might not** have time to prepare anything else.

Notice:

- **might, may** and **could** are followed by another verb in the base form.
- **might, may** and **could** stay the same with all pronouns (I, you, he, she, it, we, they).

6 Writing

Look at the photos. When might you eat this type of food? What occasion do you think is taking place? Write a sentence for each photo. Then compare your ideas with your partner. How far did you agree?

It might be a _____ cake.

They may...

It could...

They...

7 Speaking

Work in pairs. Imagine you are going to prepare a special meal for members of your family or some friends. You are going to create a role play to plan the shopping. Use Ben and Claudia's conversation from Activity 2 to help you. Discuss first:

- Who are you going to cook for? How many people?
- What dishes are you going to have? What food will you need to buy? Do you already have some food that you can use?

Read the cards for further information.

FRIEND A	FRIEND B
You are offering to do the shopping for the meal:	You are not going with your friend but you have a lot of suggestions about the shopping.
You could say things such as:	You could say things such as:
'What do we need from the shops?'	'Can you get a / some… please?'
'I'll get some...'	'Can you buy… too?'
	'Could you…?'
	'We need…'

SPEAKING TIP

In real conversation, people regularly use each other's names. They often start bits of speech like this: 'Claudia, what do we need from the shops?' or 'Ben, don't forget to take some money…'. Try opening some parts of speech like this – but don't do it too much!

If you feel confident, perform your role play for the class. Practise using modals in your speech. Listen to several role plays and decide which special meal you would like to go to.

〉 3.4 The body

In this session you will learn vocabulary about the body and how to talk about appearance.

1 Writing 📝 ABC XYZ

Draw the shape of a person. Draw the person using the words below.
Compare your drawings with a partner.

> ankle   arm   back   beard   chest   ear   eye   face   finger
> left foot   right foot   left hand   right hand   head   heart   knee   leg
> mouth   moustache   neck   nose   shoulder   throat   toe   tooth

2 Reading 📖

Read the descriptions of Zarveen and Chenhua. Which words from Activity 1 are mentioned? Read again and find one mistake in each description. Can you correct the mistakes?

This is Zarveen. He has dark eyes and a short grey beard with a moustache too. He's wearing glasses and a black hat. The weather is quite cool, so he's wearing a blue shirt and a light white coat with blue and red stripes. He's writing a message on his phone with his right hand.

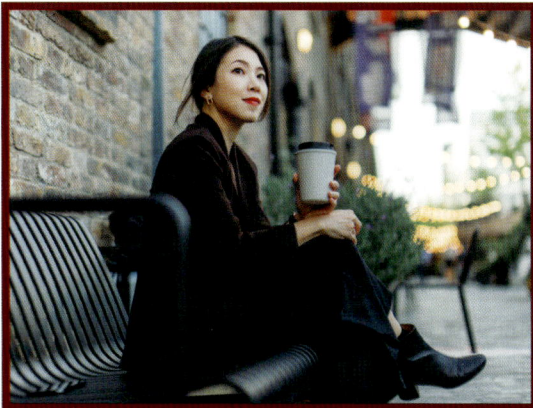

This is Chenhua. She's got brown eyes and long dark hair, which is tied back. If you look at her ears, you can see that she is wearing earrings. It's a cold day, so she's wearing a smart brown jacket and boots. She's holding a coffee cup in her right hand.

3 Speaking 💬

Work in pairs. Describe someone to your partner, but do not say their name. Describe something about their appearance and what they are doing at the moment. Include one mistake. Can your partner guess who it is and correct the mistake?

4 Reading 📖 ABC XYZ

Match the descriptions with the people in photos i-iv. Everyone has a problem with a part of their body. Which description does not match a picture?

a Hanna has short grey hair and dark eyes. She is wearing a gold wedding ring. Today she's not well because she has a toothache.

b Ian has short dark hair and a beard. He is lying down. He's normally healthy but today he's got a cold and sore throat. He can't speak loudly.

c Mick is sitting down because he has injured his left ankle. He can't stand up. You can see his blue football boots.

d Kerry has dark hair and she is wearing a white t-shirt. She's hurt herself. She was working in her garage when she cut her finger. As you can see, the skin is red.

e Bill has injured his right foot. He fell down when he was playing football and he couldn't get up easily. Now his foot hurts when he touches it. On his left leg, he is wearing one orange sock and one black boot.

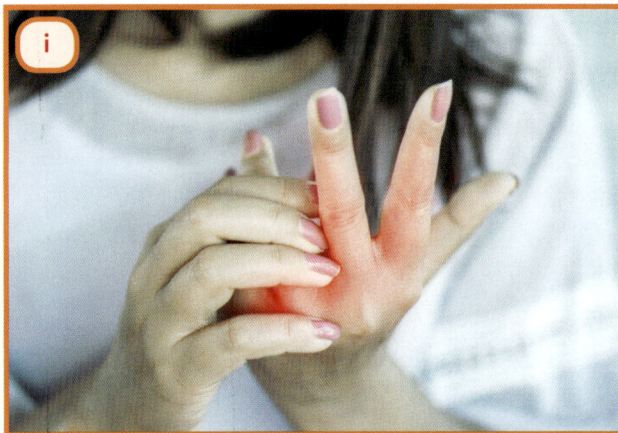

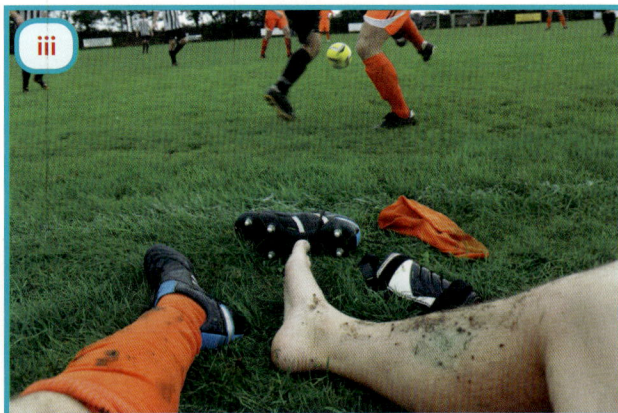

5 Listening (track 3.4) 🎧

Listen and match each conversation to a photo from Activity 4.

GRAMMAR FOCUS

Modal verbs, should, should not (shouldn't), must, must not (mustn't)

We can use **should** and **should not (shouldn't)** to give advice.

- You **should** have some soup.
- You **shouldn't** eat any hard food.

We can use **must** and **must not (mustn't)** to talk about strong obligation **(must)** or prohibition **(mustn't)**.

- …you **must** go to the dentist!
- You **mustn't** try to walk on it.

Note: all of these modal verbs are followed by another verb in the base form.

These verbs all stay the same with all pronouns (I, you, he, she, it, we, they).

---

6 Reading 📖

Match the children's problems in a-e with the most suitable advice in i-v.

a   My eyes are really sore.

b   Junaid has got a bad headache.

c   Elena has got a sore throat.

d   Arlo has had a stomach ache for two weeks now.

e   Maryam's left foot is hurting.

i   He should rest in a dark room.

ii   She shouldn't wear those trainers any more – they are too small.

iii That is a long time. He must go to the doctor!

iv   She should eat soft food, maybe some ice cream.

v   You mustn't spend any more time on your computer.

READING AND LISTENING TIP

Look out for the verb, **can** and **could**, in reading and listening texts and notice the different uses. In Session 3.3, we saw examples of **can** used to make requests; **can** and **could** are also used to talk about:

ability:

- Usually I **can** work when I have a cold.
- He **can't** stand up.   (negative)
- He **couldn't** get up easily.   (negative past simple)

possibility:

- As you **can** see, the skin is red.

permission:

- **Can** I have a look?

---

7 Speaking 💬

Work in pairs. Read the sentences about feelings. What do the underlined phrases mean? Can you give one more piece of advice to each person? Compare your answers with another pair.

a   I have been very busy today. <u>I am so tired</u>.

b   Katy was playing hockey at the weekend. Unfortunately, she <u>broke her leg</u>.

c   I'm <u>feeling very lazy</u> at the moment. I think I need <u>to do some exercise</u>.

d   I'm not feeling very well. I need <u>to get some fresh air</u>.

You should try …

Katy mustn't …

8 Reading 📖 ABC XYZ

a   Jaya is writing an email to her Aunt Bhavna with some photos from a family party. What was the special occasion? Answer the questions.

New message

← → ↻   ≡

Hi Aunt Bhavna,

I thought you might like to see some photos from Rahul's birthday last weekend. As you can see, my brother is as funny as ever. You might not recognise him because he has a bald head now. He lost his hair about five years ago. He has a young son now, Arjun. He's such a kind and loving little boy, and clever too. You can see him at the front, on the left, in the blue and white shirt.

Also to the left of the photo is Rahul's wife, Nisha, in the pink shirt. She's really nice – very creative. She has an home design business. Then, behind Rahul is Uncle Dev. He is still so serious, but he did laugh at Arjun's dancing.

Everyone else, I think, you know…

Love from Jaya

▾ | 🔗 ⬜ 🔍   **Send**

---

i   Which family members does Jaya describe?

ii   What is Arjun wearing?

iii   What information shows that Rahul's wife, Nisha, is creative?

iv   Why does Jaya think that Aunt Bhavna won't recognise Uncle Dev?

b   Here are some adjectives to describe what someone is like as a person. Which ones does Jaya use? Which adjectives can you use to describe your family members?

> kind   helpful   funny   calm   serious   strong
> loving   clever   caring   creative

WRITING TIP

When you are describing a picture or photo, adverbs of direction, **left** and **right**, can be used to say where people or things are. Look at this example from Jaya's email:

- You can see him at the front, **on the left**…
- Also **to the left** of the photo is Rahul's wife, Nisha,…

We can see the adverb, **right**, in a similar way:

- Rahul's sisters are **to the right** of the picture…
- **On the right** is Rahul's mother…

WRITING TIP

When you are describing people or objects, choose descriptive adjectives. These can be colours and patterns, e.g. *with blue and white stripes, checked shirt*; or they could be words to describe qualities, e.g. *light white coat, smart black jacket.*

9 Writing

Imagine you are writing to someone who has not seen your family for a long time. Write a description of some members of your family. If you can, choose a photograph of your family to help you describe them. Use Jaya's email to help you.

Your descriptions should include:

- what they look like
- what they are wearing
- what they are like as a person – use the adjectives you were given to help you.

> 3.5 Staying healthy

These activities will help you learn about health and illness.

1 Reading 📖 ABC XYZ

We all sometimes need help when we are ill or if something is hurt. Who can you speak to if you have a health problem? Match the jobs to the people pictured. Then match these sentences to the correct photo.

a William helps people when they have problems with their teeth. He usually wears a white coat and often looks at photographs of people's mouths and teeth. He has just started his job and is being helped by someone with more experience.

b Anika enjoys working with people. They visit her office when they have problems with their bodies. She checks people's health, gives them tests and sends them to hospital. People like Anika work in hospitals too.

c Laura knows a lot about different types of medicines. She works in a type of shop. Her job is to give out tablets and other things to help people get better. She gives people advice and usually wears a white coat.

d Tom enjoys working with people. Sometimes he checks people's health and helps them with small problems, for example, if they cut themselves or have an allergy. Tom works in a hospital. He is a friendly man and likes to help older people to stay healthy.

| chemist | nurse |
| dentist | doctor |

> **READING TIP**
>
> Notice how the present simple is used to describe **processes** and **procedures**:
>
> - He often **looks** at photographs of people's mouths and teeth.
> - She **checks** people's health, **gives** them tests and **sends** them to hospital.
> - Sometimes he **checks** people's health and **helps** them with small problems…

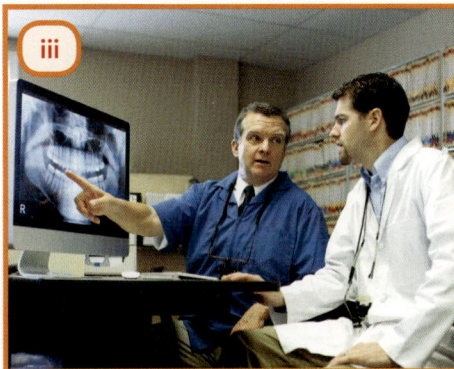

2 Reading 📖

Read about Mina's visit to the doctor. Choose the correct words for each letter a-e in the text. Then answer the questions in pairs.

A visit to the doctor

I'm usually very healthy, but last Thursday I ᵃ_____ to feel ill. I felt really tired, so I went to bed to ᵇ_____ down. The next day, I ᶜ_____ worse. I had a fever, a headache and it was hard to breathe. My stomach hurt too. I made an ᵈ_____ to visit the doctor and he told me I had the flu.

He told me that I must rest and drink lots of water. He sent me to the pharmacy to get some tablets for my headache. I ᵉ_____ five days resting at home. Yesterday, I started to feel better.

a	became	was	started
b	lie	sleep	rest
c	touched	thought	felt
d	occasion	appointment	organisation
e	gave	stayed	spent

f Have you ever had the flu? Did you have the same symptoms as Mina?

g What do you think of the doctor's advice for Mina? What other advice could you give her?

3 Writing 📝

Imagine that you go to a new doctor's office. Copy and complete the form.

High Street Doctor

Your name:
_____

Your address:
_____

Your date of birth:
_____

Telephone number:
_____

Details of any health problems:

4 Listening (track 3.5) 🎧

Listen to Matthias talking about hurting himself and then getting better.
Answer the following questions:

a What happened to make Mattias hurt himself?

b What was he doing when he got hurt?

c How did he feel at the time?

d How did Mattias feel as he was recovering?

e Name two things Matthias did to help himself get better.

f What is Matthias going to do next weekend?

5 Speaking 💬

When did you last have an illness or hurt yourself? What was it like? How did you feel?
Describe it to your partner. Use Matthias's description and the sentence starters below
to help you.

- 'Last year I …'
- 'I couldn't go out for …'
- 'I felt …'
- 'The doctor said I should …'

PROJECT

What advice would you give to people who want to stay healthy?
In groups, talk about different ways to stay healthy and keep fit.
You could discuss:

- diet – the types of food to eat
- different types of sports
- activities such as walking.

Use modals such as:

'To stay healthy, you **should**…'

'You **could** play…'

Make a poster to show your ideas. Make sure you write some clear tips for
people. Include some interesting pictures. Show your finished poster to the class.

EXAM-STYLE QUESTIONS

Speaking practice

Use this role play to practise your speaking skills. Get a partner to ask you the questions.

> A friend is inviting you to come to their house for food. They ask you these questions.
>
> a Would you like to come to my house for food?
>
> b What day and time can you come?
>
> c What food do you like to eat?
>
> d What types of food do you not like to eat?
>
> e What should we do after we have eaten?
>
> [10]

CHECK YOUR PROGRESS

How confident do you feel about what you have learned and practised in this unit? How many of the following things could you do?

1 Give four adjectives to describe the taste and appearance of food.
2 Know how to adjust verbs when writing in the third person singular.
3 Name the nine main modals.
4 Name 15 different parts of the body.
5 Describe what these following people do: doctor, nurse, dentist, chemist.

Rate yourself from 1 (not confident) to 5 (very confident).

Which things would you like to learn more about?
Which things would you like to practise again?

Share your thoughts with a partner.

> Grammar practice

Future simple

GRAMMAR FOCUS

We can use the future simple tense in several different ways.
We use **will** + verb (without <u>to</u>) for affirmative sentences and **will not** or **won't** (+ verb) for negative sentences. For example:

To talk or ask about future facts:

- In two years' time, our town **will** have a new health centre.

(We know this is true because builders are building the health centre now.)

- The café is closing down. We **won't** be able to go there again.
- **Will** your parents be at the party?
- What time **will** the train leave?

To talk about future predictions and wishes:

- If you come to our house, there **will** always be something wonderful to eat!
- I hope scientists **will** find a way to beat cancer.

To make an offer (usually in the short form, **'ll**):

- Well, have a drink now. Then I**'ll** get lunch ready.
- OK. I**'ll** also get some peppers, cauliflower and eggs. I**'ll** go to the big supermarket.
- You should rest and have a hot lemon drink. I**'ll** get you one.

If we want to make an offer or a suggestion with a question, we use **shall**. Notice that this form is usually used with **I** or **we** (1st person):

- **Shall** I get you a drink?
- **Shall** we go to that new restaurant this weekend?

Remember: we can also use **will** and **won't** to talk about a spontaneous decision (see Session 3.2).

1 Writing

Copy and complete the sentences and questions. Choose the correct verb from the word box and change to the future simple, using **will**, **won't** or **shall**. The first one has been done for you.

open	**be**	not eat
close	serve	cook

a   In the future, I hope there **will** be less pollution.

b   It's very cold in here. I _____ that window.

c   _____ we _____ a curry tonight?

d   I'm sure Jack _____ that egg salad. I don't think he likes eggs.

e   I think Maria _____ her shop soon – she is nearly 70 and wants to retire.

f   In the future, I think robots _____ customers in the shops.

2 Reading

Look at your completed sentences and questions in Activity 1.
Which sentences and questions talk about:

i   A future prediction?

ii   A future wish?

iii A future fact?

iv   An offer?

v   A suggestion?

3 Reading

Bushra and Anna are in class, discussing ideas about the future of their town. Copy the converstation and choose the correct verb form. The first one has been done for you.

Anna: What ªchanges / will change in our town in five years, do you think?

Bushra: There ᵇwill be/ is a lot more people, I think. They ᶜare building/ will build four hundred new houses just outside the town now.

Anna: I know! My cousin ᵈlives /will live nearby and she says that the building work is really noisy. She thinks her parents ᵉare wanting / will want to move house soon. They say that the traffic in the town ᶠgets / will get worse when the new houses are finished.

Bushra: Yes, could be. I think they ᵍbuild / will build a new school too. There ʰis / will be only one in our town at the moment.

Anna: And new shops maybe?

Bushra: No, I don't think so. There ⁱaren't /won't be more shops because so many people shop online now.

4 Speaking

Work in pairs. How do you think your town or city will change in five or ten years' time? Discuss your ideas with your partner, then share with your class. Use the future simple to make your predictions.

I think we will have a new...
There won't be any...

> Chapter 4
Education

IN THIS UNIT YOU WILL:

- talk about different school subjects
- find answers in a longer spoken text about school topics
- learn about different types of nouns to describe school themes
- find apostrophes to talk about possession
- write about experiences of school
- listen to people talk about studying.

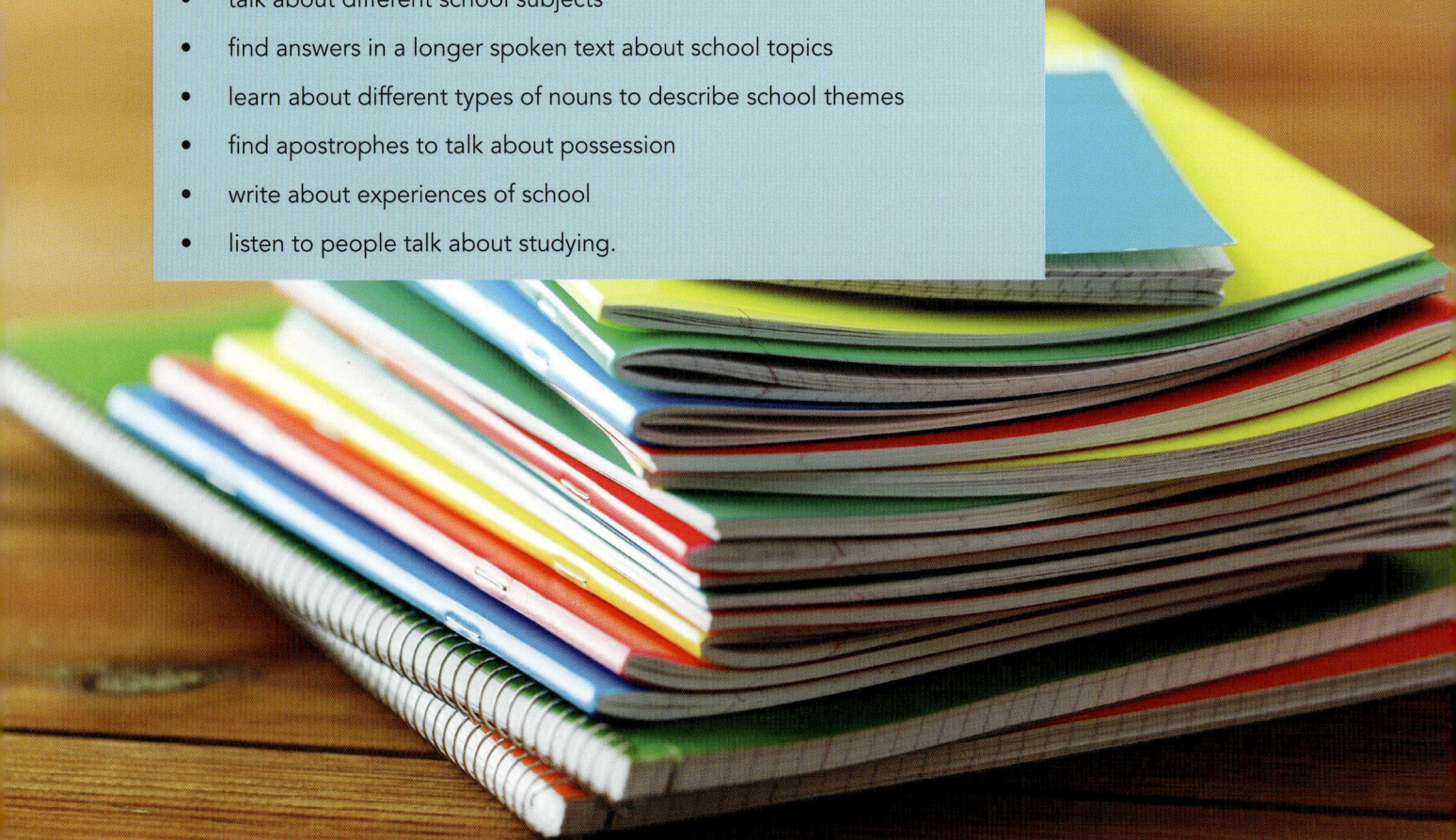

> 4.1 Lessons

These activities will help you to talk about subjects at school.

1 Reading and Speaking 📖 💬 ABC XYZ

Work in pairs. How well do you know your school subjects? Try this quiz. Match the school subjects in the box with the meanings.

In this subject…

a you could study English, Arabic, Spanish and many others.

b you study events from the past.

c you study the science of the human body and plants.

d you could learn how to play an instrument, e.g. the guitar or violin.

e you could learn how to create software.

f you could learn how electricity works.

g you learn about your environment and the Earth's properties.

h you learn about gases and liquids.

i you learn about religion.

> biology   chemistry
> physics   geography
> history
> computer science
> music   languages
> religious education (RE)

2 Speaking 💬 ABC XYZ

Look at the four pictures of school subjects. In pairs, ask your partner these questions:

a Which subjects can you see in the pictures? Match the photos to the following words:

   i art   **ii** physical education (PE)   **iii** drama   **iv** maths

b What do you do in these subjects? Use the meanings in Activity 1 or the phrases below to help you.

In art, you learn how to …
When you study maths, you …

> sports   maths problems
> draw   paint   act

3 Writing 📝 ABC XYZ

Read the subjects again and write down the ones that you study at school. Which are you good at? Which do you enjoy the most? Which subjects do you study that are not in this list?

4 Reading 📖

Read Kesha's description of one subject at school.

A school subject that I love

My favourite school subject is history. I've always loved learning about how people lived in the past. Now my favourite topic is 20th century history. I like the stories of important events in the last century and how they have changed how we live today.

In history lessons, I like listening to Mrs Smith when she explains the topic and uses interesting examples. She's a brilliant teacher because she really loves the subject and that makes us like it too. We sometimes use textbooks, but we often watch films and online videos. I enjoy it most when we work in groups, because it is interesting and fun to discuss ideas and hear everyone's opinions. We do writing exercises but also lots of projects about different times in history.

I get good grades in history, but I get better grades in maths and sciences. However, it is still my favourite subject!

STUDY SKILLS

Reading and listening activities usually require you to understand the sense of the whole text, as well as information in different parts. Therefore, read the whole text once or twice before you answer any questions. Also notice what topics are covered by the questions. This will help you understand the main topic.

Activities 4 and 5 give you practice in questions about the whole text and different parts.

Answer the following questions:

a   What is Kesha's favourite history topic?

b   Why does she like this topic?

c   Why does Kesha like Mrs Smith?

d   Which activity does Kesha like most in her history lessons?

e   Which is the best introduction to Kesha's essay?

   i   Kesha describes important events that she learns in her history lessons.

   ii   Kesha describes how she gets better marks for her history work than other school subjects.

   iii   Kesha describes the different things that make her enjoy learning history.

5 Listening (track 4.1) 🎧

Now listen to Stella talking about biology. Listen once and answer question a. Then listen again and answer b–e.

a   Stella mentions three topics in her description. Put the topics in order.

   i   her teacher   **ii**   what she learns   **iii**   her favourite part of the lesson

b   What three things does Stella enjoy learning about?

c   How does she describe the subject?

d   What part of the lesson does she enjoy most?

e   What two things does she like about the way Mr Singh teaches?

6 Speaking 💬

Compare your answers to Activity 5 with a partner. Ask your partner:

• What answers did you write down first time?

• What parts did you find more challenging?

How can you develop your skill at answering these types of questions? Copy the following techniques into your notebook. Tick [✓] the techniques that you already do. Put a star [*] by the ones that you would like to try. Compare with your partner. Can you add more tips to the list?

• Before listening, look at the topic and predict what the speaker might say.

• Before listening, read the question/s carefully.

• While listening, listen for key nouns and verbs.

• While listening, listen for 'joining words', e.g. *and*, *but*, *or*, to show where new points are.

7 Writing 📝

Write about your favourite school subject. Use these questions to build your text:

• What is your favourite subject?

• Why do you like it? Give reasons.

• What do you do in lessons for that subject?

Use Kesha and Stella's descriptions to help you. Write around 80 words.

WRITING TIP

The structure or organisation of your writing is important so you need to think about the order of what you write about. Often, writing activities have bullet points (•) to guide you. Use these bullet points to help you organise your writing. Always check that you have written about every bullet point.

> 4.2 In the classroom

These activities will help you learn vocabulary about the classroom.

1 Speaking 💬 ABC XYZ

In pairs, look at the following words. Look around your classroom.
How many of these items can you see? Which items do you use the most?

> bell   blackboard   book   desk   dictionary   eraser
> interactive whiteboard   notebook   notice   paper   pen   pencil
> pencil case   equipment   poster   ruler   whiteboard

2 Speaking 💬 ABC XYZ

Which items can you see in the photos?
What other classroom items can you add to the list?

> ### STUDY SKILLS
>
> Lots of activities in this book are about learning words. Knowing vocabulary is a very important skill in learning a language. Always find ways to develop your vocabulary. Use websites, watch films and read books.

3 Listening (track 4.2) 🎧

Listen to Yasmin and Mara's conversation. How does Yasmin help Mara? Listen again, then write the missing words in your notebook. What type of words are missing?

Mara:	Yasmin, have you got another ^apen? I've forgotten mine.
Yasmin:	Yes, I've got three ^b_____. Do you want to borrow one?
Mara:	Yes, please.
Yasmin:	You're always forgetting your ^c_____. The day before yesterday you forgot all your ^d_____.
Mara:	I know! There is always so much to carry. My school bag is so heavy. And it was worse at my primary school, because we were smaller then.
Yasmin:	Yes, it's hard for small children. It's better at this ^e_____ because we have safe places to keep things in. But there are more classes and more books – I have three textbooks just for ^f_____.
Mara:	That's right. Oh… can I borrow a ^g_____ and an eraser too?
Yasmin:	Yes, here you go! It's lucky that I've got lots of ^h_____ and two ⁱ_____!

GRAMMAR FOCUS

Nouns are used for people, places, things and ideas. **Countable nouns** are nouns that can be counted:

- Yasmin, have you got another **pen**?
- Yes, I've got three **pens.**
- Can I borrow **a pencil** and **an eraser** too?
- …I've got **lots of pencils** and **two erasers**!

Uncountable nouns can't be divided into separate things. They are always singular so have no plural form. They are usually ideas or things that are difficult to count.

- You're always forgetting your **equipment**.
- I have three textbooks just for **Chemistry.**

Here are some more examples of uncountable nouns:

- **information, education, beauty, peace** = ideas
- **rice, salt, sugar** = things that are difficult to count.

KEY TERMS

countable nouns: nouns that can be counted or divided

uncountable nouns: nouns that cannot be counted or divided

4 Reading 📖

Read the Grammar focus box. Write the correct noun forms in your notebook to complete the sentences. Which ones are true for you and your school?

a We get more **homeworks / homework** from some teachers than others.

b I always enjoy PE and have lots of **energy / energies** after the lesson.

c Many classrooms at our school have interactive **whiteboard / whiteboards**.

d In class, my friends give me lots of **help / helps** when I need it.

e We have some information **poster / posters** on the walls in our classroom.

f At school, we try to recycle **paper / papers** and plastic.

GRAMMAR FOCUS

Countable nouns have singular and plural forms. **Regular plural nouns** are made by adding -s, -es, or -ies to the noun. For example:

- The day before yesterday, you forgot all your notebooks.
- But there are more classes…
  (Add 'es' after nouns ending in 's', 'ss', 'z', 'x', sh', 'ch'.)
- Put the dictionaries back in the cupboard. Note: ~~dictionarys~~ – dictionaries
  (Add 'ies' after nouns with a consonant before 'y'.)

Irregular plural nouns are formed in different ways. There are some nouns that change quite a lot. Look at these examples of common irregular plural nouns:

- …it's hard on small **children.** child (singular) = children (plural)
- Lots of **people** attended the school concert. person (s) = people (pl)
- Brush your **teeth** before you go to school. tooth (s) = teeth (pl)
- Teaching is a popular profession for both **women** and **men.**
  woman (s) = women (pl); man (s) = men (pl)

KEY TERMS

regular plural nouns: nouns that become plural when adding -s, -es, or -ies

irregular plural nouns: nouns that follow unusual rules in the plural form

5 Reading 📖

Hassan and Josh's school have $500 to spend on new equipment. The head teacher has asked students to discuss how to spend the money. Read the boys' conversation. Which ideas do you like?

Hassan:	We have $500 to buy new school equipment. What should we buy?
Josh:	Plenty of IT equipment! How about new computers for the classrooms?
Hassan:	$500 won't buy much computer equipment. It's very expensive. But perhaps we could buy some software?
Josh:	Yes, good idea. Or we could buy new art equipment – different kinds of paints and paint brushes.
Hassan:	Mmm…maybe… Or we could spend it on trips or visits to museums? Somewhere that would help art, history or geography projects?
Josh:	Or new football shirts for all the school teams?
Hassan:	Or pay a famous coach to give lots of advice to the football teams? They haven't made much progress this year!

6 Reading 📖 🔤

a Read the conversation again. Look at the underlined words. Find words that mean:

   i   someone who trains sports players

   ii when something gets better or improves

   iii computer programmes

   iv when someone tells you what they think you should do.

b Look at the blue words. Which nouns are uncountable? Are the other nouns regular or irregular in plural form?

c Read the Study skills box. Now look for examples of uncountable nouns with amounts in the conversation in Activity 5. The first one is <mark>highlighted</mark>. Can you find three more?

STUDY SKILLS

When talking about an uncountable noun, you have to use extra words to talk about the amount of something:

- I need two **pieces of** equipment.

- There is a **pile of** work on his desk.

- There is a **lot of** information on that laptop.

---

7 Writing 📝

Imagine your school has $500 to spend on new equipment. Work in pairs. Discuss how you would spend the money.

I think we should spend the money on…

We could buy some…

a Write down four ideas each. Use singular and plural nouns. Use uncountable nouns with expressions of amount.

b Compare each other's sentences and choose the four best ideas.

c Check the use of singular, plural and uncountable nouns in your sentences.

Now present your ideas to the class. Vote on the best ideas.

STUDY SKILLS

English has many rules about grammar but there are times when these rules do not apply. For example, irregular and uncountable nouns follow different patterns. You will need to learn these differences. Keep a list of the most common differences and practise speaking and using the examples in conversation.

> 4.3 School life

These activities will help you talk about life in school.

1 Listening (track 4.3) 🎧

Maz, Dom, Anna and Asif are discussing their experiences at primary school. Asif is the leader of the discussion. Listen and decide if the sentences are true or false.

a Maz met her best friend, Amira, when she began primary school.

b She spends time with Amira once a week.

c Dom enjoyed his first day at primary school.

d Dom made lots of friends when he started primary school.

e Dom started playing football when he met his friend, Jamal.

f Football was the only activity Dom liked at primary school.

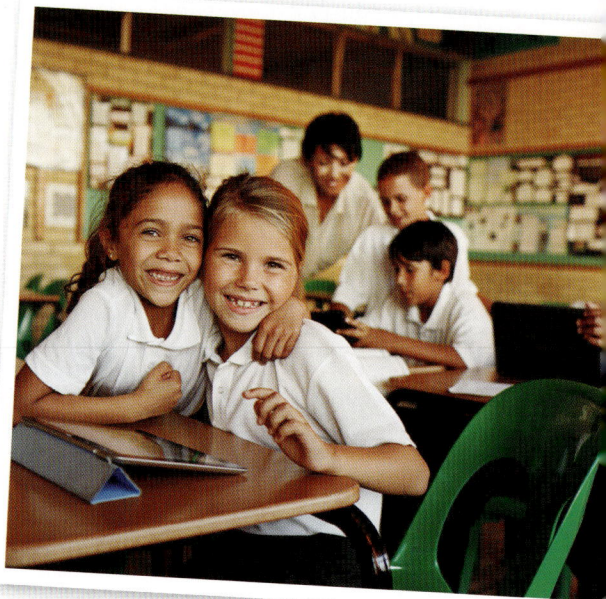

2 Listening (track 4.3) 🎧

You are going to have a group discussion. One person will be the leader and everyone will take turns to speak. First, listen again. Complete the questions from the conversation in your notebook.

a _____ your favourite memory of primary school? _____ you like to go first, Maz?

b _____ was it so special?

c What memories _____ everyone else _____?

d What _____ you, Dom?

e _____ it get any better?

f And Anna, _____ about you?

3 Reading 📖

Look at the questions in Activity 2 again.

a Which questions does Asif use to guide the discussion?

b Which questions do Anna and Maz ask to continue the discussion?

4 Reading 📖

Here are some ways to reply when you are having a conversation. Which phrases did you hear in the discussion in Activities 1 and 2?

a Great, thanks Maz.

b That's hard.

c Something similar happened to me when…

d Yes, it did. It took a while, but…

e No, it didn't.

f I agree with that.

g That's interesting.

h It was different for me...

5 Speaking 💬

In groups, talk about your own memories of primary school. Choose one person in the group to be leader. Use the following questions to guide the conversation:

• What do you remember about your first day at primary school?

• What friends did you make?

• What were your favourite activities?

Can you think of other questions to ask too? Use the conversation, questions and phrases in Activities 1-4 to help you.

On my first day, I remember playing with...

I made a friend called...

One of my favourite activities was...

6 Speaking 💬

In pairs, talk about your group discussion in Activity 5. Ask yourselves:

• How did I add to the discussion?

• What topics did I talk about?

• Did I ask questions?

7 Speaking 💬 🗣

a Read the words below aloud with a partner. Copy the table and put the words in the correct group.

| body do got often on go to |
| not low won show two |

Short 'o' sounds	Long 'o' sounds	
ɒ	əʊ	u
got	*go*	*do*
on		

b Can you add two more words to each group?

SPEAKING TIP

Active roles in group discussion activities help to develop conversation skills. Which active roles could you take?

For example:
The leader guides the discussion and makes sure everyone has a chance to speak. Encourage the group members to join in. You can do this by asking them questions directly.

The other people should take turns to speak. They can develop the discussion by asking questions too.

PRONOUNCING ENGLISH

Short and long 'o' sound

Some words with the vowel, 'o', have a short sound (for example, *got*, *on*).

There are also words with 'o' that have a long sound (for example, *do*, *sports*).

GRAMMAR FOCUS

Genitive forms (Possessive forms) in English use an **apostrophe** to show possession of something. For example:

Singular nouns (-**'s**)

- …she needed another girl to join her <u>sister</u>**'s** game.
- I go to <u>Tara</u>**'s** house at least once a week…

Notice: there is no apostrophe with the pronoun, **it**.

- Can you put the laptop back in <u>its case</u>?
- Please replace this chair. <u>Its leg</u> is broken.

An apostrophe is only used with the word 'it' to show a missing letter.

- **It's** an expensive laptop so look after it!
  (It's = it is)

Plural nouns: regular

- The <u>boy**s'** changing room</u> is over there.
  (Apostrophe after s)

Plural nouns: irregular

- <u>People</u>**'s** <u>memories</u> of primary school can be very different.
  (Irregular plural + **'s**)

Remember: we can also use possessive adjectives to show that something belongs to someone or the relationship between two people.

- What's **your** favourite memory of primary school
- …it was when I met **my** best friend, Amira…I remember playing with her and **her** sister.
- Dom met **his** friend, Jamal, at primary school.
- We are friends because **our** interests are similar.
- …**their** first day at primary school was a good experience.

KEY TERMS

genitive forms: these forms are used to show possession

apostrophe: a punctuation mark that shows possession or a missing letter

8 Reading 📖

Read the school notices. Can you add the missing apostrophes? Write the correct sentences in your notebooks. Which notice has no apostrophe?

> **a** Cleaners cupboard – keep out!

> **b** Girls changing room closed for repairs.

> **c** Please leave all essays on Mr Sharmas desk.

| d | Childrens play area – no dogs. |

| e | Womens fitness class starting Monday evening in the school hall. |

| f | After use, put the equipment back in its box. |

| g | The teachers meeting is at 3pm today. |

9 Writing 📝

What examples of possession are there in these pictures? Write two sentences for each photo, mixing up the order. Include an apostrophe to show possession.

The children's desks are all made of wood.

10 Reading 📖

Give your sentences to a partner. Match each other's sentences to the photos. Then read the Writing tip and check each other's sentences.

WRITING TIP

Proofreading your work is important. This is when you read your work and check that it makes sense, and that spelling and punctuation are correct. Sometimes, it helps to read it once to check that your phrasing is good, then a second time to check for spelling and punctuation.

> 4.4 Teachers

In this session you will discuss different types of schools and the people who work in them.

1 Speaking and Writing 💬 📝 ABC XYZ

Work in pairs. Look at the words to describe different types of school. Draw a timeline. Order the places according to when students attend them (starting with the youngest).

> university   nursery   secondary school   primary school

Who do you know who attends these types of schools? Which have you attended?

2 Reading 📖 ABC XYZ

Copy the table into your notebook. Write the words below in the correct part of the table. Can you add two more words to each group?

People at school	Places in school

> canteen   director   playground   student   teacher
> sports hall   classroom   science lab   classmate   lecture hall

3 Speaking and Reading 💬 📖

Work in pairs. Read about the work of three teachers and why they like it. Before you read, discuss what you think the teachers will say. Then read and match the teachers to photos a–c. Were any of your predictions correct?

Miss Dias

I teach history. I am very interested in my subject and I enjoy answering my students' questions. Sometimes I teach in a classroom and sometimes I teach in a lecture hall – a room with rows of seats facing me. I prefer teaching in a classroom because there are more opportunities to interact with my students.

Miss Turnbull

I teach science to groups of older students. After their studies, most of them will have careers involving science. I enjoy helping students to do well in their studies. It is very rewarding to see them learn new things and then achieve good grades. I love watching them become more confident.

Miss Gbeho

> I love working with students who want to learn. Luckily, my students are enthusiastic! I teach a lot of different subjects, but science is my favourite. Although my students are quite young, most of them understand the subject very well. I think this is because of their enthusiastic attitude – it helps them to learn.

4 Speaking 💬

Read the teachers' comments again in Activity 3.
Answer the questions with your partner.

a Where do you think each of the teachers work? Primary school, secondary school or university?

b What does Miss Dias like about her job?

c Which places does she teach in?

d Miss Dias says that she likes 'to interact with my students'. The meaning is:

    i to communicate, usually by asking and answering questions

    ii when the teacher talks and students only listen.

e What does Miss Turnbull like about her job?

f Miss Gbeho says that her students are 'enthusiastic'. The meaning is:

    i they are hard-working

    ii they have energy and interest in the subject.

STUDY SKILLS

Some activities require you to explain things in your own words. You need to show two skills: 1) that you understand what is said; 2) that you can re-phrase things. This tests your own knowledge of different words. Practise this skill as you work through the book. There are several more activities like this.

5 Reading

Read the timetable for extra activities at Parkside High School. Work in pairs and answer the questions.

a Which activity takes place early in the morning?

b How many sports clubs are there? Where do they take place?

c Which clubs could you join if you are good at music or acting?

d Which clubs on the timetable are available at your school? Does your school offer any other extra activities?

e Which teachers organise extra activities at your school? Have you joined any activities? Which ones?

Activity	Time	Place / Teacher
Year 7-10 Table tennis	After school Monday	In the Sports Hall with Miss Chang
Year 8 Science club	After school Monday	In Science Lab 2 with Mr Behrs
Year 7-10 Drama workshop	After school Tuesday	In Classroom C1 with Ms Ruiz
Year 7-10 Yoga	After school Tuesday	In the Main Hall with Mr Kapski
Year 7-10 Football	After school Wednesday	On the School Field with Mr Cole
Year 7 Computer club	After school Wednesday	In Classroom C2 with Miss Shah
Year 7-10 Basketball	Before school Thursday	In the Playground with Mr Alan
Year 7-10 School band practice	After school Friday	In the Main Hall with Mrs Patel

6 Listening (track 4.4)

Listen to Kensuke talk about his favourite teacher. Then answer the questions.

a What subject does Mr Ord teach?

b How does Kensuke describe Mr Ord?

c Which way of working does Kensuke like? Why?

7 Writing

a Listen again to Kensuke's description of Mr Ord in Activity 6.
Then write a description of your favourite teacher. Write about 90 words. Explain:

- What subject the teacher teaches.
- Why you like the teacher.
- What you do in the teacher's lessons. Why do you enjoy them?

b Exchange your work with a partner. Compare your descriptions: say something positive and give each other feedback:

- Have you followed the instructions you were given?
- Is the description clear and simple to follow?
- Check sentence structure, use of vocabulary and spelling.

I like how you describe....

Can I make a suggestion? I think you should...

How about changing this word to....

> 4.5 Studying

In this session you will talk about the different ways that people learn.

1 Reading 📖 ABC/XYZ

Work in pairs and try this quiz about school studies. Match the words with a meaning.

exercise   report   break   course   result   timetable   department   mark

a   To stop something for a short time. Schools usually have one mid-morning.

b   A set of classes which usually leads to an exam.

c   A part of a school that teaches one subject.

d   A practice activity, usually in a textbook.

e   A point you get for each correct answer in an exam or a piece of school work.

f   The grade you receive after an exam or test.

g   A teacher's written communication about a student's ability at school.

h   A plan that shows when classes at school take place.

2 Speaking 💬

Answer these questions with your partner:

a   What times do you take a break in your school day?

b   Which course are you enjoying most this year? Why?

c   How was your last school report? Did you think your teachers' comments were fair?

d   Which subject/s do you get your best marks in?

e   What do you think are the most useful exercises in your English textbook?

f   What was your best result in your exams last year?

g   Do you like your lesson timetable this year? Would you like to change anything?

h   Which is the smallest subject department in your school?

3 Listening (track 4.5) 🎧

Listen to Justin, Adah, Wang Le and Lisa talk about the different ways they like to learn. Decide if the sentences are true or false.

a   In history, Justin learns by asking the teacher questions.

b   Justin likes working on his own.

c   Adah usually watches study videos more than once.

d   Practice exams help Adah to follow his progress.

e   Wang Le doesn't think his teacher knows much about physics.

f   Wang Le makes sure that his work is correct by looking in his textbook.

g   Lisa prefers group work to pair work.

h   Lisa can't see any reason for doing homework.

4 Listening (track 4.5) 🎧

Listen again. What do Justin, Adah, Wang le and Lisa say about these ways of learning? Which views do you agree or disagree with?

a asking questions
b working in pairs
c using a textbook
d working in groups
e homework

5 Reading and Speaking 📖 💬 ABC XYZ

a Work in pairs. Match these students' comments to the phrases in the word box. Then talk about these ways of learning. Which ones do you find the most helpful and why?

i
> I like working on my own sometimes. It gives me space to think.

ii
> Coursebooks give me extra information, such as study tips, to help me understand my subjects.

iii
> I like working with another classmate because you can help each other.

iv
> I like to be active, as well as listen to the teacher. For example, working in groups or doing experiments.

v
> I like working with three or four other students because you can share ideas.

> listening to a teacher   working on your own   working in pairs
> working in groups   using a textbook

b After your discussion, make notes on your thoughts about i to v. Then join with another pair and compare your views.

SPEAKING TIP

When you consider other people's views, sometimes you agree with some things they say but not everything.

You can use phrases such as:

In some ways, I agree with Justin because… but…

You can talk about why you disagree by using phrases such as:

On the other hand, I disagree with Lisa because…

STUDY SKILLS

Look at **affixes** in words to find out what type of words they are. An affix is a part added to a word that changes its meaning. An affix at the beginning of a word is called a **prefix**; an affix at the end is a **suffix**.

Here are some words which appear in Unit 4. Their **suffixes** show that they are nouns:

informat**ion**, discuss**ion**, quest**ion**, equip**ment**, depart**ment**, experi**ment**

Look out for other words with these **suffixes** as you work through this course. Also look for other affixes which show you that a word is a noun.

KEY TERM

affix: a part added to the beginning or end of a root word, which changes its meaning

6 Writing 📝

Design a study tips poster to explain how you learn best.
First, read the examples. Which techniques do you already use?

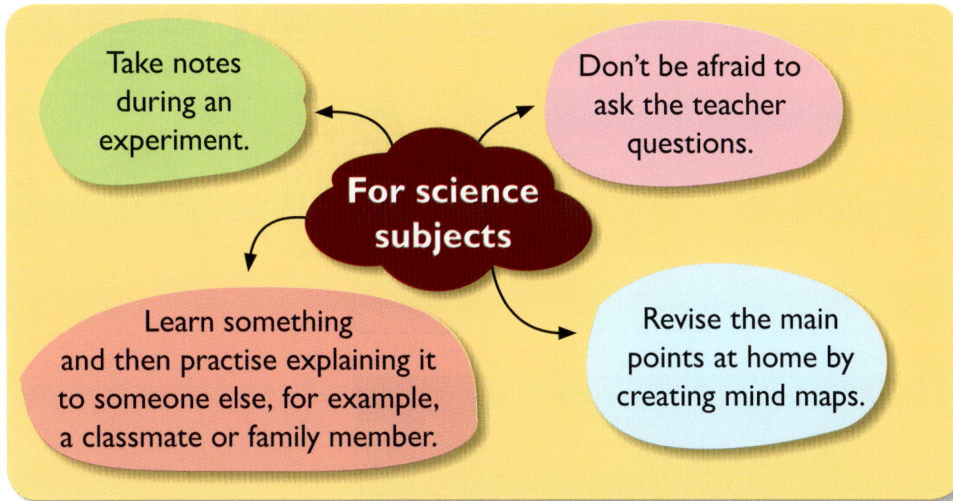

Take notes during an experiment.

Don't be afraid to ask the teacher questions.

For science subjects

Learn something and then practise explaining it to someone else, for example, a classmate or family member.

Revise the main points at home by creating mind maps.

FOR **ART** AND **DESIGN**

1 Use a book for drawing to practise your ideas.

2 Watch online videos about painting.

3 Experiment with different types of paint, pens and pencils.

WRITING TIP

Remember that using examples in your writing helps to add detail. You can introduce them by using the phrase 'For example,' at the end of a sentence.

Choose a school subject and create a list of points. Use the examples in the posters to help you. Start your points with prepositional phrases.
For example: For science subjects…

ENGLISH AROUND THE WORLD

In countries around the world, some types of university course are taught in English, even if English is not the native language. These courses are often in subjects such as science, technology, engineering and maths (STEM). In these professions, most of the information and vocabulary is in English. When students are studying these courses, they need to do all their research and exams in English.

PROJECT

Think about a design for a school. What is it like?
In groups, talk about:

- what the building is like

- what is on your timetable – any unusual lessons?

- what your school uniform is like

Make some drawings of your ideas. You can make a map of the building, write a timetable and draw your new uniform.

Share your ideas and drawings with the class. Whose ideas do you like best?

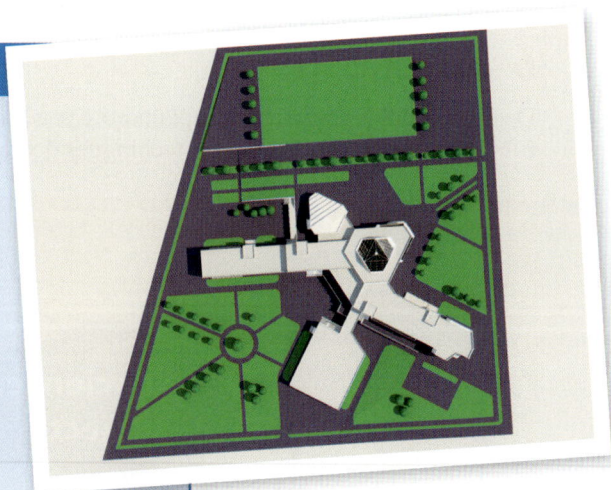

EXAM-STYLE QUESTIONS

Reading practice

Use this activity to practise your reading skills. In this text, Mr Sarkar talks about his job as a PE (sport) teacher. Answer the following questions.

Why I like teaching

I have been teaching for 25 years. I really enjoy it. My subject is PE. My favourite sports are football and running. I started teaching in a primary school, but then decided I would like to work with older students. They're funny and you can do more activities with them.

I try to help my students. Some are really good at PE, but some students don't feel confident. I try to help them by showing them ways to improve their skills. I get on well with my students. Last year, our school football team did really well. It was lovely to see the students succeed. Next year, I am changing schools. I am moving back home to India. I have a new job as director.

a   How long has Mr Sarkar worked in education?   [1]
b   What does Mr Sarkar teach?   [1]
c   Which sports does Mr Sarkar enjoy the most?   [2]
d   In what sort of school did Mr Sarkar begin his teaching career?   [1]
e   Give two reasons Mr Sarkar likes working with older students.   [2]
f   How does Mr Sarkar help students who feel they aren't good at sport?   [2]
g   When is Mr Sarkar moving to a new school?   [1]
h   Which country will Mr Sarkar live in?   [1]
i   What role will Mr Sarkar have in his new school?   [1]

[Total: 12]

CHECK YOUR PROGRESS

How confident do you feel about what you have learned and practised in this unit?
How many of the following things could you do?

1   Write down ten different subjects you study in school. Take care with spellings.

2   Give two examples of irregular nouns and explain what happens when they become plurals.

3   Write a sentence containing an apostrophe to show possession.

4   Write three sentences containing the words 'secondary school', 'timetable', 'university'.

5   Explain what these phrases mean: 'do an experiment'; 'practise my maths'; 'read my book'.

Rate yourself from 1 (not confident) to 5 (very confident).

Which things would you like to learn more about?
Which things would you like to practise again?

Share your thoughts with a partner.

> Grammar practice

Modal verbs: Have (got) to and ought to

KEY TERM

obligation: something that you must do or have a duty to do

1 Reading

Match the sentence halves to make complete sentences.

a You have to eat before you go out,
b Tara ought to check her homework
c We have to change schools
d Marcus has got to return the books by Monday
e Ismail has got to improve his science grades
f Mum says I ought to get a study guide

i to help me with my exam revision.
ii if he wants to be a doctor.
iii – it's the library rule.
iv before she gives it to the teacher.
v or you'll be hungry later.
vi when we get to Year 7.

2 Reading 📖

Read the study tips. Which ones do you agree with?

If you want to study well for exams…

a you have to get enough sleep.

b you have to be well-organised.

c you ought to drink plenty of water.

d you ought to eat less chocolate and more fruit.

e you ought to put your smart phone away.

f you have got to practise with past exam papers.

3 Writing ✎

Now write four more study tips, using any of the modal verbs, **have to, have got to** or **ought to**.

Imperatives

GRAMMAR FOCUS

When we give instructions or orders (imperatives), we put the verb first and take away the pronoun, you.

- **Come** in and **close** the door.
- (<u>not</u> You come in and close the door).
- Please **open** your books to page 25.
- **Show** me what you have written.
- **Join** the drama club! It will be fun.

Notice what happens when we want to make the instruction or order negative: we put **don't** first, before all main verbs.

- **Don't open** that window.
- (<u>not</u> You don't open the window).
- **Don't bring** food into the classrooms.
- **Don't be** so noisy!

KEY TERM

imperative: the form of the verb that is usually used to give orders or instructions

1 Reading 📖

Put the words in order to make the instructions. The first one has been done for you.

a have / Don't / barbecues / the grass /on   Don't have barbecues on the grass.

b the reading room / quiet / Be / in

c the school hall / run / in / Don't

d safety glasses / Wear / experiments / during

e your / during the performance / off / Switch / mobile phone

f wash /Please / hands / your

2 Reading 📖

Match each completed instruction from Activity 1 to a place (a–f) where you might see it. The first one has been done for you.

a   In a library
b   In a park   a
c   In a hospital
d   In a school
e   In a science lab
f   In a theatre or cinema

3 Writing 📝

Work in pairs. Choose a part of your school and write four new instructions to improve the area. Here are some places you could write about (or choose your own):

> the gym or sports hall   the library   your classroom
> the playground   the computer room   the science labs

Don't leave your bags by the classroom door.

Please leave the sports hall quietly.

Chapter 5

The world of work

IN THIS UNIT YOU WILL:

- learn vocabulary about jobs and careers
- read about the world of work
- use compound nouns to describe different careers
- practise using demonstrative pronouns in conversation
- practise form-filling for job applications
- find the main points in a text.

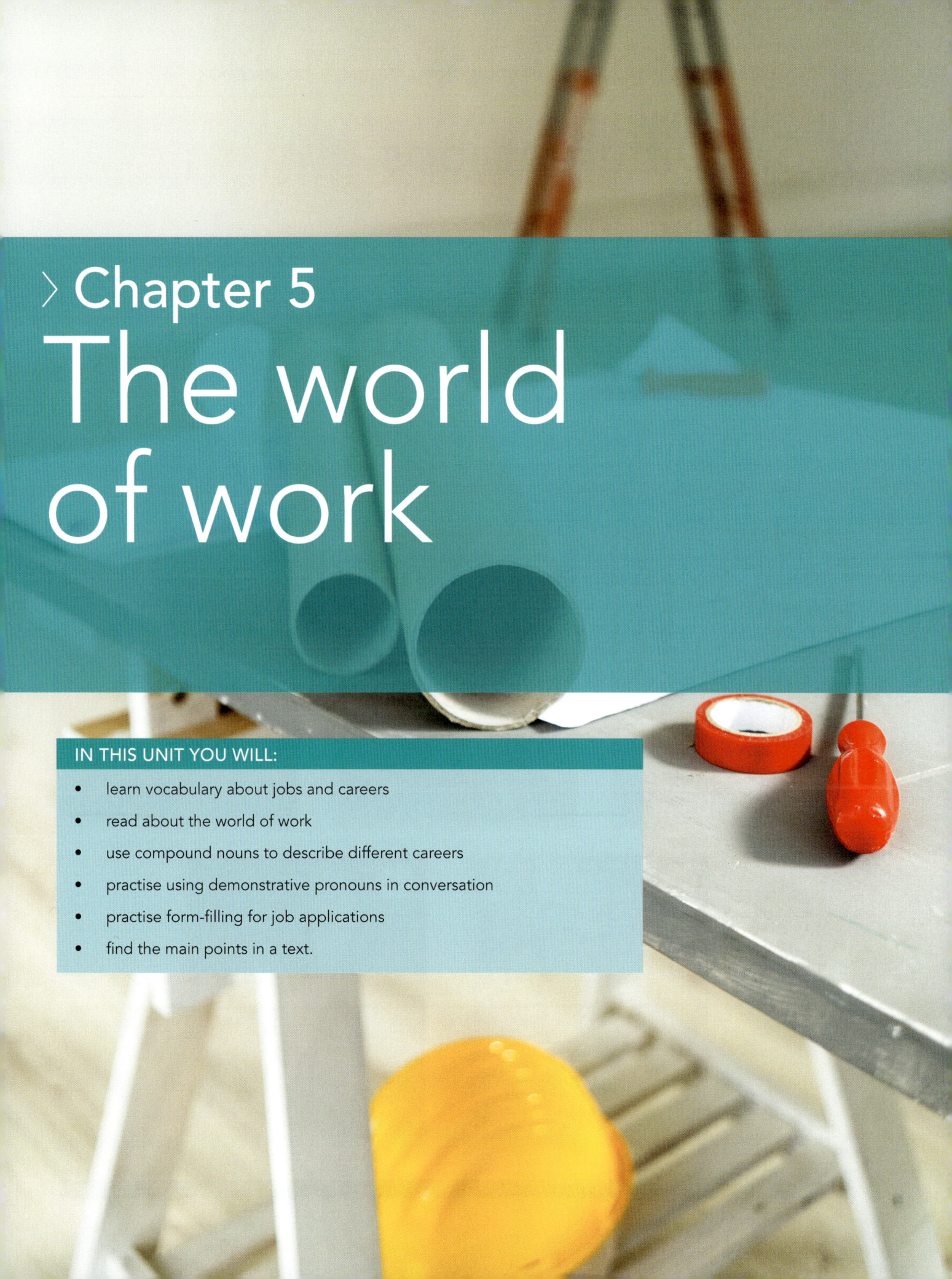

> 5.1 Different jobs

Use these activities to learn vocabulary about jobs and careers.

1 Reading and Speaking 📖 💬 ABC XYZ

Read the job titles and match them to a photo. In pairs, explain what each person does. Use the words in the word box to help you. Do you know anyone who does any of these jobs?

a pilot   **b** lawyer   **c** waiter   **d** builder   **e** farmer

> serve   build   give   grow   legal advice
> crops   buildings   planes   customers

A lawyer gives legal advice.

2 Speaking 💬 ABC XYZ

Match the jobs in Activity 1 with another job from the same profession. Can you explain the difference between the two jobs? Use the words in the word box to help you.

a flight attendant   **b** chef   **c** engineer   **d** mechanic   **e** secretary

> cook   plan   look after   organise   mend   meetings
> passengers   special dishes   machines   building projects

A lawyer gives legal advice and a secretary organises meetings.

3 Listening and Speaking (track 5.1) 🎧 💬

Work in pairs. Listen to Jose, Millie, Lorna and Jake talk about the jobs they do. Which jobs from Activity 1 do they mention?

Listen again. What does each person like or not like about their job? Tell a partner.

4 Listening (track 5.1) 🎧 ABC XYZ

a   Copy and complete the comments with the correct words you heard in Activity 3. Listen again if you need to.

> profession   career   full-time   part-time   work
> temporary   job

i   I like my _____ because I work with great people.
ii   Building is hard _____ but I enjoy it.
iii   I often work six days a week. It is certainly a _____ job!
iv   I also travel a long distance to work. In this _____, that is quite normal.
v   I work _____ three days a week.
vi   It's a _____ job though – I finish in two months' time…
vii   Eventually, I'd like a _____ in engineering.

b   Which three words mean something very similar to job?
c   Which words relate to the frequency or length of a job?

STUDY SKILLS

Job, work, profession, career are examples of **synonyms** – words that mean nearly the same as each other. Remember that synonyms don't have exactly the same meaning as each other. There are small differences in meaning and use between synonyms. It is an important skill to be able to understand these differences. When you learn new synonyms, make sure you understand the differences between them by looking at how the word is used in a sentence.

KEY TERM

synonym: a word that means nearly the same as another word

5 Reading 📖 ᴬᴮᶜ

Match the words in the word box with a definition.

a The regular work that a person does to earn money.

b Activity that needs some effort to do.

c Jobs that you do in your working life in the same type of work.

d Work that needs special training or skills and often a high level of education.

> career
> profession
> job
> work

6 Speaking 💬

Discuss these questions with your partner. Use the examples to help you.
You will then understand how these words are used.

a What careers are you interested in?

I'm interested in a career in Art and Design, but I don't know which job yet.

b What professions do people have in your family?

Many people in my family work in education. My dad is a teacher and my mum is a university professor. My uncle is a head teacher.

c Who works full-time in your family?

Both my parents work full time, and my older brother too.

d Do you know anyone with a part-time job? What do they do?

My cousin has a part-time job. He is a waiter in a restaurant. My older sister works in a clothes shop at weekends.

e Which professions do people have in your town or city?

We live in an old town, so most employment is in the tourism industry.

7 Reading 📖

What different ways are there to find a job?

a Read the job adverts.

Jobs and careers

The following jobs and careers are available: >

Teaching assistant
A large primary school is looking for a teaching assistant. You must be ready to start in September and have experience working with children of 8-11 years. This is a full-time job.

Secretary
A small company needs a secretary. You must be available to start immediately. You must have experience with computer systems. This is a permanent part-time job.

Postal worker
A person is needed to deliver post and light parcels. You must be available to work early in the morning. Some work during the night is also required. This is a temporary job for six months only.

b   In pairs, read about people who are looking for a job.
Which job do you think would be good for each person?

Kai
I'm looking for a full-time or a part-time job, but it must be permanent. I can start straight away. I have computer skills. I like working on my own.

Lynne
I am looking for a temporary job. I can do lots of things, but I'm not very good at getting up early!

Ola
I am looking for any type of job – part-time, full-time or temporary. I don't want an office job. I prefer being outside because I like the open air.

Eva
I love working with children, so I'm looking for a job in a school. I need a part-time job and can start in September. I like helping young people because I enjoy seeing them make progress.

Will
I am looking for a job working with young people. I used to work in a nursery. I would like to work full-time.

8 Speaking and Writing 💬 📝

In pairs, create a short job advert for a new job at your school.

a   Discuss together what your school needs. Think about different parts of the school.

> classrooms   playground   sports field   canteen   kitchen   science lab

For example:

I think we need a classroom assistant to help our teacher to…

The science lab needs someone to…

b   Describe the job and the things that need doing. Is it full or part-time, permanent or temporary? When do you want the person to start work?

The word box has some phrases to help you.

> …School is looking for…   **We need a… to…**
> **You must have experience with…**   You must be interested in…
> This is a… job   You must be available to start…

c   Present your adverts to your class. Have a class vote on the best idea!

READING TIP

Some real-life texts will contain words that you do not know. It will help you if you look at the words surrounding those words. This means looking at the surrounding words to help you. For example, if you didn't understand the phrase **open air**, in the last advert in Activity 6, you could look at the words around it and guess that it meant 'being outside'.

> 5.2 Working with people

Use these activities to learn more about jobs where you work with others.

1 Reading and Speaking 📖 💬 ABC XYZ

Work in pairs. Read the jobs in the word box and then put them into groups. Use the examples to help you. (Some jobs will have more than one group).

doctor   architect   baker   bus/taxi driver   businessman   businesswoman   cleaner   engineer   farmer   firefighter   flight attendant   mechanic   nurse   police officer   receptionist   salesperson   shop assistant   soldier   teacher   vet

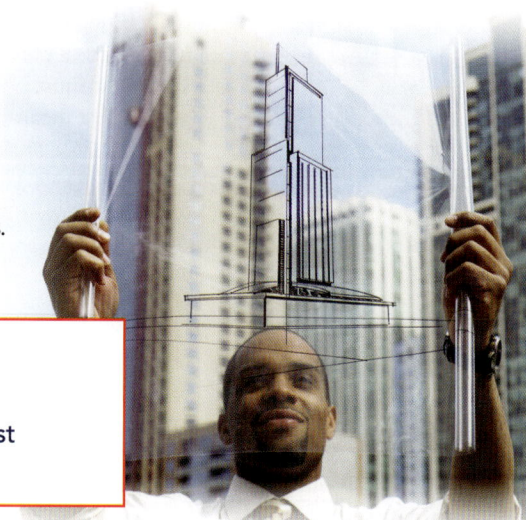

a jobs that help others get better: nurse

b jobs that require a lot of training: architect

c jobs working with lots of different people: shop assistant

d jobs with travel: flight attendant

e jobs working with your hands: mechanic

f jobs working with animals: vet

g jobs that are dangerous: soldier

Can you add one more job to each group? When you have finished, discuss the jobs that are done by people you know.

STUDY TIP

Remember to look at **suffixes** on words to help you understand the meaning.

Suffixes are groups of letters on the end of words. Suffixes make a different word and change the meaning.

For example: build**er**   act**or**   scient**ist**   employ**ment**   profess**ion**

KEY TERM

suffix: an addition to the end of a word, such as **-er** or **-ion**

---

2 Writing 📝 ABC XYZ

Read the Study tip. Here are some common suffixes for jobs:

-er	-or	-ant	-ist	-ic
baker				

Find words in Activity 1 with these endings and write them in the correct group. Can you think of more examples for each suffix? You can also add words that are not about jobs.

3 Speaking and Reading 💬 📖

Work in pairs and try this job quiz. Find words in Activity 1 to complete the descriptions in your notebook.

a   An _____ designs buildings and makes sure they are built correctly.

b   A _____ makes bread and cakes for shops.

c   A _____ greets visitors to an office or hotel.

d   A _____ looks after animals when they are sick or need care.

e   A _____ serves customers in shops.

f   A _____ or _____ owns a company and makes important decisions about the company.

g   A _____ sells products for a company.

h   A _____ stops fires and protects people and property from burning.

GRAMMAR FOCUS

Compound nouns are two (or more) words that are put together to create a new meaning.

Open compound nouns are made of two separate words:

- police officer
- flight attendant
- bus driver

Closed compound nouns are two joined words that form a single word:

- firefighter
- businesswoman

Pronunciation

When you say compound nouns aloud, put more stress upon the first word or part. For example:

- <u>fligh</u>t attendant
- <u>fire</u>fighter

A **compound adjective** or **adverb** is a two-word adjective where the two words appear to create a new meaning. The words are usually separated by a hyphen (-). Look at these examples from the text in Activity 5 below:

- I'm working **part-time** while I am still at school. (compound adverb)
- … it also gives me useful skills for when I have a **full-time** job. (compound adjective)

Compound adjectives are often used to describe lengths of time. For example:

- A **two-week** holiday / A **ten-week** school term / a **three-day** weekend.

KEY TERMS

compound noun: two or more words that are one unit (for example, postman or bus driver)

compound adjective or **adverb:** two or more words that appear together to create a new meaning (usually separated by a hyphen) (for example, part-time, two-weeks)

4 Writing ✎

a   Look at your answers to Activity 3. Which words are compound nouns?
Are they open or closed?

b   Write four more short job descriptions to test your friends.

5 Reading 📖

a   Molly is describing her part-time job. Read her description.
Where does she work and what is her job?

> Every Saturday, I work in the electrical department in the Nova department store in the city centre. I serve customers and tidy up the displays on the shop floor. I'm working part-time while I am still at school. Of course I like it because I earn extra money for myself, but it also gives me useful skills for when I have a full-time job. For example, I have to work well in a team with my colleagues and my manager. I have to be helpful, polite and patient with customers and keep calm if there are any problems. I also look after the till when customers pay for items. I don't know yet what I want to do as a career, but this job makes me more confident. It is good experience to put on a job or college application.

b   i   When does Molly work? Does she still go to school?

ii   What type of products do you think she sells?

iii   How does she think her job will help her in the future?

iv   Molly has learned important 'people skills' in her job.
Which two examples does she give?

v   What else does she do?

vi   Molly says that her job is 'good experience to put on a job or college
application'. Why do you think this is?

6 Speaking 💬

Do you or anyone you know have a part-time job? What kind of job is it?
What do they have to do?

My cousin is 19 and she works as a waitress in a café.
She serves customers and...

7 Reading 📖 ᴬᴮᶜ

The Nova department store is advertising some more part-time jobs.
Read the advert and then answer the questions.

Part-time staff wanted

The Nova department store is looking for part-time staff for the following departments:

Men and women's clothes | Sports floor |
Furniture department | Computer shop | Novita café

You must be over 16 and available to work most Saturdays and some Thursday evenings. This is a great opportunity for confident and enthusiastic young people who are able to work well with others. You need to be calm, polite and patient and able to work in a busy environment.

Download an application form from our website:
nova.com/careers/

---

a   What do you think 'staff' means?
b   Which departments are mentioned in the advert?
c   Match the adjectives from the advert to their opposite meaning:
    Copy the words below into your notebook.

confident	bored
enthusiastic	rude
calm	quiet
polite	shy
patient	nervous
busy	impatient

8 Writing

Imagine that you want to apply for a part-time job at the Nova department store.

- Decide which department you would like to work in.
- Copy and complete the form below. Take time with Section B where you need to write a paragraph.

WRITING TIP

When explaining about a specific time or period, you can start a sentence with the word 'when'.

- 'When I played for the local football team,…'.

Notice how this phrase has a comma at the end; this shows the end of the first part of the sentence (the first **clause**).

JOB APPLICATION FORM

Section A

Name _____

Age _____

Address _____
_____
_____

Section B

Describe a time when you worked with other people. It could be an example from school, a sports team or another part-time job. Write 40–60 words.

- What did you do?
- Who did you work with?
- What did you enjoy about the job? Describe anything new that you learned.

_____
_____
_____

Before you start, read Zainab's answer to Section B.

Last year, when I worked in a supermarket, I worked with six other people and my manager, Ali. I enjoyed working as a team because we all helped each other. I learned a lot from my colleagues, especially the older ones. I learned how to communicate with different customers and to stay calm if there was a problem.

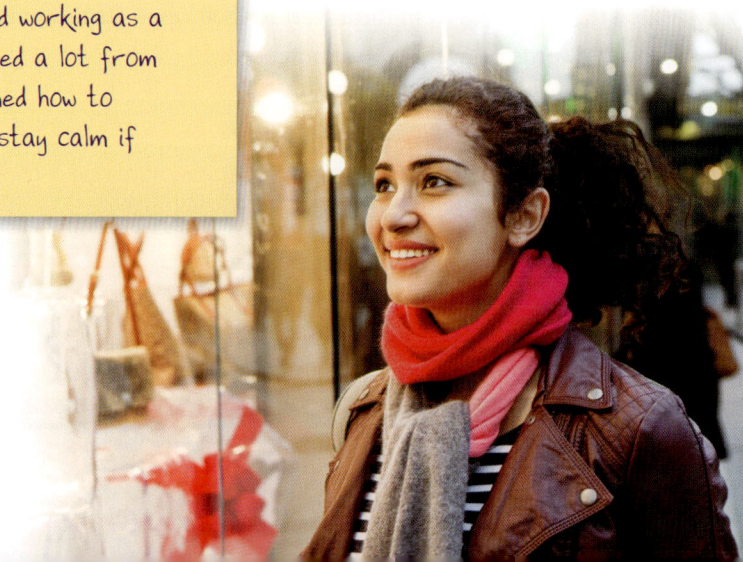

> 5.3 Creative jobs

These activities will help you learn about jobs in creative careers.

1 Reading 📖 🔤

In pairs, complete the paragraphs below by using the jobs in the word box.
Then match the paragraphs to the correct photos, i-iv.

photographer   chef
hairdresser   actor

a   I meet lots of customers every day. By the time they leave, they look quite different and they are usually pleased with the result! I enjoy chatting to them and making them feel happy. Although I work near other people, I work by myself. All of my work is indoors. I'm a _____.

b   I work in a team. Although I am the boss, I like to let other people be involved and help with the work. The place where I work is very busy and it does get hot! I don't usually get to meet our customers, but I know they like the things we create. I'm a _____.

c   I really enjoy my job. I love performing and wearing different costumes. I spend a lot of time practising and learning words. I like working with others. Sometimes I might work with one or two people and sometimes I work with many people. I'm an _____.

d   Most of my work takes place indoors, but sometimes I work outside too. I work with two assistants, but meet different people every day. I enjoy working with technology. The equipment I use in my job costs a lot of money. I'm a _____.

2 Reading and Speaking 📖 💬 ABC XYZ

What do people do in these jobs? Match the jobs with a description.

a	photographer	i	cuts people's hair
b	chef	ii	performs roles on stage and screen
c	hairdresser	iii	creates special food dishes for restaurants
d	actor	iv	takes pictures for newspapers and magazines

What other creative jobs do you know? Think of two more jobs and describe them to a partner (don't say the name of the job). Can they guess the job?

3 Reading 📖

a Read the conversation. Lucas is showing some visitors the place where he works. What job from Activity 1 does Lucas do?

Visitors: Hi Lucas. Thanks for inviting us to your studio. Can we come in?

Lucas: Yes, sure. Come and meet my assistants. This is Su Lyn and this is Travis. They help me to set up the equipment.

Visitor 1: Hello there. That's an amazing camera over there. Is it very heavy to hold?

Lucas: Yes, that one is quite heavy. But this camera here is lighter and easier to use.

Visitor 1: Which one? This one here next to me on this table?

Lucas: Yes, that's right.

Visitor 2: And those lights are huge! I'm looking at those lights over there at the back of the studio.

Lucas: Yes, we need strong lights to get good clear pictures. You really notice a difference if the lights aren't turned on! Now have a look at some examples of our work…we took these pictures yesterday…

---

b Read the conversation again and then answer the questions.

i Who helps Lucas at work?

ii Which equipment does he mention?

iii What does he show the visitors at the end?

GRAMMAR FOCUS

Demonstrative pronouns are used to talk about people or things in a sentence.

We use **this** and **these** to talk about things that are near to us.

- …**this** camera here is lighter and easier to use.
- …we took **these** picture**s** yesterday.

this = about singular nouns
these = about plural nouns

We use **that** and **those** to talk about things that are farther from us (not near).

- **That**'s an amazing camera over there.
- Yes, **that** one is quite heavy.
- I'm looking at **those** light**s** over there at the back of the studio.

that = about singular nouns
those = about plural nouns

This can be used to introduce people. Remember to use **this** for both, when talking about two people. For example:

- **This** is Su Lyn and **this** is Travis.
  (~~these are Su Lyn and Travis~~)

You can also use **this** about yourself at the start of phone calls. For example:

- Hi, **this** is Elena.

That can also be used to reply to something. For example:

- Which one? This one here next to me on this table?
  Yes, **that**'s right.

KEY TERM

demonstrative pronouns: used to talk about things near or further away (for example, this, these, that, those)

4 Reading 📖

Complete Louisa's conversation in your notebook with the correct demonstrative pronouns (you will need to use some more than once).

┌───┐
│   this   these   that   those   │
└───┘

Hairdresser:	Mmm… Your hair is very long. So which bits should I cut?
Louisa:	ᵃ This part here at the front – but not too much…
Hairdresser:	What about ᵇ_____ bits on either side of your face? How much should I cut off?
Louisa:	Just a couple of centimetres, I think. But I'm not sure… maybe I should have a shorter hair style. I'm a bit bored of ᶜ_____ hair style!
Hairdresser:	Yes, maybe time for a change! Have you seen ᵈ_____ photos over there by the window? They will give you some ideas. And we have ᵉ_____ magazines here – there are lots of styles here.
Louisa:	That's a good idea. I'll have a look at the photos first. I like ᶠ_____ photo there on the left.
Hairdresser:	Yes, ᵍ_____ style would look good on you!

5 Listening (track 5.3) 🎧

Listen to the audio and then answer the questions.

a Jhangir worked in an art gallery before he became an artist. An art gallery is:
  i a shop where you can buy paints and paper
  ii a place where artists show their work.
b What kind of places buy Jhangir's work?
c What other jobs does Jhangir do, as well as painting?
d How long has Emma worked in her profession?
e Where could you see Emma's acting work?
f Can you name one disadvantage of Emma's job?
g Emma is going to train as a music teacher. 'Train' means:
  i to study skills needed to do a job
  ii to do someone else's job.

> **LISTENING TIP**
>
> When you hear words that you don't fully understand, think how the different parts of the word might help you. For example, 'music teacher' is a compound noun and you are likely to know both words ('music' and 'teacher').

6 Listening (track 5.3) 🎧 🗣️

Listen to the words from Activity 5 again. How many syllables do the words have? Can you mark where the stress appears?

> painting   career   artist   gallery   exhibitions   buildings
> companies   offices   libraries   singer   drama   theatre
> perform   weddings   music   teacher

For example:

painting

career

7 Writing 📝

What kind of career would you like when you are older? Would you like to work in a creative profession? Or a technical job? Many careers need both creative and practical skills.

Write a paragraph about what kind of career or job you would like. Use these questions to develop your paragraph:

- What are you good at?
- What are you interested in?
- What kind of job would you like? Why?
- What things might you do in that job?

Before you start, look at Abe's paragraph first. How has he answered the questions above? Use his example to help you.

When I am older, I would like to be a photographer. I am quite creative and good at drawing. I like looking at the world around me. There are lots of interesting things to see if you really look! I love taking pictures of birds and animals. It's a great feeling when you get a good picture. Hopefully, if I become a photographer, I could sell my photos to wildlife and travel magazines and websites.

Share your paragraph with the class. Read out each other's paragraphs and try to guess who wrote each one.

STUDY SKILL

Some writing activities ask you to write about something you have done. However, some activities ask you to imagine a future situation. Before you write, spend time making a plan. You could use a set of questions like the ones in Activity 6. Spending time thinking and making a plan before you write will result in a better answer.

> 5.4 In the place of work

Use these activities to learn about being at work.

1 Reading 📖 ABC XYZ

a Look at the word box and find four words to describe places of work. Match them to the photos. Do you know anyone who works in any of these places?

> staff   office   business   factory   shop   restaurant   meeting   customer

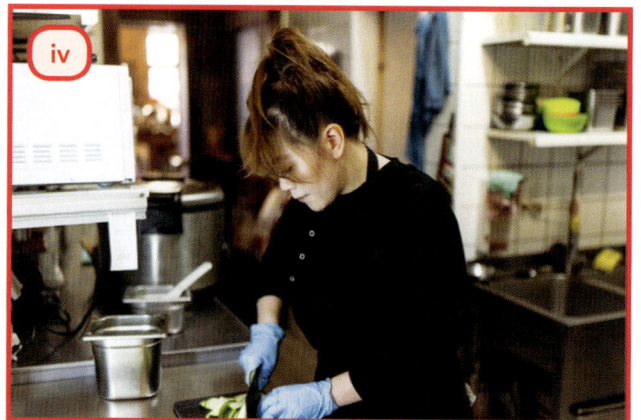

b Match the other words in the word box with the meanings below. Where can you see examples of these words in the photos?

i A company that buys and sells products and services.

ii A person who buys something from a shop or business.

iii A group of people who work for an organisation.

iv When people come together to discuss something.

v To pay money to get something.

2 Reading 📖

In some places, there is often a main industry. Read Sabrina's description of the biggest industry in her city. Which industry does she describe?

> The main **industry** in my city is producing clothes. There are lots of factories that make clothes to sell in our country and abroad. This industry is the main **employer** in our city – most people work in clothes factories or **companies** that sell clothes. One company has over 1000 **employees**. The **salary** is a bit better at that company than some of the others, so most people try and get a job there, so they can earn more money.

Read the description again. Match the words in **bold** with a meaning. The first one has been done for you.

a   Companies, factories and activities that produce things to sell. *Industry*
b   The money you earn every month for doing a job.
c   The people who work for a company.
d   A person or organisation that gives people work.
e   An organisation that sells products or services to make money.

3 Speaking 💬

Work with a partner. Answer these questions:

a   What kind of industries are shown in photos i, ii and iv?
b   Which are the main industries in the area where you live?
c   Which companies are the biggest employers in your town or city?
d   Do you know how many employees there are at the biggest companies? (Make a guess!)

4 Listening (track 5.4) 🎧

Listen to Linh talk about her job. Which photo from Activity 1 does she talk about? Listen again. Are the sentences true or false?

a   Linh works part-time in the restaurant.
b   She has done her job for less than three years.
c   She likes everything about her job.
d   Linh is in charge of the kitchen in the restaurant.
e   Linh's boss has taught her a lot of useful skills.
f   Linh would like to work for a bakery.
g   Baking is Linh's favourite type of cooking.

5 Reading 📖

Read Ernesto's description of the place where he works. Answer the questions:

Working at the airport

I work at an airport near London. It's a really busy place. There are aeroplanes landing all of the time, and there's always lots of people arriving or waiting to fly. There must be at least 1000 people who work at the airport. Some people work in cafes, some fly planes, some clean the airport and some are security guards.

I work as a mechanic. I don't really see many of our customers. My job is to make sure the aeroplanes are working properly. Most of my work is done in a large area under the main airport. There's enough space to fit an aeroplane inside. A lot of my time is spent checking aeroplanes and testing them. My job is to make sure they are safe to fly. It is a very responsible job.

> **KEY TERM**
>
> **main point:** the key idea or detail in a text

a   The **main point** of paragraph 1 is to:
   i   describe the people arriving
   ii   describe the security guards
   iii   describe the airport.

b   The staff who work at the airport:
   i   all do the same job
   ii   do lots of different jobs
   iii   all work with airplanes.

c   The main point of paragraph 2 is to:
   i   describe the customers
   ii   describe Ernesto's job
   iii   describe the aeroplanes.

d   Ernesto's job involves:
   i   flying planes
   ii   repairing planes
   iii   working with customers.

e   Most of the time he works in an area:
   i   above the main airport
   ii   in the main airport
   iii   below the main airport.

f   Can you name two things that Ernesto does in his job?

g   Why does he say that his job is 'very responsible'?

  i   He works with machines and not people.

  ii   He does things that protect passengers from danger.

STUDY SKILLS

In some texts, you can find several main points in one text. However, there will be activities where you must find just one main point in a paragraph. This means reducing the points to the one essential or overall idea.

---

6 Speaking 💬

How easy or challenging did you find Activity 5? Read the following study tips for multiple-choice questions. Copy the tips below into your notebooks. Put a tick (✓) next to ones you do already. Put a star (*) next to ones that you will try from now. Compare with your partner.

- Read the question carefully and underline key words.
- Put the question into your own words.
- Read all the options carefully, even if one seems correct at first.
- Try to answer the question, before you look at the options.
- Delete answers that you know are not correct. Then look carefully at the others.
- Answer the questions you know first.
- If you do not know, always make a guess.

Do you have any other tips for approaching multiple-choice questions? Share your ideas with your partner.

ENGLISH AROUND THE WORLD

English is the language of international business. The reason for this is simple: international companies with offices all over the world need one well-known language to communicate with each other. English is also needed if companies want to trade with companies in other countries. This is why all the senior staff in some large international companies communicate entirely in English, wherever they are in the world.

> 5.5 Having a career

Use these activities to learn ways to talk about different parts of working life.

1 Listening (track 5.4) ABC XYZ 🎧

It is Careers Day at Tam's, Reuben's and Noor's school. A careers adviser is talking to them about their interests and skills.

a Listen once.

Which school subjects does each student mention?

b Listen again and answer the questions.

  i Tam is good at communicating. Can you name three examples that he gives?

  ii What would Reuben like his future job to have?

  iii What two things would Noor dislike in a job?

  iv What type of job would she like in the future?

2 Reading and Writing 📖 📝

During Careers Day, the students listened to people talking about their professions. Tam, Reuben and Noor were each interested in the following jobs.

a Which job interested each student? Why? Give reasons.

b Which job wouldn't each student be interested in? Give two examples.

Use the examples and your notes from Activity 1 to help you.

> ### LISTENING TIP
>
> When listening to longer recordings, you will need to search for key words and ideas. You must think about what is and isn't important. Read the activity questions carefully because they will guide you to key words and ideas.

Salesperson

This career would be good for people who enjoy talking to others and selling products. Sometimes you will sell things over the phone. Sometimes you will travel to different parts of the country. To do well in this job you must be full of energy and good at persuading people to buy things.

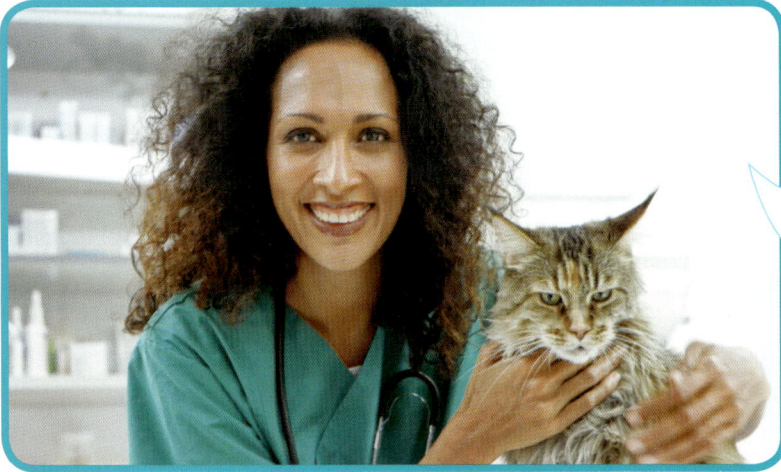

Vet

This career involves working with animals. You must have a background in science. Most of the time I work in our vet's practice. Sometimes, I travel to people's houses and farms in the local area. You always need to do some operations in this profession.

Legal secretary

This career involves working in a lawyer's office. You prepare contracts, keep records and send emails and letters. You must be able to speak to customers in a professional way.

I think Noor was interested in the…'s job because she would like a job that is…

She would like to have a job that…

She is good at…

I don't think Tam would be interested in the …'s job because…

3 Speaking 💬

In pairs, talk about the careers mentioned in Activity 2.

Ask your partner:

a   Would you like to do any of those jobs? Why / why not?

I would like to be a salesperson because I enjoy travelling.

I would love to be a vet. I love…. and I'm good at…

b   What other careers are you interested in? Why?

I would like to work as an engineer because…

4 Reading 📖

Use this activity to practise reading a longer text. Mei is explaining the different stages of her career during her life. Answer the questions below.

My career

My name is Mei. I am 66 years old and I have had a long and interesting career. When I left school, I didn't know what I wanted to do. I loved art, but my parents wanted me to become an architect. I needed some time to make the right decision, so I decided to spend a year helping a local architect and finding out about that career.

First, to earn money during that year, I got a part-time job at a sports centre in the evenings. Then, during the day, I helped the architect. I realised that I could use my art skills. Drawing and designing buildings is a type of art. We used to draw designs on large pieces of paper but now we almost always use computers.

The next year, I went to university to study architecture. It took seven years. My first job was at a large company in Canada. I really enjoyed it and after a few years, I got promoted. Then, the company closed and I was unemployed. I searched for jobs, but couldn't find anything I liked. So I decided to start my own architecture company.

I spent the next 40 years developing my company. It is very successful. Next year, I am retiring. My daughter is taking over the company. I will have a long holiday and then I will spend my days doing lots of art.

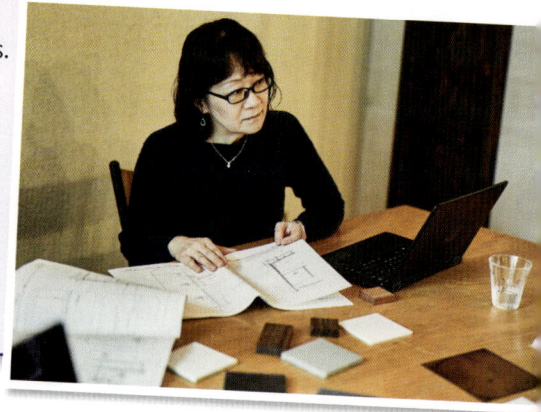

a How old is Mei?

b When she was young, why did Mei spend time with a local architect?

c At the same time, what other job did Mei do?

d How long did it take Mei to train as an architect?

e Why did Mei decide to start her own company?

f What does 'retiring' mean?

   i To stop working - usually when you are older.

   ii To continue working and move to a different job.

g What two things does Mei plan to do when she retires?

STUDY SKILLS

As you get better at English, it will help to practise reading longer texts. Reading longer texts means you must concentrate and find answers that are contained in the paragraphs. First, skim the text to understand the general sense. Then spend more time reading again until you find the right information. Make sure you read the activity questions to make sure you are looking for the important information.

5 Reading 📖

Read the important moments from Mei's career. Copy the sentences and put them in the correct order to create a timeline. Start with the first moment.

a   When she was young she also helped a local architect.

b   The Canadian company closed and Mei was unemployed.

c   Mei got a job at a large company in Canada.

d   She got a better job at the Canadian company.

e   Mei loved art as a teenager.

f   Mei started her own company.

g   When she was young, she worked part-time at a sports centre.

h   She went to university to study architecture.

6 Writing 📝

Ask a member of your family or an older friend about important moments in their working life. Create a timeline, using Activity 5 as an example.

PROJECT

In this unit, you have learned about a range of jobs and careers. However, there are some unusual jobs and careers that you haven't studied. In groups, you are going to make a display for other students about an unusual job. This might be something like an astronaut, tour guide or politician. In your display, you could include:

•   details about the unusual job

•   information about skills and training needed

•   some interesting pictures.

Start by deciding which job to write about, then do some research.
Make sure every group member does some writing.

EXAM-STYLE QUESTION

Writing practice

Imagine you want a part-time job at a cinema. The job includes collecting tickets, helping customers, serving food and drinks and cleaning.

Write a letter to the cinema applying for the job. You should say:

- why you want the job
- what experience you have
- what sort of person you are
- why you like working in a team
- when you are available to work.

You do not need to write an address. Write 130-140 words. [12]

CHECK YOUR PROGRESS

How confident do you feel about what you have learned and practised in this unit? How many of the things below could you do?

1 Write two sentences explaining what job you would like when you are older.
2 Give three examples of compound nouns.
3 Write a sentence containing a demonstrative.
4 Identify the main point of a text.
5 Give two tips for reading longer texts.

Rate yourself from 1 (not confident) to 5 (very confident).

Which things would you like to learn more about?
Which things would you like to practise again?

Share your thoughts with a partner.

⟩ Grammar practice

Modal verbs: Used to

GRAMMAR FOCUS

We use **used to** to talk about past habits and states that do not happen now in the present time. The meaning is 'was accustomed to something' or 'was familiar with something'. We use **used to**, followed by the base form. For example:

- Deepak **used to** work in a bank.
- I **used to** drive to work but now I travel by underground.
- There **used to** be a department store in New Street but now it is a supermarket.

If we want to make a negative sentence or a question, we use *didn't (did not)* or *did, followed by* **use to**:

- They *didn't* **use to** work full-time.
- The airport ***didn't* use to** be so busy.
- What job *did* Fatima **use to** do?
- ***Did*** you **use to** have a job in the theatre? (Yes, I did. / No, I didn't.)

Like some other modal verbs, ***used to*** does not change according to the person.

1 Reading 📖

Complete the sentences and questions with the correct form of **use(d) to** and a verb below. The first one has been done for you.

> not have   work   love   plan   not be   ~~travel~~

a My Granddad <u>used to travel</u> to work by bus.
b Offices _____ computers when Granddad was young.
c When Alex was an engineer, he _____ building projects.
d There _____ a restaurant in that building.
e Minh _____ science subjects at school. Now she is a doctor.
f Where _____ Martha _____?

2 Speaking 💬

Work in pairs. Ask and answer these questions about you using **use to**.
Compare your answers.

a Which school subjects did you use to enjoy at primary school?
Do you still like the same subjects now?

b What time did you use to get up in the morning when you were younger?
Do you still get up at that time now?

c Have you ever moved house? Where did you use to live?

d Have you ever changed schools? Which school did you use to go to?

Causative have / get

GRAMMAR FOCUS

The verbs, *have* and *get* are sometimes used as causative verbs. Causative verbs show that the subject of the sentence does not do the action, but someone else does it for them. Look at these examples. We use *have* + *object* + **past participle**, to show that another person does the action:

- Ollie's dad *has* his car repaired at the mechanic's garage.
- (Someone at the garage repairs Dad's car for him).
- I *am having* my hair cut on Saturday.
- (Someone is cutting my hair for me).
- I *had* my bedroom painted last year.
- (Someone painted my bedroom for me).
- Why are you going to the dentist? To *have* my teeth checked.

We can use *get* in the same structure (*get* + *object* + *past participle*); *get* is more informal than *have*.

- My grandma *gets* her food shopping delivered to her house.
- Ellie *got* her camera fixed at the weekend.

KEY TERM

Past participle: the base form of the verb + -ed. It can be used to form a verb tense or an adjective

1 Reading 📖

Match each question with an answer and write it in your notebook. The first one has been done for you.

a Why are you going to the hairdressers now? ___iv___   **i** They are having a house built.

b Why are Amir's parents meeting the architect? _____   **ii** To get a table booked for Saturday evening.

c Why did you phone the restaurant? _____   **iii** To get a cake made for Rui's birthday.

d Why did you go on the supermarket website? _____   **iv** To get my hair cut.

e Can I leave my car at the garage? _____   **v** To get some shopping delivered.

f Why did Mrs Silva call the bakery? _____   **vi** Certainly, we'll get it fixed for you this week.

2 Writing

Change the sentences to show that another person does the jobs a-f. Use the verbs in brackets and remember to change them into the correct tense. The first one has been done for you.

a   I couldn't repair my car myself so ... (have).   I had my car repaired.

b   Sara didn't want to paint her shed herself so ... (get).   _____

c   Mr Chang didn't have time to clean his house so ... (have).   _____

d   Luke couldn't repair his motorbike himself so ... (get)   _____

e   Pia didn't have time to copy the documents herself so ... (get)   _____

f   Layla couldn't make a dress for her wedding so ... (have)   _____

> # Chapter 6
Getting around

IN THIS UNIT YOU WILL:

- talk about different types of transport and ways to travel

- learn about cardinal and ordinal numbers

- find key information in texts

- write about journeys and different times of the year

- listen to information about travel

- learn about time and frequency adverbs

- talk in pairs and groups.

> 6.1 Types of transport

Use these activities to practise talking about transport and travel.

1 Speaking 💬 ABC XYZ

What do you know about different types of transport? In pairs, use the word box to answer the transport quiz.

a Find ten types of transport in the word box.

b Which types of transport are:

  i   by land?   ii   by air?   iii   by water?

c What types of transport can you see in the photos i–iv?

d What transport type takes people to hospital in an emergency? An _____.

e Who travels on transport (not driving)? A _____.

f Who operates a bus, motorcycle, train, tram or ambulance? A _____.

g A journey by plane is called a _____.

h You wait on a _____ before getting on a train.

i What's the difference between the two types of ticket?

j A system of trains, tracks and stations is called a _____.

ambulance   bicycle
boat   bus   driver
ferry   flight
motorcycle
passenger   plane
platform   railway
return ticket
one way ticket
train   tram   car

2 Speaking 💬

How do you use transport? In pairs, ask each other these questions and compare your answers.

a   What types of transport do you often use?

b   Which transport do you prefer? Why?

I often rent a bike to take my cousins round the city when they come to visit us.

| straight ahead   cross |
| leave   lost |
| get out   take |

3 Reading 📖 ABC XYZ

Jamila has travelled to meet her cousin, Sofia, in the next town. Sofia is worried because she hasn't arrived yet. Complete their phone conversation using the word box.

> Sofia: Where are you? Did you ^a take the train or the bus? What time did it ^b_____ the station?
>
> Jamila: I took the train. It left at 10.30.
>
> Sofia: 10.30! You should be here by now. Are you ok? When did you ^c_____ of the train?
>
> Jamila: About 40 minutes ago. I'm still trying to find the café!
>
> Sofia: It's very near the train station – you go ^d_____ after you leave the station exit. Then you ^e_____ the road and it's in front of you!
>
> Jamila: I can't see any cafes. I think I am ^f_____!
>
> Sofia: Oh no… How did you get lost? The café is very close!

4 Speaking 💬

In pairs, talk about the last time you used public transport.
Use the words and expressions from Activity 3 to help you.

a   Where were you going? Why?

b   What happened during and after the journey? Were there any problems?

5 Speaking 💬

In pairs, read the comments below. What transport type do the comments describe?

Sort the comments into advantages (good points) and disadvantages (bad points).

Which comments do you agree with?

| it's cheap | they can be busy | they can be delayed in traffic | they are frequent |

| you often have to wait | you can often sit upstairs and downstairs | you can use it at any age | they don't go everywhere - only to certain places |

STUDY SKILLS

One way to make your answers longer is to talk about advantages and disadvantages. You may be asked about what you do and don't enjoy about something. It might be about a small detail, such as bus travel, or it might be more general, such as ways to travel. Spend time practising ways to discuss small and larger topics.

6 Writing and Speaking 📝 💬

Choose three other transport types from Activity 1. Make notes about advantages and disadvantages. Give your notes to another pair and compare. Explain the advantages and disadvantages of each type of transport.

One advantage of a bus is that it...

A disadvantage of the car is...

Another problem with the car is...

SPEAKING TIP

When you are explaining several reasons for something, you can use words and phrases like 'Another reason is…' and 'Another disadvantage is…'

---

7 Listening (track 6.1) 🎧

Listen to Jasmine talk about different types of transport.
Answer the following questions:

a   What is Jasmine's favourite way to travel? What are the advantages?

b   What is her least favourite way to travel? What are the disadvantages?

c   Which two types of transport has she never travelled on?

d   What does Jasmine think about planes?

e   Which of Jasmine's views and experiences are similar to yours? Which are different?

PRONOUNCING ENGLISH

Short and long 'i' sound

Some words with the vowel 'i' have a short sound, for example: *in, amazing*.

There are also words with 'i' that have a long sound, for example: *like, flight*.

---

8 Speaking 💬 🗣

a   Read the words below aloud with a partner. Copy the table and put the words in the correct group.

---

did   sit   time   I   walking   is   exercise
city   traffic   think   bicycle   ticket

Short 'i' sounds	Long 'i' sounds
/ɪ/	/aɪ/

b   Can you add two more words to each group?

9 Speaking 💬

In pairs, you are going to do a role play about travel. Imagine you are making a plan to travel somewhere together for a day out. In your role play, you should ask:

a Where should we go?

b How will we get there?

c What time should we leave and return?

d What will we do when we get there?

Remember that modal verbs help you to talk about future events. You could use phrases such as:

We could go to...

We can get there by...

We should leave at...

We must return by...

When we get there, we can...

Perform your role play for the class.

› 6.2 In the air

In these activities you will listen to, read about and discuss flying.

1 Reading 📖 ABC XYZ

In the next activity, you are going to listen to two people talking about their experiences of flying. First, can you match these words with the meaning?

a An exciting activity that may be a new experience.

b A travel document that shows your identity (who you are).

c Something you use to carry your clothes when you are travelling.

d When something happens later than expected.

e All the bags and cases that you take when you travel.

f A journey to another place that is usually short.

> trip   baggage
> adventure
> passport
> suitcase   delayed

2 Listening (track 6.2) 🎧

Listen to Leah and Max talk about their experiences of flying.
First, listen for the words in Activity 1 and number them as you hear them.
Then listen again and answer these questions:

a How many times has Leah been on a plane?

b What two things went wrong the last time she travelled?

c Which family member helped Leah? How?

d How many flights has Max done this year? Why?

e What advice does he give for travelling by plane? (Two things)

3 Speaking 💬

In pairs, talk about travelling by plane. Ask your partner:

a Have you ever been on a plane?

b If you haven't, would you like to travel by plane?

c Which two countries would you like to fly to and why?

4 Writing 📝

Which two countries would you like to fly to and why?
Write your ideas, then give them to your teacher to read out.
As a class, listen and guess who wrote each idea.

Here is Luis's example to help you:

I would like to fly to Italy because I have always wanted to see Rome.
I would also like to fly to China to visit the Great Wall.

GRAMMAR FOCUS

You can use cardinal and ordinal numbers to talk about ideas and information about numbers.

Cardinal numbers talk about quantity or size. Look at these examples from Activity 2:

- I got to the airport **four** hours before the flight!
- Luckily, we only live **twenty** kilometres away
- I've been on **seven** trips already this year.

Cardinal numbers can be written as letters ('four') or numbers ('4').

Ordinal numbers talk about the position of an object in an order. Look at these examples:

- The **first** time was great – it felt like an adventure…
- …but the **second** time, it was terrible.
- …my next trip is on the **21st** of July.

Ordinal numbers can be written in letters ('second') or numbers ('21st'). Most ordinal numbers end in **-th.** We usually use this method to write dates:

- I have a doctor's appointment on **5th** May.
- The school trip this summer is on **14th** July.

Ordinal numbers that end in one (1) end in **-st** when they are written as numbers.

- Please come to Roman's party on the **1st** of August.
- The school term ends on the **31st** of March.

Notice: the number 'eleven' is different. The ordinal number is **eleventh**, so this number is written like this:

- The football match has been changed to **11th** February.

Ordinal numbers that end in two (2) end in **-nd**:

- When is the parents' meeting? **2nd** May.
- When is Nadia's birthday? **22nd** October.

Notice: the number 'twelve' is different. The ordinal number is **twelfth**, so this number is written like this:

- Saira's son was born on the **12th** of November.

Ordinal numbers that end in three (3) end in **-rd**:

- The new school year starts on the **3rd** of September.
- When do you go on holiday? On the **23rd** of April.

Notice: the number 'thirteen' is different. The ordinal number is **thirteenth**, so this number is written like this:

- The next swimming class is on the **13th** of January.

KEY TERMS

cardinal number: a number that shows quantity or size, such as one, two, three

ordinal number: a number that shows the order of something, such as first, second, third

5 Speaking 💬 ABC XYZ

Work in pairs. Ask each other these questions to practise using ordinal numbers:

a When does this school term end? When did it start?

b What date does your next school holiday start?

c Are there any school trips this year? When do they happen?

d When is your birthday?

e Do you have any important events coming up? When are the dates?

6 Reading 📖

Read Megan's text about travelling by plane, on the following page. Then match the paragraph summaries to the correct paragraph.

a After a nervous start, Megan really liked being in the air during the flight.

b Megan took a plane to spend time with a member of her family in another country.

c Before the family left at the end of their visit, they couldn't find their travel documents.

d Before flying, the family checked in their luggage and showed their travel documents.

My first trip on a plane

a On my tenth birthday, I travelled on a plane for the first time. My family was going to Canada to visit my grandmother. I was very excited to see my grandmother because I hadn't seen her for more than two years. I was also nervous because I'd never been on a plane before.

b When we arrived at the airport, we waited in a line and handed our baggage in. Then we had something to eat and a drink. It seemed like a long time before we had to wait again while an officer checked our passports. When we entered the plane, I began to feel really nervous. I wasn't sure what it would feel like to be in the air.

c As the plane started to move, it sounded like thunder. Suddenly, we were in the air and it felt amazing. I looked out of the window at the ground below. I loved it. One thing I didn't enjoy was landing – it was a bit scary!

d We had a great time in Canada. It was lovely to see my grandmother. When it was time to go home, we discovered a problem – my dad had lost our passports! For an hour we looked everywhere in the house. Then, we found them. My little brother had hidden them under his bed.

7 Reading 📖

Read the text again and decide if the sentences are true or false.

a Megan was 11 when she travelled abroad by plane.

b It was a year since she had visited her grandmother.

c Before the plane took off it made a very loud noise.

d When the plane arrived on the ground, Megan felt quite afraid.

e Before leaving, the family could not find their travel documents for quite a long time.

f They found the documents in someone's bedroom.

ENGLISH AROUND THE WORLD

Although Mandarin and Spanish are spoken by more people than English, learning English makes travelling a lot easier. That's because English is the world's most popular second language. So if you meet, for example, a Swedish person in Peru, it's likely that you will both know enough English to communicate.

〉 6.3 Cycles and motorcycles

These activities will help you to find out more about cycle transport.

1 Speaking 💬

Before you read the text below, discuss these questions with a partner:

a   Do many people own motorcycles where you live? Have you ever been on one? What's it like?

b   What are the advantages and disadvantages? Think of two points for each.

2 Reading 📖

Read the following email where Tian describes his motorcycle. First, read the text quickly. Does he mention any points that you talked about in Activity 1?

Subject: New motorcycle

Hi

How are you? I'm sorry I haven't been in touch for a while. I've just started a new job and so I've been really busy. I'm working six days a week and sometimes 10 hours a day.

I'm writing to tell you that I've finally bought a motorcycle. It's amazing. The best thing about it is the way it makes me feel free. It feels like I can go anywhere I want to. It's so much better than travelling by public transport. It's also much easier to park than a car because it's not as wide and can fit into small spaces.

My mother wasn't pleased when I bought it. She says it's loud and dangerous. I disagree – I'm very careful, but on my first trip out, I did feel a bit nervous. It also rained and I got very wet – I wasn't expecting that! There are only two problems with owning a motorcycle. First, it's expensive to buy and second, when it rains, you get wet!

Next time you visit me, I'll take you on a journey to the coast. You'll love being my passenger!

See you soon,

Tian

Read the text again. Write down:

a   three reasons why Tian likes travelling by motorcycle

b   two disadvantages of owning a motorcycle.

3 Reading 📖

Look again at Tian's email and then answer the following questions:

a Why hasn't Tian contacted his friend recently?

b How do you know that Tian doesn't have much free time?

c Who doesn't like Tian's motorcycle? Why?

d Where does Tian plan to go with his friend when he comes to see him?

4 Speaking 💬

In this unit you have now read two longer texts - Megan's journey to Canada in Session 6.2 and Tian's email. In pairs, discuss these questions:

a What are the challenges of reading longer texts?

b What techniques help you to understand longer texts?

c Now read the following study tips for reading longer texts. Which tips have you already mentioned? Which ones will you try from now? Compare your ideas with another pair.

Study tips
1 Before you read, think about what you already know about the topic.
2 Read the activity questions first, so you know what information to look for.
3 First read the text quickly to get the main idea (skimming).
4 Then read the text more slowly to find details.
5 Look for important words.
6 Pay attention to titles and pictures (to help you find main points).
7 Look carefully at the first sentence in each paragraph. This often tells you the main topic of the paragraph.
8 Work out an unknown word from the rest of the sentence.

5 Writing 📝

Now write your own description of a journey. For example, your first memory of travelling, or a more recent journey. Use the questions to plan the order of your writing. Write a short paragraph for each question.

- How did you travel? What type of transport?
- Where did you go? Why?
- What did you enjoy and not enjoy about the journey?
- Did anything interesting, strange or funny happen? What happened?

Start by making a plan of what you will include in your description. Try to write at least 100 words.

Before you start writing, look again at Megan's description in Activity 6 of Session 6.2.

WRITING TIP

When writing, always think about who you are writing to and the **tone** to use. Descriptive texts can be quite **informal**. When you write informally, it can sound more like spoken English, but make sure that you still use accurate grammar and spelling.

KEY TERMS

tone: the way that someone speaks or writes that suggests mood and feelings

informal: more relaxed – the type of English used in more casual written texts, such as emails to friends

6 Reading 📖

Give your book to a partner and read each other's work. Together, check that you have covered the questions in Activity 5. Is there anything your partner could improve? For example:

* spelling and grammar
* the length and detail of their writing
* descriptive nouns, adjectives and verbs
* correct use of ordinal and cardinal numbers.

7 Listening (track 6.3) 🎧

Chen blogs about transport in her city. Listen to her talking to a local radio station about the benefits of cycling and walking.

a   Before listening, what benefits do you think she will mention?

b   Now listen. Which of your points does Chen mention?

c   Listen again. Answer the questions below.

   i   What are two benefits of cycling according to Chen?

   ii   What does Chen say are two benefits of walking?

8 Speaking 💬

What do you think of Chen's views about travel? In pairs, discuss these points. Then share your views with the class.

* Is it possible to live without a car? What could be the advantages?
* Are there enough cycle paths and bus lanes in your town?
* What changes could you make to the ways you travel?

> 6.4 Talking about time

In this session you will talk about time, seasons, months and days of the week.

1 Reading 📖 ABC XYZ

How well do you know your times in English? Choose the correct option in the sentences. Compare your answers with a partner.

a   There are 60 / 100 seconds in a minute.

b   There are 60 / 100 minutes in an hour.

c   If you have a break for 'half an hour', it is 30 / 60 minutes long.

d   We put a.m. after the time (e.g. 10 a.m.) to show morning / afternoon or evening time.

e   We put p.m. after the time (e.g. 8 p.m.) to show morning / afternoon or evening time.

f   The part of the day called 'morning' starts at 6 am / 12 am.

g   'Morning' finishes at 11am / 12 pm. Then 'afternoon' starts.

h   An alarm clock rings loudly to tell you when to get up / go to sleep.

i   5 o'clock is very late / early in the morning.

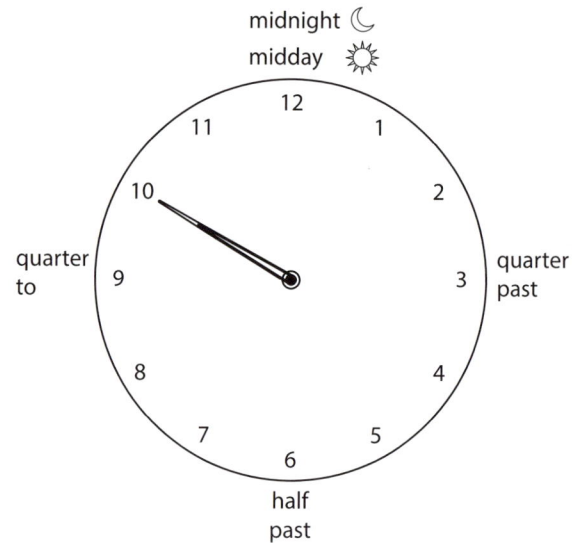

2 Reading 📖

a   Read Eva's story about when she arranged to meet her cousin, Hans. What time of the day does she describe?

Early

I'm terrible at getting up in the morning. Normally I'm late for everything. Usually I turn on my alarm clock for 7 a.m., but often I'm still in bed at 8. But today, I got up at half past four because I had arranged to meet my cousin, Hans. He was arriving at six on a train from Germany. I caught the 5 o'clock bus into town. The bus was empty! I arrived at the station at quarter past five – 45 minutes early. I had a coffee and half an hour passed. The station clock showed it was now quarter to six. I waited. The train came, but he didn't get off. Several minutes passed, then an hour. He wasn't on any of the trains. So I decided to call him. He had just woken up. He laughed. 'You're early. I'm on the train arriving at 18.00!'

b Read the story again. Copy the clock for each question and draw the correct time.
   i   What time did Eva get up today?
   ii   What time was the bus she caught into town?
   iii What time did she arrive at the station?
   iv   What time did the station clock show half an hour later?
   v   What time was Hans' train due at the station?

WRITING TIP

When we write the time in English, it appears like this:

Usually I turn on my alarm clock for **7 a.m.**

a.m. = before 12 o'clock in the day time

p.m. = after 12 o'clock in the day time.

Sometimes **'o'clock'** is used.

o'clock is an abbreviation for 'of the clock', which is no longer used in English.

• I caught the **5 o'clock** bus into town.

24-hour clock

We use the 24-hour clock system in travel timetables.

• I'm on the train arriving at **18.00**!

18:00 is 6 p.m. in the evening

But 06:00 is 6 a.m. in the morning.

In informal texts or conversation, you can use the number alone to talk about the time. For example:

• ...often I'm still in bed at **8**.

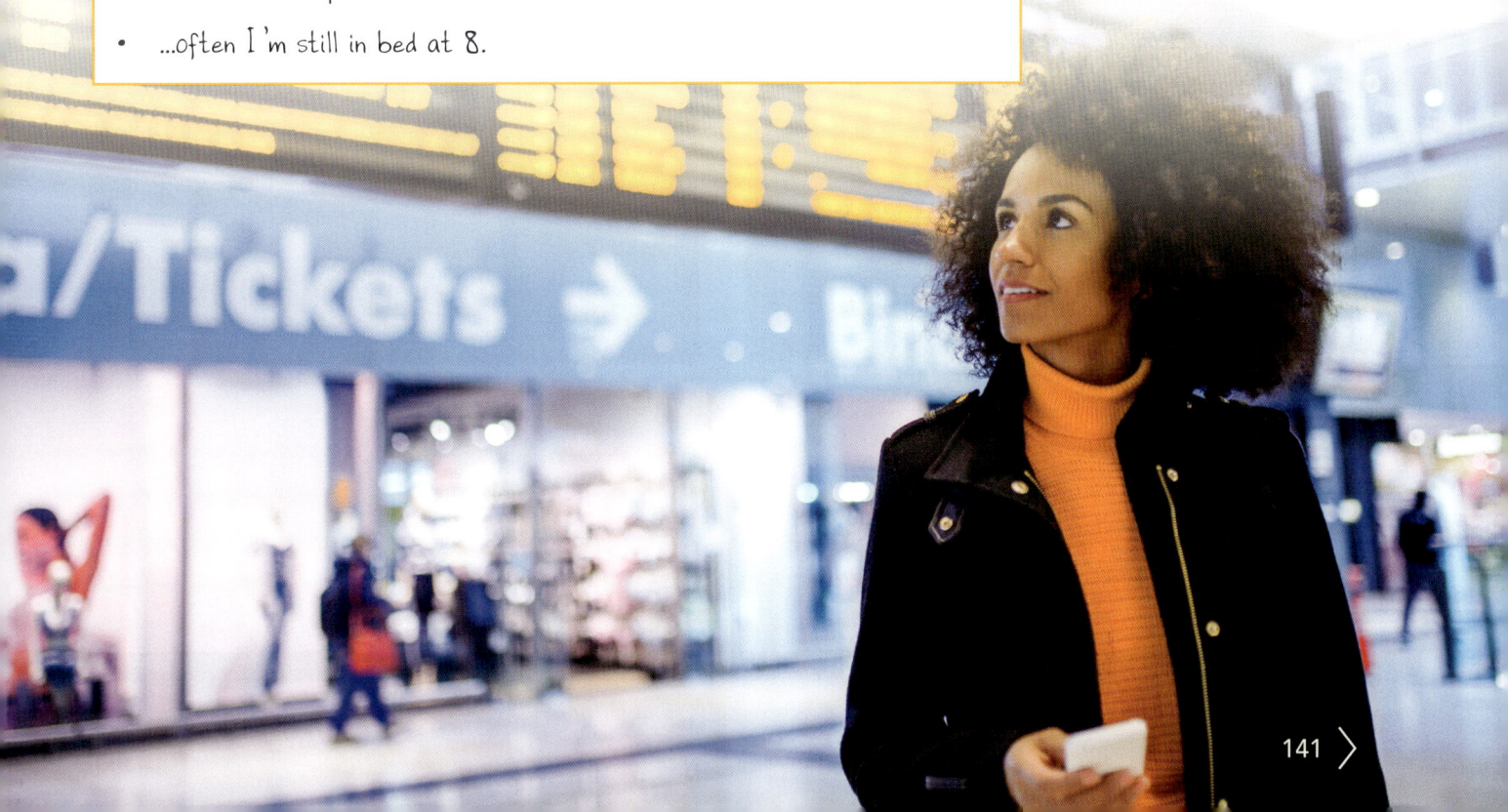

3 Reading 📖

In pairs, match photos a–d with the sentences below.

i   The train was due at 11 a.m., but there was a delay so it was late.

ii The 2 p.m. bus was coming up the road.

iii He just missed the 9 a.m. train.

iv He ate quickly – he had to leave at 8 a.m.

Write all the times in the sentences above as 24-hour clock times.

4 Listening (track 6.4) 🎧 ABC XYZ

a   Finn and Aron are arranging a day when they can go swimming.
Listen to their conversation. Which days of the week do they mention?

b   Listen again. Which activities from the word box does Finn plan to do this week?
When does he arrange to meet Aron? Copy and complete his diary.

	Monday	Tuesday	Wednesday	Thursday	Friday	Saturday	Sunday
a.m.							
p.m.							

> grandma's house
> for dinner
> swimming with Aron
> football practice
> cinema with dad
> science club
> maths class
> visit my cousin

5 Reading and Speaking 📖 💬 ABC XYZ

Work in pairs. Read the following seasons and months:

> summer   autumn   winter   spring

> January   February   March   April   May   June   July   August
> September   October   November   December

- What season is it in your country at the moment?
- What's the weather like?
- Which months match the seasons where you live?

6 Reading 📖

Read Olivia's description of the seasons in Australia and compare with your country.
Can you find one thing that is similar and one that is different?

Where I live in Sydney, Australia, we have four seasons: summer, autumn, winter and spring. Here, our summer months are December, January and February. It gets really hot! I love it because I spend lots of time on the beach with my friends. It's a time for having fun but there is also a negative side: in some parts of the country, there are a lot of dangerous fires because the plants and trees get so dry.

For us, the autumn months are March, April and May. The weather gets cooler and some trees turn red and yellow. It's beautiful! In Australia, the football season also starts in autumn.

The winter season is June, July and August. The weather can be freezing and there is rain, snow and storms in a lot of places in Australia. My little brother loves playing in the snow in winter.

Spring comes in September, October and November. These months are warmer but there is often a lot of rain too. I love spring because the flowers on the trees looks so beautiful!

Now answer these questions:

a Which are the warmest months in Australia?
b What activity does Olivia enjoy doing?
c What problem do some parts of Australia have in summer?
d When are the coldest months? What kind of weather is there?
e What does Olivia's brother enjoy doing?
f What does Olivia enjoy about spring?

7 Speaking 💬

In pairs, discuss the things that are similar and different between Olivia's description and your country.

- Which are the hottest months in your country?
- Which are the cooler months?
- What kind of activities and events happen during these months?
- Are there any problems that happen in the different seasons? What happens?

8 Speaking 💬

In pairs, talk about these questions and give reasons for your answers.
Compare your answers with each other. How similar or different are your views?

- Which is your favourite month or season? Why?
- Do you have a favourite day of the week? Why? What happens on that day?

I like summer because I like hot weather. I like going to the... and playing...

I like Saturdays because I play football. After football we always...

I like December because my birthday is in that month.

> **SPEAKING TIP**
>
> Justifying an opinion means giving reasons for a view. When you justify your opinion, try to think of more than one reason for your view. This will help you extend your speech and use a wider range of grammatical structures.

> 6.5 Order of events

This session will help you to talk about when things take place.

1 Listening (track 6.5) 🎧

Ethan is making a video call to his Aunt Jen, who lives abroad.
Listen to the conversation. What does Aunt Jen want to know first?

Listen again and answer these questions:

a Put Ethan's activities in the correct order:
  i   Then he went to a café.
  ii Finally, he arrived home.
  iii First, he had football practice.
  iv Next, he went shopping.

b How often does Ethan have football practice?
  i Every day of the week.
  ii Once a week.

c What is special about Ethan's plans for tomorrow?

GRAMMAR FOCUS

Time adverbs show the **order** or **sequence** that things happen. For example:

- **First**, I got up at 7 a.m.
- **Then** we went to the café to eat.
- **Next**, we went into town…
- **Finally**, we got home

Time adverbs also show **when** something happened. For example:

- What have you been up to **today**?
- We spent the **afternoon** on the computer.
- Have you got any plans for **tomorrow**?
- Dad bought a new car **last week.**
- I thought your dad bought a new car **last year**.

Time adverbs also show **how often** something happened. For example:

- Football practice is **weekly**.

Time adverbs also give information about what happens in a period of time or how long something lasts. For example:

- I've been with this club **for a year**…
- …dad hasn't bought a new car **since 2010**.

STUDY SKILLS

In a listening exercise, you often need to listen for key information. Sometimes, the key dates and events you are listening for are linked to time expressions. Take careful notice of time and frequency adverbs (see later in this session) in questions and recordings – they are often essential parts of the activity.

KEY TERM

time adverb: a word that shows when something happens (for example, 'first', 'today', 'weekly', 'last year', 'since 2010')

2 Speaking 💬

Work in pairs. Imagine you are on a video call with a family member or friend.
Tell each other about something you have done recently. For example:

- What did you do at the weekend?
- What did you do after school one day last week?
- Describe one day in the last school holidays.

Remember to use time adverbs to show the order of events and when things happened.
Use Ethan's conversation to help you.

One day we went to... It was really good. First we... then we...

Last week after school I...

3 Reading 📖

a Now read Ben's description of family celebrations. Which type of celebration is he talking about?

In our family, we always celebrate each other's birthdays. Usually, we have a special meal together, often at home or sometimes in a restaurant. For the younger children, we normally have a party at home. Some of the older family members love a party too and they are rarely the ones who go home first! Last year, there were 25 family members at my grandfather's celebration. Next year, when my grandfather is 70, we are going to do something different. We are all going to go on holiday to celebrate it. We have never celebrated a birthday with a holiday before and I'm really looking forward to it. Meanwhile, I am going to enjoy my grandfather's party this year at home.

b Read the description again. Are the following sentences true or false?
   i   It is most common for Ben's family to celebrate birthdays with something to eat.
   ii   They always have the birthday dinner at home.
   iii This is the same for young children.
   iv   The older family members often leave birthday parties early.
   v   Last year, the family celebrated Ben's grandfather's birthday with a holiday.
   vi   They have celebrated birthdays with holidays before.

GRAMMAR FOCUS

Frequency adverbs tell you how often something happens. For example:

- …we **always** celebrate each other's birthdays.
- I **often** travel by train.

Adverbs of frequency are usually placed at the beginning of a sentence.

If the adverb comes first, it indicates that the speaker wants to emphasise the adverb.

- **Usually**, we have a special meal together…

In other sentences, the adverb is placed between the subject and the verb…

- …we **normally** have a party at home.

…except with the verb, **to be**, where the adverb comes after **am/are/is**:

- …they are **rarely** the ones who go home first!

KEY TERM

frequency adverb: a word that shows how often something happened

4 Reading 📖

Choose the correct frequency adverb to complete these sentences in your notebook.

a   We **always / often** celebrate birthdays with a meal, but sometimes we have a party instead.

b   Talia's first birthday party is tomorrow – she has **sometimes / never** had one before.

c   My uncle **sometimes / rarely** goes on holiday with his friends – about three or four times a year.

d   Maria **normally / rarely** goes to parties because she prefers smaller celebrations.

e   I **always / never** send birthday messages to my friends – I haven't forgotten one so far.

f   My sister **rarely / usually** celebrates her birthday at home, but this year was different because she is studying abroad.

5 Writing ✍

What kind of celebrations do you have with your family and friends? Write a paragraph about a special celebration. Use these questions to build your paragraph and Ben's description as a guide:

- When does the celebration happen?
- Who do you celebrate with?
- What activities do you do to celebrate it?

Use time and frequency adverbs where necessary.

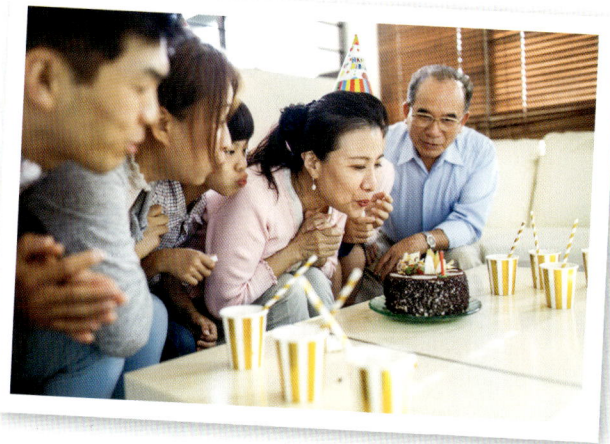

PROJECT

In groups you are going to prepare and give a presentation to your class on a type of transport. You could choose something familiar like the car or bicycle, but it might be fun to choose something really unusual. The aim of your presentation is to present information in a clear way.

Start by choosing the type of transport you want to learn more about. You could:

- collect some fun facts about it
- find out when it was first made
- collect some interesting pictures.

Make sure you all speak and practise your presentation before giving it. Help each other with pronunciation and decide if you want to use **visual aids**.

Your presentation should last around two minutes.

KEY TERM

visual aids: pictures and other images to help with a presentation

EXAM-STYLE QUESTION

Reading practice

Use this reading activity to help you practise the skills and knowledge you have learned during this unit. Remember to read the text and the questions carefully.

In this passage, Jenny describes a trip to Fiordland National Park in New Zealand.

A day out

Most years, I go on holiday with my family. We usually travel away for a week and stay somewhere in our own country, New Zealand. Last year, we went to Lake Wakatipu, then Auckland later in the year. This year was different. My dad was very busy at work, so we could only have one day out together.

There are six of us in our family – me, my two brothers, mum, dad and grandmother. Normally, we would all travel in my dad's car, but this year we decided to travel by coach for a change. Another difference was that we decided to take my friend, Nellie, and her brother. That meant eight of us were travelling together.

After some discussion, we all decided that we should visit the Fiordland National Park. I'd been before on school trips, so it would be the third time I'd visited, but I didn't mind. It's a beautiful place.

We left at 8.30 a.m. The coach journey was long and the coach stopped frequently – there were lots of vehicles travelling to Milford Sound that day. But that didn't bother me – it was lovely having my friend sitting next to me. We chatted all the way. We finally arrived at 10.30 a.m.

Fiordland National Park is amazing, but I enjoyed the journey best of all! It was nice being able to spend time with my friend – we rarely get to sit and chat for hours at a time. We arrived back home at 7.45 p.m. Before that I was full of energy, but then I was so tired that I went to bed at nine. I don't often do that!

CONTINUED

a   Where do the family live?   [1]

b   Where did the family go on their last holiday?   [1]

c   Why could the family only have a single day out?   [1]

d   How many people are there in Jenny's family?   [1]

e   What type of transport do the family usually use to go on holiday?   [1]

f   How many people went on the day out?   [1]

g   How did Jenny visit the National Park before?   [1]

h   What time did they begin their journey?   [1]

i   Why did the coach have to stop often?   [1]

j   When did they get to the National Park?   [1]

k   What was Jenny's favourite part of the trip and why?   [1]

l   How did Jenny feel when she got back?   [1]

[Total: 12]

CHECK YOUR PROGRESS

How confident do you feel about what you have learned and practised in this unit?
How many of the things below could you do?

1   Write a definition for the following words: journey; passenger; luggage;
    passport.

2   Explain the difference between cardinal and ordinal numbers.

3   Draw three clock faces and show the following times: 1.45 p.m.; 6.45 a.m.;
    3.30 p.m.

4   Using examples, explain what time adverbs are.

5   Using examples, explain what frequency adverbs are.

Rate yourself from 1 (not confident) to 5 (very confident).

Which things would you like to learn more about?
Which things would you like to practise again?

Share your thoughts with a partner.

> Grammar practice

Present tenses with future meaning

GRAMMAR FOCUS

We can use the present continuous tense to talk about arrangements for the future. For example:

- …on Wednesday evening, I'**m going** to the cinema with my dad.
- We're meeting after school at 4pm.
- They **aren't having** basketball practice on Saturdays anymore.

They have changed their plans.

- What **are** you **doing** next Monday?

We can use the present simple for events in the future which are certain because they are facts, or because there is a fixed schedule.

- The bus **leaves** early on Saturday morning…
- The new sports centre **doesn't open** until next year.
- What time **does** Jon's train **arrive** this evening?

See Unit 2, Session 2.2, for more details of the present continuous.

---

1 Reading 📖

Jack and Leon are arranging to meet at the weekend. Choose the correct tense to complete their conversation.

Jack: Hi, what time [a]**do we meet / are we meeting** on Saturday?

Leon: Sorry, I can't make it. [b]**I play / I'm playing** football. I've got football practice for the Red Stars team on Saturday.

Jack: Are you sure? Football practice for the Red Stars always [c]**starts / is starting** on the second Saturday in September. I'm sure of it! My brother used to play for them.

Leon: Well, it's not really 'practice'. [d]**I go / I'm going** for a trial – you know, a test to see if I'm good enough for the team. The trials [e]**happen / are** happening this Saturday.

Jack: Oh ok. Good luck with that! What about Sunday then? [f]**We watch / We're watching** the big match at 2pm at Jermaine's house. Want to come?

Leon: Yes, sounds good. I'll get the bus, but I might be late. The timetable [g]**changes / is changing** after the summer and the buses don't run so often.

---

2 Writing and Speaking 📝 💬

In your notebook, make notes about your plans for each day next week. Then work with a partner and talk about your plans. Find a time when you are both free and arrange to meet.

What are you doing this week?

On Sunday we're having lunch with my cousins...

On Monday after school, I'm going swimming...

Are you free on Saturday afternoon?

Verbs with dependent prepositions

GRAMMAR FOCUS

Some verbs are followed by a specific preposition in a sentence. These types of verbs are called **prepositional verbs**. The preposition often comes before the object of the verb. For example:

*   When did you **get** off the train?

*   I **agree** with him.

*   Arlo **looks** like his dad – they have the same big eyes.

In sentences with a verb and a dependent preposition, the verb and the preposition cannot usually be separated.

*   I agree ~~him with~~ – I agree **with him**.

Notice how the meaning of verbs with dependent prepositions is very similar to the meaning of the verb on its own. This makes prepositional verbs different from phrasal verbs, where the meaning is often very different from the original single verb.

KEY TERM

prepositional verb: a verb that is followed by a dependent preposition in a sentence

1 Reading and Writing 📖 📝

Complete these sentences with the correct dependent prepositions.

> up   to (x2)   for   on   after   down   in

a   On a plane, you can listen _____ music on your headphones.
b   Can you look _____ my suitcase while I get a coffee?
c   When we left the station, we got _____ a bus to the city centre.
d   I can't find my car keys – can you help me look _____ them?
e   That's not your passport – that passport belongs _____ Ella.
f   Before we travel, we need to fill _____ this visa form.
g   Before we leave, we must tidy _____ this room.
h   If you want to go to sleep, you can lie _____ on the back seat.

> Chapter 7

People and places

IN THIS UNIT YOU WILL:

- read about different countries

- learn how to use direct speech, reported speech, reported commands and questions

- write conditional sentences about directions and travel

- give directions on a world map

- talk about the weather using degree adverbs

- write about your own country.

❯ 7.1 Countries

Use these activities to learn words to describe different places around the world.

1 Speaking 💬 ABC XYZ

Look at the map. In pairs, find the following continents and areas. Which continent do you live in?

Africa   North America   Central America South America   Antarctica   Asia Australasia   Europe   The Arctic

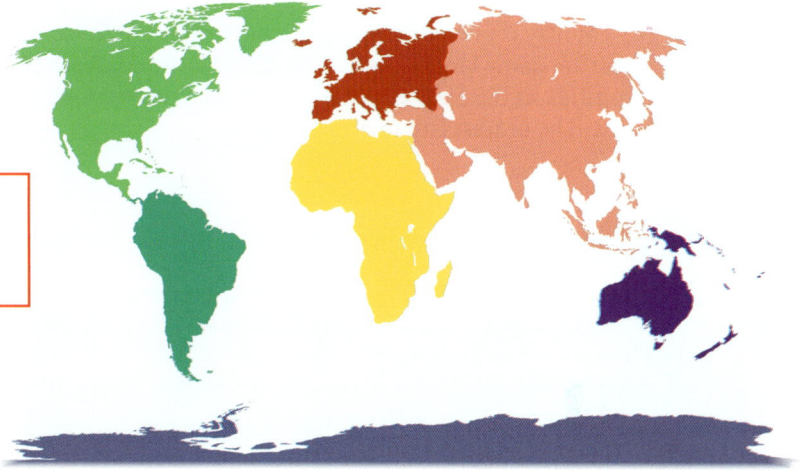

2 Speaking 💬 ABC XYZ

What can you see in the following photos?

forest   desert   waterfall   beach   river   mountain   sea   coast   snow

3 Reading 📖 ABC XYZ

a Here are four people describing their countries. Match their description to the national flags.

Mason

My country is one of the largest in the world. There are many different **regions**. There are many large cities but I live in the countryside. The **landscape** is beautiful. At the back of my small **village** is a large forest. There's a river in the forest. The nearest city to me is Ottawa.

i

Jacob

I live on an **island**. Most people think it is a beautiful island and I agree. My country has two main islands and many smaller ones all separated by the sea. There are some amazing waterfalls, lots of cold, fresh, clean **air** and even black beaches, with sand from volcanoes. If you love **nature**, it's a lovely place to live, but it is very cold in winter and we get plenty of snow and ice.

ii

Bandhini

My country is on the tip of a larger country and is surrounded by sea. There are lots of interesting animals that live here, including elephants and crocodiles. Our country produces a lot of tea and sells it to the rest of the world. The highest mountain is called Adam's Peak.

iii

Ruby

I live on an island, but it is a very large one. There are eight states in my country and the **climate** changes. There are four seasons, but the climate in the northern region is different because it only has a wet season and a dry season. In the summer, it can be very hot. I live in a busy city near the coast, but my country also has ten very dry deserts.

iv

b Look at the words in bold in the texts. Can you understand their meaning by reading the sentences around the words? Now match the words with a description.

i A group of houses that is smaller than a town

ii A land surrounded by water

iii The weather conditions over a long time

iv The things you can see in an area of land

v An area, usually part of a country

vi Animals, plants, oceans and landscapes

vii A gas that we breathe to stay alive

> region
> landscape
> village
> air
> nature
> island
> climate

4 Reading 📖

Look again at the four descriptions in Activity 3 and answer the questions below.
Use these questions to practise answering multiple-choice activities.

Select the correct answer:

a   Who has a lot of trees behind their home?

   i   Mason   **ii**   Jacob   **iii**   Bandhini   **iv**   Ruby

b   Who mentions a product from their country that other countries buy?

   i   Mason   **ii**   Jacob   **iii**   Bandhini   **iv**   Ruby

c   Who says that they live by the sea?

   i   Mason   **ii**   Jacob   **iii**   Bandhini   **iv**   Ruby

d   Who says that the weather in one part of their country isn't the same the weather in other parts?

   i   Mason   **ii**   Jacob   **iii**   Bandhini   **iv**   Ruby

e   Who says that their country has freezing temperatures?

   i   Mason   **ii**   Jacob   **iii**   Bandhini   **iv**   Ruby

> **READING TIP**
>
> Multiple-choice questions ask about different information in the text but usually use different words to the text. The questions test which details you understand in the text. You should read the text carefully and notice first which answers you are sure are not correct. When you think you know the answer, check it again.

5 Speaking 💬

Work in pairs. Imagine you are talking to a tourist. Take turns describing the country you live in. Ask your partner:

- What kind of landscapes are there in your country?
- Which natural places are well-known or popular?
- What kind of natural places do you enjoy visiting? Why?

In our country, there are beautiful mountains in the... region ...

The...   waterfall is popular because...

I love visiting the... because...

> **STUDY SKILLS**
>
> Build your conversation skills by learning facts and details about world topics you explore in this course. These are common topics for tests, as well as useful for social situations. Keep notes in a conversation notebook to help you remember facts and details.

6 Writing 📝

Write about the country you live in. Use the sentences in Activity 3 as guides.
Use these questions to help you:

- What is the capital city?
- Do you live on an island? If not, which countries border (are next to) your country?
- What is the climate like?
- What is the landscape like in your country?
- What types of nature and animals are there?

I live in Singapore, which is in South East Asia... Our capital city is called...

> 7.2 Favourite places

In this session you will learn to talk about different places and regions.

1 Listening (track 7.1) 🎧 ABC XYZ

a   Listen to Lee describe life in Naples. He uses the word 'eruption'. This is when fire and rocks come out of a volcano.

Put the topics he mentions in the correct order:

> **i places to eat   ii the climate   iii something from nature   iv buildings**

b   Listen again and answer the questions:
   i   In which country is Naples?
   ii   How long has Lee lived in Naples?
   iii   What is his job?
   iv   What positive things does he say about Naples?
   v   Why does he say Naples is a dangerous city?
   vi   Why is the year 2021 important?

LISTENING TIP

Many listening activities require you to understand information connected with **years.** Make sure you can understand how years are said. Look at how these years in Activity 1 are said:

2021: twenty (20) twenty-one (21)

1992: nineteen (19) ninety-two (92)

---

2 Speaking 💬

Think about the positive things Lee said about Naples. Do you like the same things about towns or cities? What different things do you like? Tell a partner.

I like old places too.

I prefer places with cooler weather...

3 Reading 📖

Read Kim's description of her Aunt Emily's favourite place. Answer the questions below.

My favourite place

My Aunt Emily has travelled all over the world. She had an important job working for an international charity. She is retired now, but still enjoys travelling. One day, when I was visiting Aunt Emily, I asked her what her favourite place was. I was quite surprised by her answer.

She told me to go and get her book of photos from the book shelf. 'Open the book,' she said. I opened it and saw lots of old photographs. She took one out. Then I shut the book.

'This is my favourite place,' she said, 'the town of Blyth in England. I went back last summer, you know. In many ways, it's a very ordinary town – it's not a rich place and it is far away from the capital city. But the people are very friendly, and it has a spectacular coast'.

'Blyth was where you lived as a child, wasn't it?' I replied.

'Yes, that's right. I loved growing up in Blyth. We lived right next to the beach. I spent most evenings playing with my friends on the beach, running on the sand and watching the waves hit the seashore. It was a very pretty place'.

'When I returned last summer, it still looked lovely, but it seemed much busier. There were a lot more cafes and restaurants. I walked along the beach again and all my lovely memories came back! It was lovely to be out in the sun, thinking about those happy times'.

Then she asked me, 'Now, what place do you like best …?'

a   What kind of work did Aunt Emily do? Does she still work now?
b   Look in the third paragraph. Can you find two things that she likes about Blyth?
c   What kind of activities did Aunt Emily do when she was young?
d   How has Blyth changed since Emily was young?
e   Do you think Emily likes these changes or not? Explain why.

seashore	sand	wave

GRAMMAR FOCUS

When we write down a conversation, we use speech marks to show exactly what people say. This is called **direct speech**. For example:

- 'This is my favourite place,' she said, 'the town of Blyth in England'.
- 'Blyth was where you lived as a child, wasn't it?' I replied.

Reported speech is used to describe what someone says without using speech marks.

Notice how the tense often moves back in reported speech from the tense used in direct speech. For example:

- 'This **is** my favourite place.'
  Aunt Emily said that this **was** her favourite place
- '…the people **are** very friendly.'
  She said that the people **were** very friendly.
- 'It **has** a spectacular coast.'
  She told me that it **had** a spectacular coast.

Reported commands are when we report a command or order. We use **told + pronoun + to + verb**. For example:

- 'Go and get my book of photos from the book shelf'.
  She told me to go and get her book of photos from the book shelf.
- 'Open the book,' she said.
  She told me to open the book.

KEY TERMS

direct speech: quoting the exact words someone says using speech marks

reported speech: a description of something someone says

reported command: a description of something someone has been told to do

4 Speaking and Writing 💬 📝

Work in pairs. Can you change the comments into reported speech? Write them in your notebook. Then read the comments again. Which ones are true for you?

a Imani: 'One of my favourite places is by the sea.'

Imani said that one of her favourite places was by the sea.

b Faisal: 'I love the town where I grew up.'

c Wei: 'I enjoy visiting modern cities with tall glass buildings.'

d Sofia: 'I don't like new buildings, I prefer old places with lots of history.'

e Maya: 'My favourite place has amazing views of the beach.'

f Zak: 'Tell me about your favourite place.'

5 Speaking and Writing 💬 📝

Work in pairs, taking turns to ask each other about a favourite place. Take notes as your partner speaks. Ask your partner:

- What is the name of your favourite place?
- Where is your favourite place?
- What can you do and see there?
- Why do you like this place so much?

Now report some of your partner's answers to your class.

Imran said that his favourite place was…

Dana told me that she liked this place because…

GRAMMAR FOCUS

Questions can also be described in reported speech. Notice again how the tense usually moves back in reported questions from the tense used in direct speech. For example:

- Direct question: 'Aunt Emily, what is your favourite place?'
- Reported question. I asked Aunt Emily **what** her favourite place *was*.
- Direct question: 'What place do you like best?'
- Reported question: she asked me **what** place I **liked** best.

Notice how the auxiliary verb, **do**, is removed in the reported question and the verb moves into the past tense.

Look what happens with questions that start with **do** or **does**:

Direct question: …do you like Blyth best of all?

Reported question: she asked her if she **liked** Blyth best of all.

Notice how pronouns change when speech is reported and that the verb, ask, is usually followed by an object:

- **I** asked Aunt Emily…
- **she** asked me…
- **she** asked her…

---

6 Writing

Dimitri has prepared these questions to ask his classmate, Pavel.
Change his questions into reported questions, using the correct pronouns.

a Do you ever go abroad?

He asked him if he ever went abroad.

b What's your favourite way of travelling?

c What's your favourite place in your country?

d What do you like best about it?

e Do you have a favourite place to relax?

f What do you do there?

WRITING TIP

When you use reported speech in a description, try to use different phrases. For example, 'he said', 'he explained that', 'he told me'… Remember to follow **told**, with an object, for example: He told me…

---

7 Speaking

Choose three questions from Activity 6 to ask your partner.
Make notes about their answers. Then report their answers back to your class.

I asked Lena if she ever went abroad. She said…

Then I asked her what her favourite way of travelling was…

She told me that…

> 7.3 Travelling

These activities will help you learn to talk about directions and journeys.

1 Writing

Copy the image of the compass into your notebook.
Can you write the following words in the correct position:

South   West   East

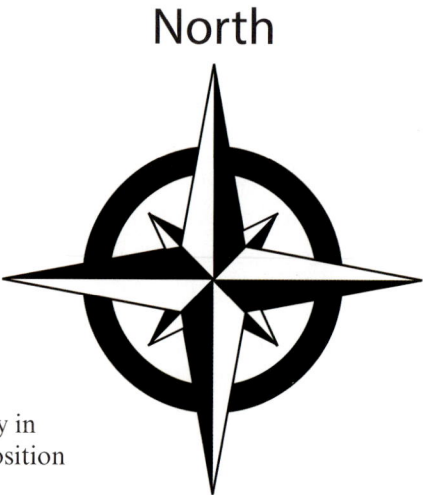

2 Writing

Find your country on a world map. Then find Australia. Where is your country in relation to Australia? Use the words in Activity 1 to describe your country's position on the world map.

I live in India. My country is north-east of Australia on the world map.

3 Reading 📖

In pairs, decide if the sentences below are true or false. Can you correct the false sentences?

a   If you travel south of Canada, you arrive in the USA.

b   When a plane flies north from South Africa to Egypt, it flies over at least seven countries.

c   If you travel to the far east side of Canada, you can visit another US state.

d   When you travel south of Singapore, you get to Malaysia.

e   When you fly west from Kenya to Gabon, you cross three countries in between.

GRAMMAR FOCUS

We use the **zero conditional** to talk about things that are generally true. We form the zero conditional with *if / when + present simple*. For example:

- **If you *travel* to the far east side of Canada,** you *can* visit another US state.

- **When you *fly* west from Kenya to Gabon,** you *cross* three countries in between.

Conditional sentences contain a <u>main clause</u> (in blue) and a <u>conditional clause</u> (in **bold**). In many cases, the order of the clauses can be reversed.

- You can visit another US state, **if you travel to the far east side of Canada.**

We often use the zero conditional to talk about rules: For example:

- **If you *are* a UK citizen,** you *need* a visa to visit India.

KEY TERMS

zero conditional: talks about things that are true

conditional sentence: a sentence about possible future events, often starting with 'If'

---

4 Reading 📖

Copy the sentences below in your notebook. Match the sentence halves to make five travel rules.

a   When people travel abroad,

b   You need a ticket,

c   You need to wear a seat belt

d   If passengers are under fifteen,

e   When you take a passport photo,

i   you can't wear a hat.

ii   they can't travel alone on many airlines.

iii   when a plane takes off.

iv   they must carry a passport.

v   if you travel on a plane,

5 Writing and Speaking 📝 💬

In pairs, write two more travel rules for planes or other types of transport. Use the zero conditional. If you are not sure that your rules are correct, ask your classmates to check.

When you learn to drive in the UK, you must be eighteen. Is that right?

No, I don't think so. You can learn to drive at seventeen.

6 Reading 📖 ABC XYZ

Class 9 are going on a geography trip. Copy and complete the email from their teacher, Mr Chang, with the missing words.

socks	cream
raincoat	hat

Farley Beach

Ⓜ Miriam

Hello Class 9,

As you know our trip to Farley Beach is on Friday. I hope you are all prepared! Remember the weather can change. Here is a list of important items to bring:

- Sun ª_____: this will protect your skin, when we are at the beach all day.

- A sun ᵇ_____: you'll need to protect your heads if the sun is strong.

- A ᶜ_____: if the weather is wet, you'll need it!

- A change of ᵈ_____: if your feet get wet, they will get sore. You will need to change to dry socks.

Let me know if you have any questions.

Mr Chang

GRAMMAR FOCUS

We use the **first conditional** to talk about future situations that are possible – things that might happen. We form the first conditional with **if / when** + **present simple** for the main clause and will/won't + base verb, for the conditional clause. For example:

- **When we are at the beach,** you will be in the sun all day,

- **If it rains,** you will need it.

- **If you don't wear loose clothes,** you won't be comfortable.

As with zero conditional sentences, the order of the clauses can usually be reversed.

- **you'll need to protect your heads,** if the sun is strong.

Notice how the form of the verbs in the <u>conditional clause</u> do not change when the pronoun changes.

- **If it rains,** the students will need suitable clothes.
- **Tara will put on her sun cream when** she arrives at the beach.

KEY TERM

first conditional: talks about possibilities, things that are likely to happen

7 Reading 📖 🔤

Will and his family are having a day trip. Choose a verb from the word box to complete each sentence. Remember to change the verb into the correct form.

a   If there are lots of people, there <u>will be</u> queues for the rides.

b   They _____ buy food there, if they are hungry.

c   They _____ the rollercoaster, if they are nervous.

d   If the family wants to have an exciting time, they _____ this place.

e   When Will is on the rides, he _____ to take a selfie.

f   Where do you think the family are going for their trip?

    i   to a museum   ii   for a picnic   iii   to an adventure park

love	~~be~~	be able to
want	not enjoy	

8 Reading 📖

Read Artem and Nina's conversation about the best holiday they can imagine. Which ideas in their conversation do you like?

Artem:	If you had a lot of money, where would you go?
Nina:	I'd visit every country on earth!
Artem:	Really? Would you? I wouldn't want to visit every country. It would be impossible anyway…
Nina:	No, maybe not *every* country… So what about you? Where would you go?
Artem:	If I had a lot of money, I'd go on holiday to a beautiful Caribbean island.
Nina:	That sounds great, but I'd prefer an adventure holiday. If I could go anywhere, I would go on safari in Tanzania. I would love to see lots of amazing animals in their natural homes.
Artem:	I would probably do that too, if I could.

GRAMMAR FOCUS

We use the **second conditional** to talk about situations that aren't real or that are less likely to happen. We form the second conditional with **if + past simple** for the main clause and would/would not (wouldn't) + base verb, for the conditional clause. For example:

- **If I had a lot of money,** I'd go on holiday to a beautiful Caribbean island.
- **If I could go anywhere,** I would go on safari in Africa.
- **If you had a lot of money,** where would you go?

As with zero and first conditional sentences, the order of the clauses can usually be reversed.

- I would probably do that too, **if I could.**

KEY TERM

second conditional: talks about things that are not real or less likely to happen

---

CONTINUED

Notice how 'would / would not' is most often <u>contracted</u> when we speak

- I'<u>d</u> visit every country on earth!
- I would<u>n't</u> want to visit every country.

Notice how the form of the verbs in <u>each clause</u> do not change when the pronoun changes, except with the verb be in the main clause.

- If Artem was rich, **he would like to visit the Caribbean.**
- They would love to go on safari, **if they went to Tanzania.**

---

9 Reading 📖

Copy and complete the sentences with the correct form of the verbs in brackets.

a If I <u>could</u> (can) travel anywhere, I <u>would go</u> (go) to the moon.

b They _____ (visit) as many countries as possible, if they_____ (have) the money.

c If you _____ (can) go anywhere, where _____ you _____ (go)?

d Nina _____ (like) to take her family, if she _____ (travel) abroad.

e If they _____(be) rich, they _____ (prefer) to have an adventure holiday.

f We _____ (love) to have a long beach holiday, if we _____ (get) the opportunity.

10 Speaking 💬

In pairs, ask each other these questions. Remember to use the second conditional structures as you speak (because you are talking about situations that aren't real). Compare your answers with each other. How similar or different are your ideas?

a Which places would you like to visit in the future? Why?
Are the places in your own country or abroad?

b Which countries would you like to visit in the future? Why?

11 Writing 📝

Now write a description of a place that you would like to visit in the future. It could be a place in your own country or somewhere abroad. Imagine you have talked to the tourist information office. Use these questions to guide you:

- What place would you like to visit?
- Who would you go with?
- Why would you like to go there?
- What would you like to do there?

Write about 90 words.

When you have finished, give your description to another student to read and check. Compare your ideas and check each other's conditional sentences to make sure they are correct.

> **WRITING TIP**
>
> Remember that the clauses in conditional sentences can be reversed, separated and presented in different ways:
>
> I would probably do that too, if I could.
>
> Where would you go?
>
> I'd prefer an adventure holiday.
>
> As you write, practise different ways of phrasing these types of sentences.

> 7.4 Weather and climate

These activities will help you practise vocabulary about the weather.

1 Speaking 💬 ABC XYZ

In pairs, group the words for weather conditions into the groups on the diagram.
Which words can fit into more than one group?

clouds   fog   heat   ice
lightning   rain   rainbow
snow   storm   sunshine
thunder   humid   cold   fog

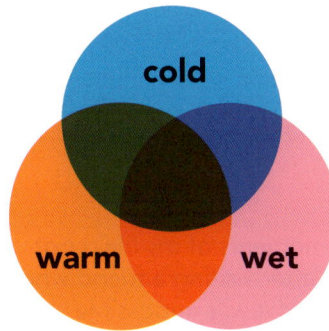

2 Speaking 💬 ABC XYZ

Work in pairs. Look at the picture.
Which words in the word box describe the weather?

3 Listening (track 7.2) 🎧 ABC XYZ

a   Listen to the weather forecast. Put the words in the order they are mentioned.

storm   sunshine   clouds   thunder   fog   lightning   rain

b   Then listen again. Decide if the sentences are true or false.
   i   There was a lot of sunshine today.
   ii   Tomorrow, it might be difficult to see early in the morning.
   iii   It will get warmer later in the day.
   iv   The weather will stay warm tomorrow.
   v   There will be strong winds and rain after tomorrow.

4 Listening (track 7.2) 🎧 🗣

a   Listen to the words from Activity 3 again and copy them in your notebook.
Underline the words with the hard 'th'. Circle words with the soft 'th'.

b   Work in pairs. Write down five more words with 'th' and practise saying them
aloud. Does the 'th' have a hard or soft sound?

PRONOUNCING ENGLISH

'th' sound

The 'th' sound in
English can be hard ð
or soft θ, for example,
father (hard 'h');
theatre (soft 'th').

5 Reading 📖 ABC XYZ

Read the five comments about different weather conditions. In pairs, match the paragraphs to photos a–e .

Natasha

One of my favourite feelings is being awake early on a sunny morning. This morning I'm driving down the coast to stay with a friend for a week. I love driving in bright sunshine in the early morning.

Ahmed

I'm lucky to live in a country with a rainforest. I work as a rainforest guide. I take visitors through the rainforest, looking at the different plants and animals. The rainforest is very hot and humid – some visitors feel very tired at the end, due to the heat. By the time we finish the tour, we are usually very wet!

Liu

Last week I had one of the scariest moments of my life. I got caught in a very bad snowstorm. I was driving home after visiting a friend when it started to snow. Very quickly, lots of snow fell and it was impossible to drive, due to the amount of snow on the road. I wasn't far from home, so I left my car and walked back.

Marios

I absolutely love crazy weather. There's something very exciting about being outside in a storm. Listening to the sound of thunder and lightning is amazing. When the storm clouds open and the rain pours down it makes me feel alive!

Stephane

Yesterday I travelled thirty miles. I usually ride on the road and it feels very safe, but yesterday was quite cold and there was a lot of fog, so it felt too dangerous. Sometimes in autumn there's a lot of fog about. This is due to the temperature difference between the ground and the air.

STUDY SKILL

Look out for phrases that are often used in texts about certain themes.
For example, the prepositional phrase, **due to**, is often used to give reasons
for specific weather or climate conditions.

- …some visitors feel very tired at the end, **due to** the heat.
- …it was impossible to drive, **due to** the amount of snow on the road.
- This is **due to** the temperature difference between the ground and the air.

GRAMMAR FOCUS

Degree adverbs show how intense something is (to what degree).
Here are some examples from Activity 4:

- The rainforest is very **hot** and **humid.**
- …it's too **humid** for some of the visitors.
- …yesterday was quite **cold.**

These degree adverbs intensify the adjectives that follow in the sentence.
This helps to make the sentences more descriptive.

KEY TERM

degree adverbs:
words that show
how intense an
adjective is

6 Speaking 💬

In pairs, look again at the comments in Activity 4 again.
How many degree adverbs can you find?

7 Speaking 💬

What is the weather like in your country? Discuss these
questions in pairs, using degree adverbs:

- What is the best time of year for weather in your
  country? Why?

  April is the best time because the weather is
  quite sunny, but temperatures are quite cool.

- Do you ever have unusual weather conditions?
  What happens? How do you feel?

  In my country, it gets very hot and humid.
  Then we get bad storms with too much rain.

- What kind of clothes or other items do you need for your country's climate?

  I always carry an umbrella in my bag.

8 Writing ✍️

Think about a time when you were outside in unusual weather. Use your discussion from Activity 6, to write a paragraph about the experience. Use the paragraphs in Activity 4 as examples. Use these questions to guide you:

* What was the weather like?
* What happened?
* How did you feel?

Use degree adverbs where appropriate and write around 40 words.

9 Reading 📖

When you have finished, give your description to another student to read and check. Compare your weather experiences. Then check each other's texts for:

* Descriptive vocabulary: how clear is the description?
* Degree adverbs: have they used these correctly?
* grammar and sentence structure
* spelling and punctuation.

Give feedback and help each other to correct the descriptions.

› 7.5 People and languages

These activities are about people and languages around the world.

1 Listening (track 7.3) 🎧

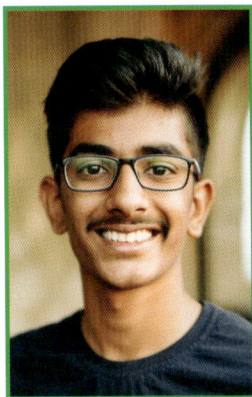

Listen to Joseph, Evi and Aesha talk about learning English. Answer the following questions.

a   Why has Joseph started learning English?
b   What does he enjoy about it?
c   When did Evi begin to learn English?
d   What do her parents think about her English skills?
e   What does Evi want to do in the future?
f   What does Aesha enjoy about learning English?
g   What does she find hard about the English language?

2 Speaking 💬

In pairs, discuss your English skills. Ask your partner:

• Which parts of learning English do you enjoy? Why?
• What do you feel you are good at?
• What do you want to improve?
• How might you use English in the future?

3 Writing 📝

Write a paragraph about your progress in English and areas you could improve. Use the comments in Activity 1 and your discussion from Activity 2 to help you.

I started learning English when I was... I have always enjoyed...

I would like to improve my... skills because...

> **STUDY SKILL**
>
> One of the most useful things for a student to do is think about their own learning. It is important to be honest about your strengths and areas where you need to improve. This helps you understand more clearly what you need to do in the next part of your studies and helps you to set goals for the future.

> **READING TIP**
>
> When you are reading a longer text, start by reading quickly to understand the gist of it – the main point and ideas of the text, rather than the details. This is called *skim* reading. Try to understand the general sense of each paragraph before you look at the smaller details.

4 Reading 📖

In this text, Adamu tells us about life in Kenya. He talks about his country and its culture – the history and its ways of life.

In pairs, read the text quickly first to get the gist of it. Match these titles with a paragraph:

a Kenyan people

b Things in nature

c National celebrations

d Sport

My country

[1]I'm very proud to live in Kenya. It is a beautiful country with amazing landscapes. Many people around the world think of wildlife when they think of Kenya. Kenya has many types of animals and birds. All over the country, you can see lions, monkeys, elephants and many other wonderful animals. Our government has created national parks to protect our wildlife.

[2]Our biggest city is our capital city, Nairobi, followed by the cities of Mombasa and Kisumu. We have over forty different cultural groups amongst our population. Although English and Swahili are the languages that are used most often in business and government offices, there are many more African languages spoken in Kenya. Traditional culture is important to many Kenyans, who use music, songs, poetry and storytelling to talk about our country's history and customs.

[3]Sport is very popular in Kenya. Kenya produces excellent athletes, famous for long distance running and other athletic events. We also love football: it is probably the most popular sport in Kenya, although rugby is becoming popular too.

[4]Each year, Kenyans celebrate Jamhuri Day (Independence Day) on 12 December, when we remember becoming free from control by the United Kingdom in 1963. We remember the day with celebrations in the street, special food and dinners and dancing.

5 Reading 📖

Read 'My country' again and answer the questions.

a   According to Adamu, what do people outside Kenya often think about when they think of his country?

b   What are Kenya's national parks for?

c   How do people often tell others about Kenya's traditions?

d   Which type of sport is Kenya well-known for?

e   What do Kenyans do on 12 December?

6 Speaking 💬

Make a list of things you like about your own country. Here are some topics to help you:

- music
- sports teams
- cities
- important days

Compare your list with a partner. Have you included similar details?
What different things have you added?

7 Writing 📝

Write about what you like about your country. Use your notes from Activity 6 and Adamu's description in Activity 4 as a model.

Start by making a plan of your writing. Decide what you will write about and the information you want to give. Try to write around 120 words.

ENGLISH AROUND THE WORLD

Although most coursebooks teach standard English, there are many other varieties of English. In countries such as the UK, USA, Australia and New Zealand, you can find differences in accent, pronunciation and even some vocabulary. And in some countries, you can hear varieties of English with sounds or words from the other languages of that country. For example, Singlish, spoken informally in Singapore, has expressions from Mandarin Chinese, Tamil and Malay.

PROJECT

In groups you are going to look at countries around the world. Each group should choose a country that they want to find out more about. Choose a country that you don't know very well. Start by reading and making notes about the country. You could find out about:

- major cities and places

- any important dates or events in the country's history

- things the country is well known for making or producing

- famous people from that country.

Present what you found out as a leaflet that gives information in a quick and colourful way. Your audience is your classmates. Include some pictures.

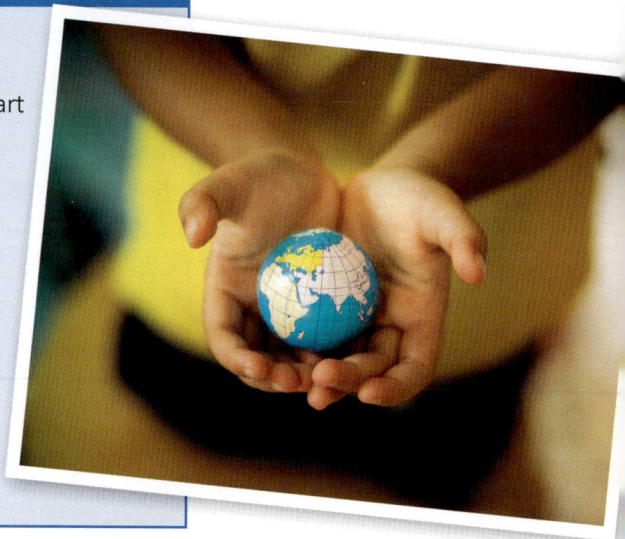

EXAM-STYLE QUESTION

Speaking practice

Conversation topic: your home country

In pairs, take turns performing this conversation about your country. Use these questions.

a Which country do you live in?

b What do you like about living in your country?

c Describe a typical food dish from your country.

d What is the best time of year to visit?

e If you could change one thing about your country what would it be?   [10]

CHECK YOUR PROGRESS

How confident do you feel about what you have learned and practised in this unit? How many of the things below could you do?

1 Give three facts about the country you live in.

2 Using an example, explain what reported speech is.

3 Write three conditional sentences about travel or weather.

4 Write down six words to describe different types of weather.

5 Describe some of the traditions of your country.

Rate yourself from 1 (not confident) to 5 (very confident).

Which things would you like to learn more about?
Which things would you like to practise again?

Share your thoughts with a partner.

› Grammar practice

Prepositions of direction

GRAMMAR FOCUS

We use prepositions of direction to show where something is or how to get there.

- How do I get **to** the train station?
- From here, you walk **towards** the post office and turn left.
- The train station **is on the right, opposite** the bank.

We often use prepositions of direction in imperative sentences.

- **Go** out of the café and **walk** across the road.
- **Turn** right and **walk** towards the station.

---

1 Reading 📖

Finn is giving his friend, Emil, directions to the science museum in his town.
Look at the map and complete Finn's directions.

Finn:	You must visit the science museum! It is my favourite place in my town.
Emil:	How do I find it? I am ᵃon / in the Star Café.
Finn:	Ok, from the Star Café, you turn left. Walk ᵇalong/ behind the road, towards the bank. Then turn right ᶜat/of the corner. Walk ᵈup/from that road ᵉacross/ towards the beach. The science museum is ᶠin/on the right. It is also ᵍnext to/opposite a shopping centre. The science museum entrance is ʰopposite /along a restaurant.

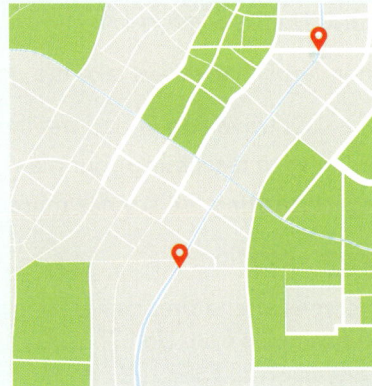

2 Writing 📝

In your notebook, write directions to a place near your school.
Draw a map to show your instructions.

Go out of the school and walk across the road. Then turn right...

Gerund (verb + ing forms)

GRAMMAR FOCUS

Gerunds are formed with the base of a verb + **ing**. They are used in several ways in English. Gerunds can be the subject or object of a sentence.

Gerunds as nouns

Although gerunds are made from a verb, they are used as nouns. Look at these examples from Unit 7:

- **Listening** to the sound of thunder and lightning is amazing.
- What's your favourite way of **travelling**?
- I spent most evenings *playing* with my friends on the beach, **running** on the sand and *watching* the waves hit the seashore.

Gerunds after verbs

Gerunds (and not the base form of the verb) are usually used after some specific verbs. Look at these examples from Unit 7:

- I loved **growing up** in Blyth.
- I enjoy **visiting** modern cities with tall glass buildings.
- I like **being able to** speak English because my cousins are English…

Notice that these verbs all describe likes and dislikes. Other verbs in this group, such as **prefer**, **don't mind**, **can't stand** and **hate**, follow the same pattern. See also Unit 1, Session 1.4.

There are other verbs that always take the gerund form. For example:

- Now Liu avoids **travelling** in bad weather… (~~Liu avoids to travel~~….)
- Have you finished **discussing** your plan?
- Finn suggests **visiting** the science museum.

Gerunds after prepositions

When a verb comes after a preposition, it is always in the form of a gerund. Look at these examples from Unit 7:

- I was driving home after **visiting** a friend when it started to snow.
- the hardest bit about **learning** English is learning irregular verbs.

1 Reading

Read Leah's description of her favourite place. Find and write down nine examples of the gerund. The first one has been highlighted for you.

> If you visit the north-west of England, I really recommend going to the Lake District. It is very famous for its beautiful lakes, mountains and forests. If you love walking and looking at beautiful views, it is the perfect place for a holiday. There are lots of other outdoor activities too; horse-riding and mountain-biking are also popular.
>
> I have lovely memories of staying in the Lake District with my family when I was growing up. I was interested in learning about nature, so I really enjoyed watching animals and birds in the forests. We usually stayed in a hotel, but once I remember camping in a field. It rained all night and the whole family got very wet and cold. We didn't do that again!

2 Writing

Answer the questions about the description in Activity 1.

a   Which gerunds are used as nouns?
b   Which gerunds come after a verb? Highlight the verbs.
c   Which gerunds come after a preposition?

3 Writing

Write a short paragraph describing your favourite place. How do you feel about it? What activities can you do there? Use Leah's description to help you.

> Chapter 8

The natural world

IN THIS UNIT YOU WILL:

- learn vocabulary about animals and nature

- practise using quantitative adjectives and pronouns to describe the natural world

- practise using manner adverbs to talk about how nature changes and develops

- write emails to friends about the natural world

- learn ways to understand and write about climate change

- practise role play skills about topics connected to nature.

〉 8.1 Animals

These activities will help you to describe animals.

1 Reading and Speaking 📖 💬 ABC XYZ

a Copy the table in your notebook. In pairs, put the animals in the word box into the correct group. Mammals are animals that feed their babies with milk. Reptiles are animals (not birds) that produce eggs.
Can you add one more word to each group?

> ~~bear~~ bird cat ~~chicken~~ cow dog duck elephant ~~fly~~ horse insect
> lion monkey mouse rabbit rat sheep ~~snake~~ spider tiger

Mammals	Birds	Reptiles	Insects
bear	chicken	snake	fly

b Which animals can you see in the four photos?

2 Listening (track 8.1) 🎧 ABC XYZ

Listen to Farhan, Ajua, Aliti and Jack talk about their feelings for different animals.
Decide if the sentences are true or false. Can you correct the false sentences?

a Farhan learned to ride a horse when he was a teenager.

b Farhan doesn't like it when his horse moves quickly.

c Ajua watched monkeys for the first time in a park near her home.

d Ajua likes monkeys because they make her laugh.

e Aliti had a bad experience with a bird recently.

f Aliti doesn't like the way birds look.

g A lot of people are afraid of Jack's favourite animal.

h Jack thinks rats are wonderful and very clever.

3 Speaking 💬

a Talk in groups. Do you agree with any of the opinions from Activity 2?
Which views surprised you? Why?

I was surprised about… because…

I agree / don't agree with…

b Now choose two of the following questions to discuss:

- Do you have any pets? Are there any pets you would like? Why?
- Which wild animals would you like to see? Why?
- Are there any animals you are afraid of? Why?

I already have some fish but I would like to own a…

I would love to see a lion because I think they are so…

I am afraid of horses because…

4 Speaking 💬 ABC XYZ

Work in pairs. Which animals do you think of when you hear the word farm?
Look again at the animals in Activity 1. Copy and complete the table below.
Some animals could fit into both groups.

Wild animals	Farm animals
bear	chicken

5 Reading 📖

Read Alwin's description of working on a farm in Wales. Which animals does he mention?

In the hills

I've been a farmer all of my life. I was born on the farm and was taught how to do the job by my father. He has retired now, so me and my brother, Dylan, are in charge now.

I love living on the farm and looking after the land and animals. It's a hard job, but each different time of the year is special. At the start of each year, we get the land ready for planting. We plant crops that are used to make important food such as bread and oil for cooking.

In April, lambs are born. It's hard work but I love watching them playing in the fields with their mothers. There are lots of different working animals on the farm, including dogs and horses. We keep chickens too, and sell their eggs in our farm shop.

By September, you can see the colours on the trees change to orange and red. It's the prettiest time of the year. Winters can be long and cold, but it's not long before we start over again.

Now read the description again and answer the questions.

a   Who are the managers of the farm now?

b   What do the farmers do at the beginning of the year?

c   What do you think a 'lamb' is?

d   Which month is the most attractive, according to the writer?

e   Which sentence tells us that the farmers follow the same actions each year?

6 Reading and Writing 📖 📝

a   Read the description. Which animal in Activity 1 does it describe?

> This animal is a type of reptile. It has no legs and its body is covered in patterns, often in beautiful colours. It lives in forests, fields and deserts. It produces eggs and eats other animals, such as rats, birds and mice. Its teeth can't break its food, so it eats other animals whole and breaks them down in its stomach!

b   Now find the parts of the text that answer these questions:

   i   What does the animal look like?

   ii   Where does it live?

   iii   What does it eat?

   iv   What interesting fact is described at the end?

c   Now find out and write about another animal in the same way. You could choose an unusual animal or even a dinosaur! Use the questions to build your text. Include an interesting, unusual or fun fact at the end. Present your description to your class. Do not say the name of the animal. Can your classmates guess what it is?

> 8.2 Outdoor spaces

These activities will help you learn vocabulary about nature and outdoor spaces.

1 Reading and Speaking 📖 💬 ABC XYZ

Work in pairs. Can you match each word group to a photo? Then find the words in the photo.

a | branch **stick** stone wood river

b | forest hill mountain **top** view dust

c | sky **island** sand sea shore

d | **star** lake shadow

2 Reading 💬

Choose the correct word to complete the definitions. Which is the best word to describe the photos in Activity 1?

a This **landscape / environment** is a large area of countryside, often describing a view or a picture.

b The **landscape / environment** is the air, water or land where people, animals and plants live.

3 Speaking 💬

In pairs, talk about the places shown in the pictures in Activity 1.
If you could choose, which place would you visit? Why?

I would like to visit the island because…

4 Listening (track 8.2) 🎧

Listen to Zane describe living in the countryside.
Where did he live before? What kind of place is Pilton?
Then listen again and answer the questions.

a   When did Zane's family move to Pilton?
b   Why did his family move to Pilton?
c   How did he feel about Pilton at first?
d   What did he miss about his old home?
e   Why does Zane feel much better now?
f   What does Zane like best about the countryside?
g   What other advantages are there?

PRONOUNCING ENGLISH

Weak forms

When we speak English, some words are pronounced in their full form and some words are pronounced as weak forms. Weak forms, such as auxiliary verbs, prepositions, linking words and articles are often lost. This can make it more difficult for the listener to understand.

Learning to recognise weak forms in sentences can improve your listening and speaking skills.

STUDY SKILLS

The adverbs, **here** and **there**, are used to talk about near and far places. Look at these examples from Zane's description:

When we first moved here, I didn't like it.

Here, we have more space at home and a big garden. (here = this (near) place)

I missed the noise of London and all the different activities you can do there. (there = that (far) place).

5 Listening (track 8.2) 🎧 🗣️

Listen to some sentences from Activity 4. Can you circle the weak forms in each one?
Then practise saying the sentences again with a partner.

a   I lived (in) London.
b   I've made new friends.
c   There's lots of fields.
d   we don't have to travel far.
e   The air is fresher and we all feel healthier.
f   we moved to a village.
g   I missed the noise of London.

6 Speaking and Writing 💬 📝

In pairs, talk about the advantages and disadvantages of living in the city and the countryside. First, look at Zane's comments below.

There were lots of different activities to do.

All my friends live nearby.

I liked the noise!

I love the space.

The air is fresher.

We all feel healthier.

a Was each of Zane's comments about the city or the countryside?

b Copy the table into your notebook. Which comments do you agree with? Add these comments to the table in the correct space.

	Advantages	Disadvantage
City		
Countryside		

c Add your own thoughts to the table.

d Now join with another pair and share your thoughts.

7 Speaking 💬

You are going to perform a role play in pairs. You are taking part in a podcast discussion about the best places to live.

Student A: the presenter who does the interview

Student B: the person in the interview.

You could start the interview like this:

Student A: Hello everybody, and welcome to our show. We are talking about the best places to live! Hello… I'd like to ask you…

When you have finished the interview, change roles and do it again.

Role play conversation topic: the countryside

Student A

Ask Student B the following questions.

a What is the name of the place where you live?

b How long have you lived there?

c Why do you think some people like living in the countryside?

d What are the disadvantages of living in the countryside?

e If you could live anywhere else, where would it be? Why?

STUDY SKILLS

In role play activities, the first questions are often easier. They are used to help you become more confident. Later questions often ask you to explain your ideas and speak for longer. Make sure that you can recognise these questions and spend time practising your answers to them.

I think people like the countryside because…

One disadvantage could be that there is less public transport…

I would like to live in… because…

8 Speaking 💬

In pairs, talk about how well you performed the role play in Activity 6.
Ask your partner:

- Which questions did you find easiest to answer?
- Which questions did you find hardest to answer? Why?
- Which language or vocabulary did you need to improve your answers?

9 Reading and Speaking 📖 💬

a Read the 'Countryside visit' activity below.

Countryside visit

Last month, you visited a place in the countryside. Write an email
to a friend about your visit. You should write 130-140 words and:

- say where you went
- explain why you decided to visit this place
- describe what the place looked like
- explain one thing you enjoyed doing there and why
- explain why your friend should visit the place.

b Here is Marim's answer to this activity. Read it and find the parts in the email that
answer the 'Countryside visit' activity.

County Down

Ⓜ **Marim**

Hi Aaron

How are you? Sorry for my late reply! Last month I went to County Down in Ireland.
I went there to visit my grandmother. I haven't seen her for a year. County Down
is a beautiful place. There are mountains, hills and forests and lots of nice views.
It also has a coast with sandy beaches and lots of rocks and stones. The sea is
really beautiful and there are islands too. You can do lots of outdoor activities –
we went hiking and swimming with Grandma's friends. I was surprised at how
much I enjoyed it. I didn't miss the city at all. If you like beautiful countryside and
outdoor activities, you should go there!

Marim

c Work in pairs. Now look at Ilsa's answer and discuss:

- What are the good things she mentions?
- What has Ilsa said about each of the things listed in Activity 8a?
- What could she add to improve her email?

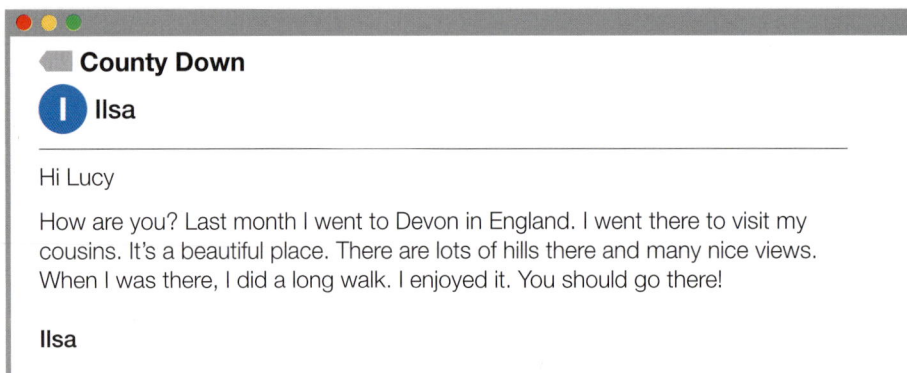

County Down

I **Ilsa**

Hi Lucy

How are you? Last month I went to Devon in England. I went there to visit my cousins. It's a beautiful place. There are lots of hills there and many nice views. When I was there, I did a long walk. I enjoyed it. You should go there!

Ilsa

10 Writing

Now write your own email answer to complete the 'Countryside visit' activity. Follow the list in Activity 8a. Use your discussions and the model emails in Activity 8b and 8c to help you. Write about 130 words.

> **WRITING TIP**
>
> Always think about who you are writing to. When writing an email to a friend, you can use casual, friendly language. Look again at how the writers started and ended their emails.
>
> Even if your text is for a friend, it is still important to use language and punctuation correctly.

> 8.3 Sights and sounds

Use these activities to learn how to describe the natural world.

1 Reading

Read the descriptions of interesting natural places by Elenoa, Matt and Brian.
In pairs, match each description to photos a, b and c.

Elenoa

I live in Viti Levu. It is one of lots of amazing islands that are part of Fiji. Most people live in Suva, which is the capital city. There are some spectacular landscapes in Fiji: we have mountains, rainforests, beaches and around eight volcanoes. The volcanoes in Fiji are quite safe because there have not been any serious eruptions for a very long time.

Matt

Although we live in a busy city in South Africa, every year my wife and I visit our favourite part of our country – the Tugela Falls, a spectacular waterfall one kilometre deep! We love adventure, so we hike to the top and watch the water crash down the rocks and into the river. Both of us love this place. The hike is hard work, but the view is amazing. We find it so peaceful and it makes us forget all our worries!

Brian

I was born in Alberta in Canada and I love living here. There are several big lakes and open spaces to explore. The thing I enjoy most is visiting the lakes with some friends, sitting at the edge and watching the sun go down and the moon rise. It's such a romantic place. You can forget your busy life and get a bit of peace!

GRAMMAR FOCUS

Quantitative adjectives describe amounts of something – the quantity. Like other types of adjective, they provide more detail about a noun. Look at these examples; they show approximate amounts of something:

- **Most** people live in Suva…
- It is one of **lots of** amazing islands…
- There are **some** spectacular landscapes in Fiji…
- There are **several** big lakes…
- …it makes us forget **all** our worries!
- **Both** of us love this place…
- You can forget your busy life and get **a bit of** peace!
- …there have not been **any** serious eruptions for a very long time.

Numbers are quantitative too and tell you the exact amount of something, but adjectives tell you approximately how much. For example:

- There are **some** spectacular landscapes in Fiji… and around eight volcanoes.

Quantitative pronouns describe amounts of something too. They can replace nouns in sentences describing:

1   an amount that is not known:

- *There are some volcanoes in Fiji but we haven't seen **any** yet…*

2   one thing within a group of the same thing:

- *…but we are going to visit **one** tomorrow.*

Countable and uncountable nouns

Remember: Some quantitative adjectives and pronouns can be used with both **countable and uncountable** nouns. However, other quantitative adjectives can only be used with either **countable** or **uncountable nouns** (not both). For example:

Both countable and uncountable nouns: **lots of**; **some**; **any, enough, no.**

Countable nouns only: **most**; **several**; **both, few, one.**

Uncountable nouns only: **much; a bit of, little.**

KEY TERMS

quantitative adjectives: adjectives that describe the amount of something

quantitative pronouns pronouns that describe amounts of something

2 Reading 📖

Read the three descriptions in Activity 1 again. Copy the sentences below in your notebook. In pairs, correct the sentences using a quantitative adjective. One sentence is accurate. Which one?

a   There are one or two islands in Fiji.

   There are lots of islands in Fiji.

b   A few people live in Suva, the capital city of Fiji.

c   The volcanoes on Fiji sometimes create serious accidents.

d   Only Matt loves the Tugela Falls.

e   There are more than two big lakes to see in Alberta.

f   Bryan enjoys going to the lakes on his own.

3 Writing 📝

Write three sentences about a place that you like to visit. Use quantitative adjectives in your sentences.

Every year my family visit…

There are lots of…

The thing I enjoy most is going to…

> most   all   no
> enough   whole
> any   many   none
> few   little

4 Reading and Speaking 📖 💬

In pairs, read each other's sentences. Are any of your ideas similar? Check that your partner has used a quantitative adjective correctly in each sentence.

5 Reading 📖

Emre is describing a special place to his friend.
Read their conversation and answer the questions.

> hill   branch   shade

Under the Tree

Emre: Look, here's a photo of the place I was telling you about.

Friend: Oh that's beautiful. Is that where you go to get a bit of peace and quiet?

Emre: Yes, exactly! In the summer, I like walking on my own in these fields near my house. It's such a quiet peaceful place – it's not crowded at all. You can just hear the birds singing. There are only three or four old stone houses nearby. At the top of the hill is an old tree. Usually, I climb to the top of the hill and sit under the tree. Its branches are covered in thick leaves, so it provides perfect shade. It's nice and cool on warm days. Over the years, I have sat under the tree and read a lot of books.

Choose the right answer.

a When does Emre like to go walking?
   i during all the months of the year
   ii during a few months in the year
   iii during most of the year

b Where are the fields where Emre walks?
   i near where he goes on holiday
   ii near where he works
   iii near where he lives

c How many houses are nearby?
   i several
   ii a lot
   iii none

d Why does Emre sit under the tree?
   i because he can feel the sunshine
   ii because the light is good to read
   iii because the tree protects him from the sun

6 Writing

Write your own description based on the picture below. Use Emre's description in Activity 5 as an example. Try to write 75 words and call it 'On the Island'. Here are some words to help you:

| coast | sea | waves | sea shore | sand | stones | rocks | sky | view | clouds |

Last summer I went...

In the spring, I like...

I love walking on the island because...

WRITING TIP

When you write descriptively from a picture, make sure that you help your reader imagine the scene. Tell them about objects and things you can see. Remember to use adjectives to give details about these objects.

> 8.4 Changing nature

Use these activities to talk about how nature changes and develops.

1 Listening (track 8.3) 🎧

Listen to Alastair describing the four seasons in the United Kingdom. Make brief notes on the main things that happen in each season. Copy and complete the table to organise your notes.

Season	What happens in the UK?
Spring	...gets warmer, plants start to grow
Summer	
Autumn	
Winter	

2 Speaking 💬

In pairs, discuss your notes from Activity 1. Ask your partner:

- What are the main conditions in each season in the United Kingdom?
- How similar or different are the seasons in your country?

Our summers are much hotter than in the UK.

We also have four seasons...

Our winters are not as cold as winters in the UK.

We have less daylight during summer.

3 Reading 📖

The natural world changes over time. Read the following article about climate change.

What is climate change?

Climate change is a way to describe the way the temperature and rainfall change over long periods of time. The earth's climate always changes, but scientists have noticed unusual patterns recently. These include:

- The earth's temperature is increasing more quickly.

- Sea levels are rising – the level is the height of the top of the sea.

- Ice in the Arctic and Antarctic regions is disappearing more quickly than usual and land ice is starting to break and go into the sea.

- There are changes in the way plants and flowers grow.

Many people are worried about climate change. Even a small change of two degrees can badly damage plants and animals. Climate change can also create more storms, very hot weather and lack of rain.

The way humans live and work certainly adds to climate change. Burning things like oil and gas and destroying forests damages the environment. Nowhere will be safe. Maybe you can help to change this. Every one of us must help.

climate change
environment

Read the questions below and then look for the answers in the text.

a What can happen over many years because of climate change?
b What are some strange changes that scientists have noticed recently?
c Which three things could happen because of climate change?
d Can you find two human habits that hurt our natural world?

READING TIP

When you answer questions that ask you to find several bits of information, remember that the key details for each question are often close together in the text. The questions usually follow the order of the text.

GRAMMAR FOCUS

Manner adverbs describe a verb. They give more information about how the action is done. We use manner adverbs before or after the verb. For example:

- In spring, the temperature **slowly** starts to get warmer.
- …leaves **quickly** start to fall from the trees.
- Sometimes, it snows **lightly**…
- …a small change of two degrees can **badly** damage plants…

Note: in the last example, the adverb is describing the verb, damage, not, *can*.

Most manner adverbs are based on adjectives, with -ly added to form the adverb. Look at the examples above:

Adjective	Adverb
slow	slowly
quick	quickly
light	lightly
bad	badly

Some manner adverbs are irregular. For example:

- The climate change presentation went **well**. (adjective = good)
- Natural environments all over the world are changing **fast**. (adjective = fast)
- It was raining **hard** last night. (adjective = hard)
- In June, the sun sets **late** in the day … (adjective = late)

Remember: These adverbs always come after the verb.

KEY TERM

manner adverbs: adverbs used to describe the way in which an action is done or happens

4 Speaking 💬 ᴬᴮᶜ
         ˣʸᶻ

Work in pairs. Look at the adverbs below:

> happily   sadly   excitedly   quickly   slowly   loudly   quietly

Now practise saying the following sentences in the manner of each adverb.

- 'Summer will be here soon.'
- 'We're going to the beach.'
- 'Look, it's snowing!'
- 'It's raining hard outside'.

5 Writing 📝

Work in pairs. Show each other photos (for example, on your phones) or look at the photo above. Write three sentences using manner adverbs to describe what you see.

Compare and check your sentences together.

Lena is laughing loudly because Raul has just told a joke.

6 Writing 📝

How do the seasons in your country compare with the United Kingdom? Write a description that compares the seasons in your country to the seasons in the United Kingdom. Use Alastair's description from Activity 1 to help you. Use your notes and discussion from Activities 1 and 2. You should write around 80 words.

My country has fewer seasons, compared to England.

Our countries are similar, but the summers are hotter where I live.

> 8.5 Taking care of the planet

In this session you will learn ways to help the natural world.

1 Speaking and Reading 💬 📖 ABC XYZ

a   What do you know about fossil fuels? Work in pairs. Match each photo i–iii to one of the fossil fuels in the word box.

gas   coal   oil

b   Now do this quick quiz.

Quiz

i   Which fossil fuel do you need to drive a car, bus or motorcycle?

ii   Which fossil fuels are used for heating?

iii   Which fossil fuel is used to make plastic?

iv   Which fossil fuel is used to make the metal, steel?

v   Why are fossil fuels bad for the environment?

STUDY SKILLS

Some activities might ask you about your knowledge of the world. The more you know about big issues, such as recycling and different lifestyles, the easier you will find these types of activities. Make sure you find out about the world around you by reading online news and talking about these issues with family and friends.

2 Listening (track 8.4) 🎧

Now listen to Dr Iqbal talk about how humans can help the planet by using solar energy. Answer the questions:

a What is solar energy?

b What does the light from the sun make?

c When do scientists think that fossil fuels will finish?

d Which three countries produce the most solar energy?

3 Reading and Speaking 📖 💬

In pairs, read the information about ways to help the environment. Talk about how many of these things you do.

Use less water: have shorter showers and only boil as much water as you need.

Stop eating animal products: farming animals causes climate change.

Stop using plastic: don't buy so many things wrapped in plastic.

Walk or cycle more: these ways of travelling do not use petrol. Traffic from cars that are not electric pollute the air and add to climate change.

4 Reading 📖

Read this article about a serious environmental problem. Which problem does the article discuss? Then read again and answer the questions.

Every little bit helps

Most of us now know that plastic damages our environment. But are we taking enough action to prevent the damage? There is one important thing that you can do to help – decrease the amount of plastic you use.

Walk along any beach and you'll still see plenty of plastic bags. Animals and sea creatures die when they eat plastic. Seabirds, dolphins, whales and turtles are among the many creatures who suffer.

500 billion plastic bags are used every year around the world. They are difficult to recycle. Every bag that is blown into a river or goes down a toilet ends up in the sea.

Lots of countries have stopped making bags that are only used one time, including Italy and China. You can help by not using plastic bags. Every little bit helps! Too many people still use plastic bags without thinking about what happens when they throw them away.

a   What can people do to help with the problem of plastic?

b   There are often many plastic bags by the sea. How does this hurt sea animals?

c   A huge amount of plastic bags are used every year. Why is this a problem?

d   What is the main purpose of this article? Choose one option:

   i   To inform readers about different countries that use plastic bags.

   ii   To describe how to recycle plastic bags.

   ii   To persuade the reader to stop using plastic bags.

e   Which facts in the article did you find surprising or shocking?

READING TIP

The purpose of a text is the reason the writer has written it. What is it trying to achieve? When you think about the purpose of a text, look at the title and last section of an article. Sometimes these parts can give you an extra idea about purpose.

STUDY SKILLS

Look out for **expressions of quantity** in reading and listening activities. These phrases often guide you to important information. For example:

Solar energy never finishes. This means that there is **enough** to make the electricity we need…

But are we taking **enough** action to prevent the damage? (enough = as much as necessary).

Notice how we can intensify the quantity adjectives, **much, many, little, few**, with adverbs, **too** and **so**:

- …don't buy **so many** things wrapped in plastic
- …stop using **so much** plastic.
- **Too many** people still use plastic bags…

5 Speaking 💬

In pairs, perform the following role play.

Student A: you are an expert on the environment.

Student B: you are a journalist. You are interviewing the expert about climate change for a website, Click Climate.

You could start the interview like this:

Student B: Hello Dr…Thank you for agreeing to this interview. I'd like to ask you…

When you have answered the questions, change roles and do it again.

Role play: the environment

Ask your partner the following questions:

a   What does 'the environment' mean?

b   What is climate change?

c   What is solar power?

d   Why are plastic bags harmful to the environment?

6 Writing 📝

Write a blog for the Click Climate website, giving advice about helping the environment. Use the information you have learned in this session. You should:

- write about the problems that the environment faces
- advise readers what they can do to help.

Write around 80 words.

WRITING TIP

When you give advice, choose the words you use carefully – think about the way you 'speak' to your readers or listeners. Make sure you give advice that is clear and polite.

ENGLISH AROUND THE WORLD

If you speak English very well and you would like to travel, you could work as a translator. There are many types of translation work: for example, you could work for an international company or a charity organisation. As well as excellent language skills, you need to be an expert in the area that you are working in (for example, law or science). Translators also need to understand the local culture and be able to tell the difference between formal and informal language.

PROJECT

As a class, you are going to produce a display called 'Beautiful nature'. Imagine that it will be shown to your parents and wider family. You will work in groups to produce different sections of the display.

As a class, start by deciding the different sections you will include. For example, you could have sections on different seasons, animals and places around the world. Each group should then choose one of these sections to produce.

In your group, look online to find facts and pictures for your section. Make sure you provide information and details. Work as a group to produce an attractive and interesting section of the display.

EXAM-STYLE QUESTION:

Writing practice

Use this activity to test your writing skills.

Helping the environment

Your friend wants to know how to help the environment. Write an email to your friend giving advice on the topic. You should write 130-140 words and:

- give several reasons why it is important to help the environment
- explain what climate change is
- describe one thing you do to help the environment (for example, at home, in school, in your community)
- suggest one other thing your friend could do to help the environment.
- explain how to persuade more people to help the environment.   [28]

CHECK YOUR PROGRESS

How confident do you feel about what you have learned and practised in this unit? How many of the things below could you do?

1   List the names of ten different animals.
2   Write down two advantages and two disadvantages of living in the countryside.
3   Write three sentences containing quantitative adjectives.
4   Give five examples of manner adverbs.
5   Explain what these terms mean: the environment; climate change; solar energy.

Rate yourself from 1 (not confident) to 5 (very confident).

Which things would you like to learn more about?
Which things would you like to practise again?

Share your thoughts with a partner.

> Grammar practice

Comparative adverbs

GRAMMAR FOCUS

We can use comparative adverbs with verbs to show change or compare things. Look at how each adverb changes in these examples from Unit 8. All the adverbs are regular.

- The air is fresher, and we all feel **healthier**. (healthy)
- In autumn, the weather gets **colder**. (cold)
- Ice in the Arctic and Antarctic regions is disappearing **more quickly** than usual. (quick)

Look at the different meanings of comparative adverbs in the following sentences:

- In mountain areas, it usually snows **more heavily** than in valleys. (heavy)
- In the south of England, it usually snows **less heavily** than in Scotland.

Irregular adverbs often completely change in the comparative form. For example:

- Climate change is getting **worse** in the 21st century. (bad)
- The oceans are rising **more.** (a lot / much)
- Schools are educating students **better** than before in climate change issues. (good)

We use the same rules for comparative adverbs as for comparative *adjectives*.

Base adverb	Comparative
1 syllable: slow	slower
cold	colder
2 syllables: quickly	*more / less* quickly
often	*more / less* often
Irregular: well	*better*
bad / badly	*worse*

We can also compare things with these phrases, without changing the form of the adverb:

- It is not raining **as much** today **as** yesterday.
- Are we trying **hard** enough to change our eating habits?
- You can't play outside – it is snowing **too heavily**.

1 Reading 📖

Copy and complete the sentences by changing the words in brackets into comparative adverbs. (Careful! There is one that doesn't change.) The first one has been done for you.

a   In the UK, the weather starts to get <u>warmer</u> (warm) in spring.

b   The climate is _____ (hot) near the equator.

c   We should all try to use _____ (little) plastic.

d   Nowadays, it seems to rain _____ (often) than before.

e   We couldn't see anything because the sun was shining too _____ (bright).

f   In Australia, if you travel _____ (far) north, you'll feel a change in temperature.

g   Are we changing our habits _____ (fast) enough to stop climate change?

Superlative adverbs

GRAMMAR FOCUS

We can also use superlative adverbs with verbs to compare things.
Look at these examples with regular adverbs:

• Trees and plants grow **fastest** in spring.
• The sun shines **brightest** in the middle of the day.

To make a superlative adverb stronger, we often use **the** + superlative adverb.
Look at this example from Unit 7, using an irregular adverb.

• At the moment, the three countries who produce and use solar energy <u>the most</u> are China, Japan and America.

Look how the meaning changes when we use a superlative adverb with the opposite meaning:

• The temperature changes <u>the least</u> between spring and summer.

We use the same rules for superlative adverbs as for superlative adjectives.

Base adverb	Superlative
1 syllable: fast	(the) fast**est**
cold	(the) cold**est**
2 or more syllables: quickly	(the) **most / least** quickly
_____ beautiful	(the) **most / least** beautiful
Irregular: well	(the) **best**
badly	(the) **worst**

1 Reading 📖

Copy and complete the sentences by changing the words in brackets into superlative adverbs.

a   During winter in the UK, it often snows _____ (heavy) in Scotland.

b   Out of all the classes, Class 9 worked the _____ (hard) on their climate change project.

c   Compared to other types of energy, fossil fuels pollute the air the _____ (much).

d   Fossil fuels will also last the _____ (short) time.

e   Out of all the seasons, I like spring the _____ (good).

f   Which do you do the _____ (often)? Travel by car or walk?

g   I hate cold weather! I find cold temperatures the _____ (comfortable).

2 Reading 📖

Copy and complete the quiz questions with the correct form of the adverb. Then choose the correct answer.

a   Which animal can run the faster / fastest?
   i   a camel
   ii   a horse
   iii a monkey

b   Which animal lives long / longer?
   i   an elephant
   ii   a lion

c   Which of these English-speaking cities gets colder / the colder in winter?
   i   Ottawa (Canada)
   ii   Wellington (New Zealand)

d   What type of rubbish is recycled the most often / oftenest in the UK?
   i   glass
   ii   paper and cardboard
   iii plastic

e   Which continent uses solar energy the more / most?
   i   Africa
   ii   Europe
   iii Asia

f   Which type of transport pollutes the environment the least/little?
   i   cars
   ii   trams
   iii motorbikes

Chapter 9

Buildings and technology

IN THIS UNIT YOU WILL:

- describe buildings and forms of communication using prepositions
- practise using the present perfect simple to talk about the world around us
- practise using the past perfect simple tense to tell narratives about shops or shopping
- do role plays about shopping and phone use
- write a formal letter
- discuss different views about phones.

> 9.1 The built environment

These activities will help you describe the buildings we see around us.

1 Reading 📖 ABC XYZ

a All buildings have a purpose. Can you match a purpose to a meaning?

A	entertainment	i	producing things in large quantities
B	manufacture	ii	this might include music, art, history, performance
C	culture	iii	things that you are interested in or enjoy

b In pairs, look at the words for buildings and think about their *purpose*. Can you put the buildings into these groups?

Entertainment or culture	Health services	Learning
Manufacture	Services	Eating
Shopping	Travelling	Sport

c Now write down the buildings you can see in the town where you live.

bank   bookshop   bus station   butcher   café   castle   cinema   clinic   coffee shop   college   factory   gym   hospital   hotel   library   museum   petrol   station   police station   post office   restaurant   service station   sports centre   stadium   swimming pool   theatre   train station   university

2 Speaking 💬 ABC XYZ

The photos below show the inside of different buildings. In pairs, discuss:

- What buildings from Activity 1 could they be?
- What are the people doing?
- What are these buildings used for?
- Which buildings have you been to? Why?

3 Listening (track 9.1) 🎧

a Listen to Paul, Zulema, Millie and Habib describe the buildings where they work
   and what they do there. Copy and complete the table.

	Paul	Zulema	Millie	Habib
Where they work	train station	museum	a	b
What they do at work	____help customers to find their c____	____sell d____ and give e____	____ make f____ for a famous clothing g____	____ meet h____ and welcome them to the hotel.

b Do you know anyone who works in these places?
   What job do they do?

4 Reading 📖

a Read Fabiana's description of the place where she works.
   Can you match the underlined words with a meaning?

   i   The floor of a building at ground level.

   ii A place where films are shown.

   iii A way out of a building in an emergency.

   iv A small room that transports people between floors. It moves up
       and down.

   v   A door, where you go in to a place.

The cinema

On Saturday, I work in my local <u>cinema</u>. It's next to a large supermarket in my home
town. The cinema is an attractive old building with three floors. The <u>entrance</u> to the
building has a large glass door with a flag and the cinema's name above it.

Inside the cinema, there is a box office. This is a kiosk where you can buy tickets
for films. The tickets cost $4. The cinema has four rooms where we show different
films. The largest of these rooms is on the <u>ground floor</u> next to the box office. One
of the things I do is collect tickets from people as they enter this room. Also on
the ground floor is a <u>lift</u> that takes you up to the second and third floors. Rooms 2
and 3 are on the second floor. Room 4 is on the third floor. The toilets are next to
room 4. Every floor has a <u>fire exit</u>. It is important that people can leave the building
quickly if there is a fire or another emergency.

Now read the text again and decide if the sentences are true or false.
Can you correct the false sentences?

b The cinema is opposite a big food shop.

c When you go in, you see the name of the cinema.

d The cinema has three places where they show films.

e The biggest room is on a floor upstairs.

f There are two lifts.

g There is a toilet on every floor.

h All three floors have a fire exit.

STUDY SKILLS

Some texts contain
numbers or details
that sound similar.
These types of texts
and questions test
your close reading
skills (when you read
more slowly and pay
close attention to
the words, ideas and
the purpose of the
text). Always check
your answers to
these questions.

5 Reading 📖 ABC XYZ

You are going to describe a place in your town or school. First read Dayab's description of Main Street in his town. Which buildings from Activity 1 does he mention?

Main Street

The largest building on Main Street is the supermarket. There is a large car park <u>under</u> the supermarket. There is a medium-sized café <u>next to</u> the supermarket. I sometimes go to this café with my family. In the café there are a few tables. <u>Across</u> the road is an office block where my dad works. The office block has its own gym. There are lots of shops on both sides of the street. At the top of the street is the museum where I sometimes go when it rains. It is made from beautiful old stone and has a shiny floor made from wood. My favourite building is the sports centre. It's <u>behind</u> Main Street and is very popular with my friends.

> supermarket
> car park   gym
>   museum

GRAMMAR FOCUS

Prepositions are used with nouns and pronouns. They show where things are, in relation to each other.

- There is a large car park **under** the supermarket.

Look at the preposition **under** in this sentence. It is part of a prepositional phrase:

- …**under** the supermarket.

A prepositional phrase shows the object which the preposition is talking about. The preposition always comes before this object. The object is usually a noun (supermarket), sometimes a <u>pronoun</u>:

- The café is **behind** <u>you</u>…

KEY TERM

preposition: words that show where things are

6 Reading and Writing 📖 📝 ᴬᴮᶜ

Look at the prepositions underlined in Dayab's description in Activity 5. Now look
at the diagram of Main Street. In your notebook, write down the correct prepositions
and buildings to complete the labels.

| sports centre   café   supermarket   office   car park   museum |

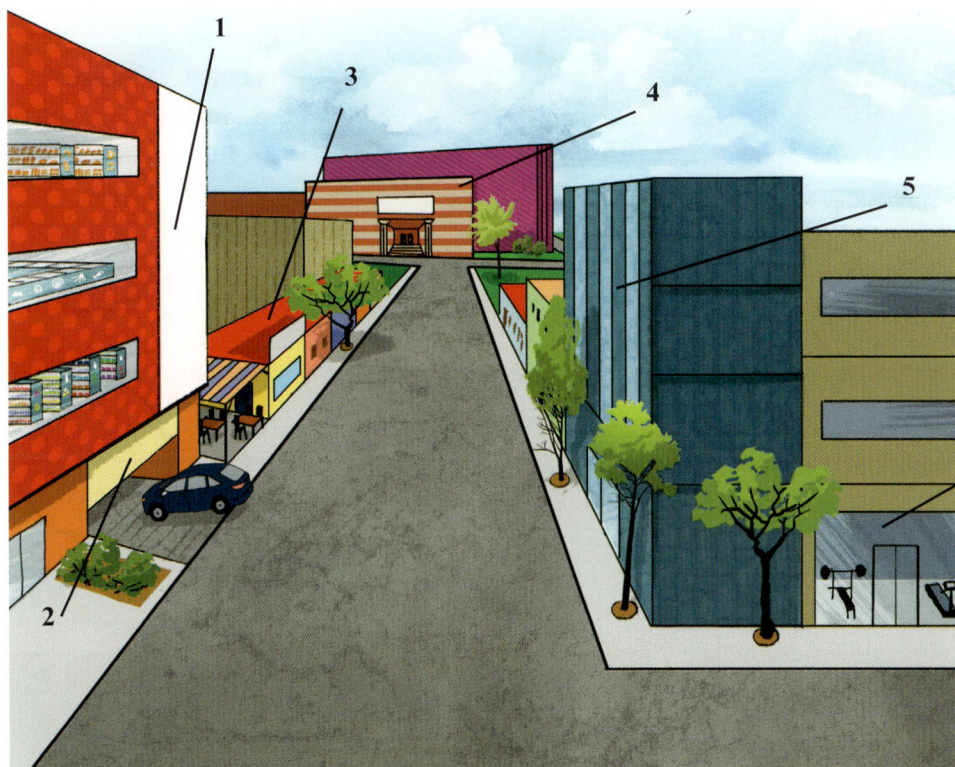

7 Writing 📝

Now write your own description of an area in your town or school.
Write around 100 words. You should:

- describe where the buildings are in relation to each other, using prepositions from
  the word box

  The sports centre at our school is between the main school building
  and the playground...

- describe how you use some of the buildings.

  The café is by the park. I always meet my friends there...

above   along
behind   below
beside   between
by   in
near   under
within

> 9.2 Moving around town

These activities will help you to talk about other things we see around us.

1 Reading and Speaking 📖 💬 ABC XYZ

When you move around a town or city, you use a transport system.
All the words in the word box describe parts of a transport system. Work in pairs.

a   Can you match the words to a meaning?

   i   A road or path that allows you to cross another road or river

   ii   The point where two roads meet

   iii   A type of transport for travelling on water

   iv   A wide road for traffic to move fast

   v   A system of trains, tracks and stations

   vi   A word for all types of transport that move along a road

   vii   A car with a driver that you pay

   viii A place where several roads join and move in a circle

b   Can you match the words in the box to the ones below to make a compound word?

   i   bus   ii   car   iii   pedestrian   iv   traffic

   Which of these things can you find near your school?

c   In pairs, find all of these things in the photos below.

boat   bridge
bus stop   car park
corner   motorway
pedestrian crossing
railway   roundabout
taxi   traffic
traffic lights

crossing   lights
stop   park

2 Listening (track 9.2) 🎧

Listen to Katherine describe the town where she lives.
Which problem does she describe?

Then listen again and answer the following questions.

a   Katherine says she lives in a 'built-up area'. What does this mean?
b   How does Katherine get to work?
c   What sometimes makes Katherine late for work?
d   How does her friend travel to work?
e   What is sometimes a problem in the car park where she works?
f   Where would Katherine prefer to live? Why?

GRAMMAR FOCUS

We use the **present perfect simple** tense when there is a link between the present and the past. Look at the sentences Katherine uses:

For example:

- For an action that started in the past and is still happening, with for (number of years) and since (starting at a point in time):
  - I**'ve lived** in a big town for 10 years.
  - I **have worked** there since I finished university.

- To talk about experience in an indefinite time that hasn't finished. This indefinite time also started in the past and is still happening:
  - I **have** always **driven** to work.
  - I **have** never **tried** public transport

- To talk about something that has happened in the recent past (but we do not know the exact time):
  - One of my friends **has** just **started** cycling to work.

We form the present perfect simple with **have / has** + the **past participle:**

- I **have worked** *there since I finished university.*
- She **has not arrived** early since she started work.
- **Have** you **seen** the traffic in the city? (Yes, I **have**. / No, I **haven't**.)
- How long **has** Katherine **lived** in the town?

Notice: we often contract *have* and *have not* in present perfect sentences:

- I**'ve lived** in a big town for 10 years.
- She **hasn't used** public transport yet.
- No, I **haven't.**

Notice: look at the adverbs and preposition (for) used in the examples above. These words are often used with the present perfect simple tense. We can also use yet and already:

- **Has** Katherine **arrived** at work yet?
- She **has** already **missed** her first meeting.

KEY TERM

present perfect simple: used to describe present events that are connected to the past, e.g. I have always taken the bus to school

3 Reading 📖 ABC XYZ

a Choose the correct verb to complete the sentences and change to the present perfect simple. Remember that these verbs are all *regular*.

> visit study achieve invite borrow not work

i Bea has invited us to her birthday party next week. Shall we go?

ii I think Helios _____ 20 countries.

iii Ravi _____ at the bank for two years.

iv I can't find my pen. _____ you _____ it?

v I _____ here since last year.

vi In her life, Zainab _____ good exam results.

b Look at your completed sentences. Which sentences describe:

i experiences in an indefinite time that has not finished?

ii something that has happened in the recent past?

iii an action that started in the past and is still happening?

4 Reading 📖

a Copy and complete the sentences by changing the verb in brackets () into the present perfect simple. Remember that these verbs are all *irregular*.

i In my life, I have won (win) several art competitions.

ii Our teacher _____ (give) us a lot of homework this week.

iii My family _____ (be) to the same place on holiday for five years.

iv I _____ (sing) at a lot of school concerts.

v I _____ never _____ (break) something expensive at home.

vi Our school _____ (buy) new equipment this year.

vii Sula _____ (forget) her ruler so I lent her mine.

b When you have completed the sentences, tick (✓) the ones that are true for you. If they are not true, change them to make them true!

In my life, I have never won an art competition or I haven't won an art competition.

STUDY SKILLS

Learning about irregular verbs is important. It is a common mistake to choose the wrong ending for irregular verbs. There are lots of irregular verbs in English, so start by learning the common ones. Find information online and in books that categorise the irregular verbs in tables and lists. Print a copy and keep it in your notebook or make your own personal list.

5 Reading 📖

Read Esme's description of living in a city. In your notebook, write down all the examples of the present perfect simple tense. Then read again and answer the questions on the next page.

In the city

I have lived in London since I was born. It's a very busy place. I have lived with my husband and two children in the north of the city for about six years now. It's a really nice neighbourhood and is much quieter than the city centre. We live in a square where there are plenty of trees, so it usually feels peaceful, but sometimes you can hear traffic noise. It's never silent! My children have always loved playing in the nearby playground. They have made a lot of friends there.

I work in the centre of London in an office. It's quite difficult to drive in London as there is a lot of traffic, so I usually take the underground train to work, or the 'tube', as we call it in London. The nearest underground station is five minutes' walk from my house. To get there, I have to cross a busy road, but fortunately there's a pedestrian crossing which makes it much easier!

My office is on the fifteenth floor of a skyscraper called The Shard. I've worked there for about three years now and I have always enjoyed the view from high up. From there, I can see many places in the city. There is green space in London as well as busy roads. The river looks beautiful from above. There are plenty of boats on the river. Some people say negative things about city life, but I love living here. It's never dull!

READING TIP

Remember that some words have more than one meaning. Look at these examples with the word, **square**:

- We live in a **square** where there are plenty of trees.
  (Buildings that are built in a square shape, on a piece of land)

- Draw a **square** on the paper.
  (A flat shape with four equal sides)

When using a dictionary to check words, always make sure you choose the correct meaning that makes sense within the sentence.

neighbourhood   playground
metro   pedestrian crossing
underground

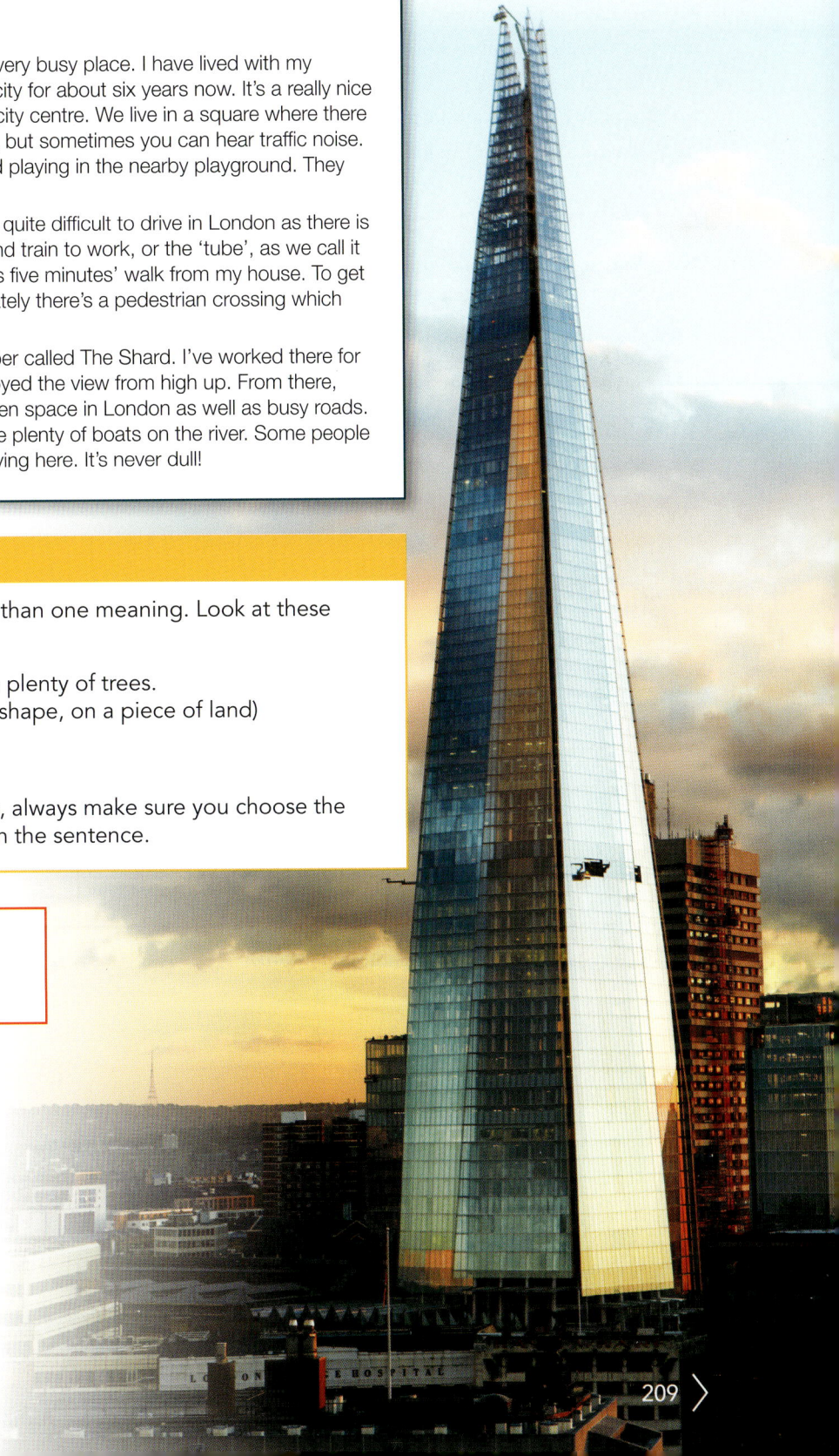

a What is the main point of paragraph 1? Select the right option:
   i to describe the traffic noise
   ii to explain where Esme lives
   ii to persuade the reader to move to London

b How long has Esme lived in her family home?
c Why has the playground nearby been good for her children?
d How does Esme get to work? Why does she choose this transport?
e What is The Shard?
f What has Esme always liked about her office on the fifteenth floor?
g What does Esme's office look down on?

6 Writing and Speaking 📝 💬

Write four sentences about your life, using the present perfect simple. Make one sentence false. Now read your sentences to a partner. Can they guess which sentence is false?

I have won a singing competition.

I think that is false!

That's right! What about you?

I've owned a cat for ten years.

That sounds true...

> **WRITING TIP**
>
> Remember that irregular verbs don't end in -ed. Make sure when you write in past tense that you use the right form of the verb.

7 Speaking 💬 🗣️

a Read the words below from Activity 2 aloud with a partner.
   Copy the table and put the words in the correct group.

| ~~small~~ **space** ~~have~~ has maybe that than days walk |

Short 'a' sounds	Long 'a' sounds	
æ	eɪ	ɔː
have	space	small

b Can you add two more words to each group?

> **PRONOUNCING ENGLISH**
>
> **Short and long 'a' sounds**
>
> Some words with the vowel 'a' have a short sound (for example, *has, an*).
>
> There are also words with 'a' that have a long sound (for example, *small, space*).

〉 9.3 Shopping

These activities will help you learn vocabulary about shops and shopping.

1 Reading 📖 ᴬᴮᶜˣʸᶻ

Read the posts from a local website where people review the shops in their town. The posts are about a shop called Drapers in the town of Hexford. In pairs, read the sentences that follow and decide if they are true or false. Can you correct the false sentences which are on the next page?

store	cotton
sale	expensive
	cheap
	customers
	credit card
	market
changing rooms	

5:40 AM 📶 37% 🔋

www.ureview.biz/hexford/drapers

✎ Customer reviews   🛒 shopping   ⚡ Hexford   ⠿ **Drapers**

Topic: Drapers – the best!

M **Mandy:** This is my favourite store in Hexford. I was there three times last week. I bought a lovely cotton dress and some gold leather shoes in the sale. The price before the sale was really expensive, but I saved a lot of money. Drapers have great sales!

👍 Like   💬 Comment   ↩ Reply

🔻 Replies:

J **John:**
I agree. It's not cheap, but Drapers sell nice clothes. I bought a jumper made from lamb's wool three years ago and it still looks new. Their clothes are great quality. They have great customer service too - they're always very friendly and helpful with customers.

👍 Like   💬 Comment   ↩ Reply

A **Abeed:**
The manager and staff are very helpful. I lost my wallet in the store last week. It contained cash, coins and my credit card, so I was quite upset because I thought it had been stolen. The staff were great – they helped me find my wallet.

👍 Like   💬 Comment   ↩ Reply

M **Maz:**
It is expensive, but you do get better quality items. You can find similar items on the market outside at half the price that Drapers charge. For example, I bought a battery charger for a third of the price, but it broke after a week.

👍 Like   💬 Comment   ↩ Reply

W **Wendy:**
It's a nice store, but there are better. I paid a lot for a shirt last year and have already had to sew on a new button. The changing rooms are tiny and they are closed on Sundays.

👍 Like   💬 Comment   ↩ Reply

a   Mandy thought that the clothes she bought in Drapers were very expensive.

b   Someone stole Abeeds's wallet in Drapers.

c   Maz was pleased with the item she bought at the market outside Drapers.

d   Wendy was not happy with something that she bought in Drapers.

e   Drapers is open every day of the week.

f   Most of the people give positive reviews of Drapers.

2 Reading 📖

Abeed is telling the story of his lost wallet to his friend, Tom. Where did they find it? Where did they look before they found it?

Abeed:	I was in Drapers last week and I lost my wallet!
Tom:	Oh no! How did you do that?
Abeed:	Well, I had taken it out of my pocket to pay for something when I decided to try on a shirt. So I went into the changing rooms. When I had tried the shirt on, I looked for some trousers to go with it. When I had found some trousers, I went to pay for everything and couldn't find my wallet!
Tom:	Oh no! What happened next?
Abeed:	Well, I told a sales assistant, who was really helpful. He had seen me go into the changing rooms, so we looked there first. But it wasn't there! So more staff came to help and they looked everywhere. Then someone found my wallet. It had dropped on the floor.
Tom:	That's lucky! Were all your cash and credit cards still there?
Abeed:	Yes, fortunately my money hadn't fallen out.

STUDY SKILLS

Remember that some items are bought by length or weight, so learn and practise words for measuring such as 'centimetre', 'gram', 'kilogram' and 'litre'. Other number or shape terms such as 'kilometre', 'circle' and 'square' are helpful ways to describe distances and objects.

GRAMMAR FOCUS

We use the **past perfect simple** to talk about an action that happened before another action in the past. We often use it when we are telling a story to explain a sequence of events that happened in the past. The past perfect simple helps the listener understand the order of events.

Look at these examples from Abeed's conversation:

Past perfect simple   Past simple

• When **I had tried** the shirt on, I looked for some trousers to go with it.

• When **I had found** some trousers, I went to pay for everything...

1   **The action in bold happened**   2   the action in blue happened

We form the past perfect simple with **had** or **had not (hadn't)** + **past participle**. The form stays the same when the pronoun changes.

• **He had seen** me go into the changing rooms, so we looked there first.

• ...fortunately my money **hadn't fallen** out.

The sentence or clause in the past simple can also go before the **past perfect simple**.

• Then someone found my wallet. It **had dropped** on the floor.

KEY TERM

past perfect simple: used to show events in the past

3 Reading 📖

In pairs, read Rachel's story about her shopping trip. Choose the correct verbs.

The sales

Last Saturday, I ªarrived / had arrived at the shopping centre by 7 a.m. because I wanted to be early for the sales. I had just parked the car when I realised something – I ᵇleft / had left my money at home! I was so angry with myself. So I ᶜdrove / had driven back home to get my wallet.

I had been at home for almost an hour when I ᵈfound / had found my wallet. It was on top of a cupboard. I was confused because I remembered I ᵉput / had put it by the door. Then my eldest son said, 'Mum, Alfie has got something to tell you …' 'Sorry, mum,' said my youngest son. Then he told me that he ᶠhid / had hidden my wallet for a joke.

4 Writing 📝

Do you have any funny or interesting stories about shopping trips?
Write your story using past simple and past perfect simple sentences.

- First, write down events that happened before the shopping trip.
- Then, write events that happened on the day of the trip.
- Write your story. Write at least 50 words. Look at the examples below to help you.

Before shopping

I saved some money
I wanted to buy some new trainers
I arranged to meet my cousin there

On the day of the shopping trip

We arrived at 10 am

We arrived at the shopping centre at 10am. I had saved some money and I wanted to buy some new trainers. We had arranged to meet my cousin at…. but she….

5 Listening (track 9.3) 🎧

Listen to Fred, Petra and Isaac talk about shopping. Who likes looking in shops? Who prefers online shopping? Then listen again and answer the questions.

a   What does Fred like spending money on?
b   What happened during his last shopping trip?
c   Why does he prefer online shopping?
d   Why didn't Petra buy the trousers?
e   Why does she prefer buying in a shop?
f   What did Isaac buy?
g   Why did Isaac complain to the shop?
h   What did the shop give Isaac?
i   What does Isaac wish he had done? Why?

6 Speaking

In pairs, perform the following role play.

Student A: You are a radio presenter. You are presenting a discussion about advantages and disadvantages of online shopping.

Student B: You are a member of the public. You have phoned into the radio programme. You don't like online shopping and want to keep the town centre shops open.

Before you start, read the questions and prepare your answers. Use the points made by Fred, Petra and Isaac to help you. Then perform the role play.

Role play: shopping in shops or online

Student A, ask your partner the following questions.

a   What are the advantages of shopping in a town centre?

b   Why don't you like online shopping?

c   Online shopping is better for some people. Who could benefit from online shopping?

d   What will happen to shops if everyone shops online?

e   How can shops attract more customers to visit shops again?

You could start the role play like this:

Student A: And we have another caller on the line … Hello … Welcome to the programme. I believe you don't like online shopping! So what are the advantages of …?

After you have answered the questions, swap roles and do it again.

7 Writing

Write two paragraphs explaining the advantages and disadvantages of shopping online. Use your ideas from the role play in Activity 4.

*   Start by making a list of advantages and disadvantages. Put the points into the two groups, then arrange the points into a sensible order.
*   Write a paragraph explaining the advantages.
*   Then write a paragraph explaining the disadvantages.
*   Write about 90 words.

> **WRITING TIP**
>
> When you are writing a paragraph containing connected points, use linking phrases. Linking phrases allow the reader to follow your points in a sensible order. For example:
>
> One of the advantages of online shopping is that…
>
> Another reason is…
>
> A further reason is…
>
> However,…

> 9.4 Computers

Use these activities to practise reading and writing about computers and technology.

1 Speaking 💬

In pairs, talk about the ways you use computers and digital technology.
Ask your partner:

- What digital equipment do you use at home and in school?
- What do you use them for?

I use my tablet to message my friends, download music and watch films...

2 Reading and Speaking 📖 💬 ABC XYZ

Here are some key words to help you talk about computers.

> app   blog   digital camera   document   email   file   game   group chat
> internet   keyboard   laptop   message   mouse   password   printer
> program   selfie   social media   tablet   website   wifi   memory stick

a   Copy the table in your notebook. In pairs, put the words into these groups. Remember that some things might go in more than one group.

Equipment	Things you produce	Parts of a computer	Entertainment or information
digital camera	email	keyboard	game

b   Now discuss where you use these things. Copy and complete the table.

At school	At home	Both

3 Speaking 💬

Now join up with another pair. Share your thoughts from Activity 1. Then talk about what you think life might be like without computers. Think of three points.

Share your answers with the class.

STUDY SKILLS

Working with a partner can be a good way to learn words and phrases. You can share your knowledge of vocabulary and teach each other words you don't know. Practise pronouncing new words together and giving each other feedback. You can also test each other to help you memorise new words.

SPEAKING TIP

Remember that you can use **2nd conditional** sentences to talk about future or imagined events. For example:

- **If** computers **didn't exist,** then communication **would be** slower.

[If + past simple]   [would + base verb]

4 Listening (track 9.4) 🎧

Gill and Mike are older users of digital technology. Listen to them talk about how they use computers in their lives. Which user is more confident?

Then listen again and choose the correct answer.

a   When did Gill first use a computer?
-   i   When she was 30 years old.
-   ii 30 years ago.

b   How did she feel the first time she used a computer?
-   i   She found it difficult to understand.
-   ii She thought it was a positive experience.

c   How does she feel now?
-   i   She still finds it difficult.
-   ii She finds it useful.

d   As a photographer, she also uses her computer to:
-   i   communicate with customers
-   ii create her photos.

e   What is Mike's attitude when he uses a computer?
-   i   He sometimes feels quite angry.
-   ii He likes using them.

f   What does Mike find difficult to do when using technology?
-   i   communicating with other people
-   ii finding information.

g   What advice could you give Mike. Discuss your ideas with a partner.

5 Speaking 💬

Some schools around the world don't have computers in their classrooms. Some schools have a lot of computers that students use every lesson. What do you think are the advantages and disadvantages of using computers at school? In pairs, talk about this topic.

Ask your partner:

-   How can computers help people learn?
-   How might computers make learning more difficult?

Keep notes as you talk, then share your views with another pair.

LISTENING TIP

Some activities ask you to recognise an attitude. Sometimes the speaker will tell you directly what they feel. Often, you will need to find key details and think of a word that describes the speaker's overall view. For example:

-   here are some ways to describe attitudes to computers:

-   She finds computers useful… They annoy him… She thinks they are essential.

6 Writing ✎

You are going to write an email to your headteacher about computers in school. Use your ideas and discussions from Activity 5 to help you.

Read the following activity.

Computers in school

Your headteacher is thinking about buying new computers for students. They want to know students' views about how they use computers in school. Write a letter to your headteacher explaining your views. You should write 100-120 words and:

- say which lessons you would use a computer in
- explain the advantages of using computers
- explain the disadvantages of using computers
- give your view on whether the school should buy new computers.

a Read your notes from Activity 5, then make a plan of points for each bullet point in the activity.

b Think about the person you are writing to to decide the tone you write in.

c When you write your letter, work through each bullet point in order.

Here is the opening of a student's letter. Notice how the opening line introduces the reason for writing in the present continuous.

Dear Headteacher,

I am writing to give my views on using computers in schools.

Working with a partner, check each other's work.

WRITING TIP

When writing a formal letter, remember to greet your reader in the appropriate way in the opening line. If you write to a headteacher, you should write in a formal way.

DATE

Opening: for example:

Dear Sir, Dear Headtecher or Dear Mrs Smith,

Introduction + lessons you would use a computer in

Advantages of using computers

Disadvantages of using computers

My opinion.

Closing:

Yours sincerely (if you have used your reader's surname)

Yours faithfully (if you have used 'Sir', 'Madam' or 'Headteacher').

7 Reading and Speaking 📝 💬

With a partner, read each other's answer to Activity 6. Check they have included the following:

- an appropriate greeting and ending
- a line at the start that introduces the reason for writing
- the information in the four bullet points above.

ENGLISH AROUND THE WORLD

English has always been the common language of computing because the early computer systems were developed in English. Today, the UK and USA continue to develop information technology, computer systems and popular software products that are used all over the world. You can even find computer terms in English changed a little to work in other languages; for example, 'mejl' in Polish (email), 'rebooter' in French (to reboot), 'downloaden' in German (to download) and 'blogg' in Norwegian (blog).

〉 9.5 Communication

Use these activities to understand ideas about mobile technology and different ways of communication.

1 Reading 📖 ABC XYZ

The words below describe forms of written communication. Which ones can you see in the photos?

> article   bill   book   brochure   certificate   comic   form   guidebook
> letter   magazine   newspaper   note   passport   postcard   ticket

Now copy the table and sort the words into the group. Which items are usually electronic or printed (on paper), or both?

Document/text	Usually printed	Usually electronic	Both
Article			✓

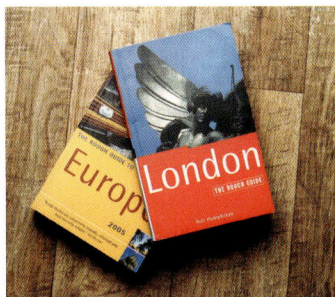

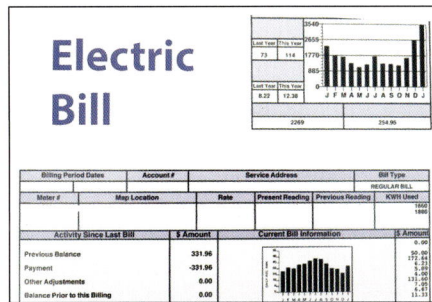

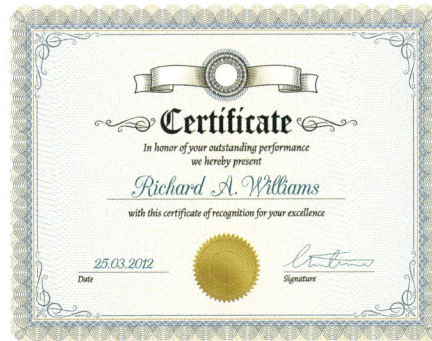

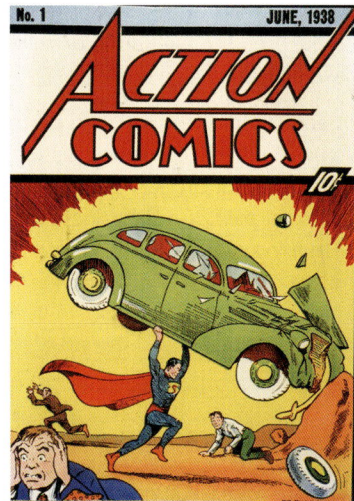

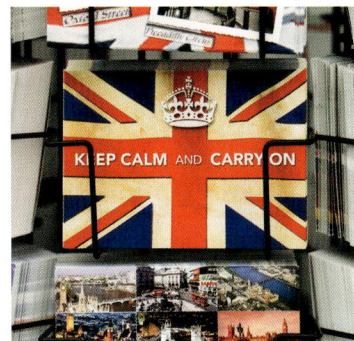

2 Reading 📖 ABC XYZ

Thandi runs her own company selling houses. The following words describe important parts of her work. Can you match the words to a meaning?

> website   screen   computer   blogs   mail   uploading

a A machine for storing and processing information
b A type of written communication
c A place where things are displayed on a computer
d Adding something on a computer
e An online place storing information
f Written articles generated online

3 Reading 📖

Complete Thandi's description of her working day with words from Activity 2.

A day in the office

My work starts at 7.30 a.m. when I arrive at the office and switch on the ᵃ**computer.** I make a coffee and then start by checking ᵇ_____ and messages. I would say more than half of my time at work is spent looking at a ᶜ_____. Five years ago, people used the telephone or called into the office, but most of our customers first make contact online these days.

I spend some of my day with customers showing them houses. The rest of the time I'm usually at my computer ᵈ_____ pictures of houses, or writing descriptions of them to put on our ᵉ_____. Social media and ᶠ_____ are an important part of our business too because we can contact a lot more people through these things. We tell them about our business, give them the latest news about housing and get to know them. Communication is an essential part of our business.

4 Reading 📖

In pairs, answer the questions on 'A day in the office'.

a How do most of Thandi's customers first contact her?
b What other examples of communication can you find in the text?
c Why do you think communication is a very important part of Thandi's business?
d Which of these ways of communicating do you use?

READING TIP

When you answer questions that need you to explain the meaning of long phrases, use synonyms to help explain it. Choose the words you need to explain in a text then use a thesaurus to find suitable synonyms.

5 Reading and Speaking 📖 💬

Mobile phones are an essential part of life across the world. Read these four opinions about phone use. Discuss in pairs. Which one is closest to your opinion?

a

Amir, 15

I use my phone for messaging mainly. It's my favourite way to keep in touch with friends. Phones are essential – it's not possible to live in the modern world without a phone.

b

Ishani, 16

I use my phone a lot, usually to message friends, watch videos and play music. I sometimes think that I use it too much. I feel nervous if I don't have my phone with me. I don't think it's very healthy to use a phone as much as I do.

c

Li Jun, 45

I use my phone for business calls during the day. I couldn't run my business without it. When I get home, I switch my phone off. Phones are not good for family life – they take your attention and stop you talking to each other.

d

Pru, 70

I use my phone to listen to music and radio when I'm walking. My family live abroad now, so phones are a great way to keep in touch. We do video calls and message each other all the time. Some of my older friends don't have phones and they don't see the benefits, but I think they're a brilliant way to stay in touch with my family.

6 Reading and Speaking 📖 💬

In pairs, read the opinions in Activity 4 again. Copy the table in your notebook and find points to complete it. Can you think of any more points to add?

Advantages of a mobile phone	Disadvantages of a mobile phone
You can message your friends all the time.	A lot of people don't know how to stop using their phones – they feel bad when they are away from their phone.

7 Speaking 💬

You are going to perform the following role play in pairs. First, discuss these questions together:

- How many people in your family own a mobile phone?
- Do you own a phone? If so, how often do you use it? What do you use it for?

Now prepare for the role play.

Student A: You are trying to persuade your parent to buy you a new phone. You want a model with the latest technology.

Student B: You are the parent. You are worried that a lot of phone use will be bad for your child. You think that there are disadvantages to owning a smart phone.

Before you start, use the points from Activity 5 to help you prepare your roles. Then perform the role play. Remember to swap roles after the first turn.

You could start the role play like this:

Student B: So …you would like a new phone. Tell me why you think you need a new phone.

Student A: I need it to… I will use it for…

Role play: mobile phones

Student B: Ask your partner the following questions.

a Why do you need a new mobile phone?

b What will you use it for?

c How can we control how much you use it?

d How do I know that you will look after it?

e It's very expensive. What will you do to help with the cost?

---

8 Speaking 💬

Discuss your answer to the role play with your partner. Answer the questions and give each other some feedback.

- Which questions did you answer well?
- Which vocabulary and language structures did you use?
- Which parts were the most challenging? Why?
- What do you need now to improve your role play skills?

PROJECT

Your class is going to take part in a letter-writing project. Personal letters are not as common as they were in the past, but most people love to receive handwritten letters.

Each person in a class should choose someone to write a letter to. It might be a letter to someone in your community, a friend or a family member. You can decide the purpose of your letter – it might be to say thank you, to find out information or to keep in touch.

Remember to think carefully about who you are writing to – choose your words carefully. Plan your letter and spend time writing it, making sure you pay attention to spelling and handwriting. Share any replies you receive with class members.

EXAM-STYLE QUESTIONS

Listening practice (track 9.5)

Use this activity to test your listening skills.

Listen to Kim talking to her friend about her family and their use of technology. Answer the questions below by ticking the correct box.

a   What does Kim say about working with computers?
  i   She finds them hard to understand
  ii   She finds it exciting
  iii She finds it uncomfortable   [1]
b   What does Kim use her computer for?
  i   Sending emails
  ii   Writing documents
  iii Online meetings   [1]
c   How long does Kim spend working on her computer each day?
  i   Two hours
  ii   Three hours
  iii Four hours   [1]
d   What do Kim's children use their computers for?
  i   Doing homework
  ii   Playing games
  iii Watching films   [1]
e   When can Kim's family use their phones?
  i   When they are eating
  ii   Before 10 o'clock at night
  iii When they have visitors   [1]

[Total: 5]

CHECK YOUR PROGRESS

How confident do you feel about what you have learned and practised in this unit? How many of the things below could you do?

1   Name ten types of buildings you might find in a town or city.
2   Write a sentence using the present perfect simple.
3   Write a sentence using the past perfect simple.
4   Give three tips for writing a letter.
5   Name five types of documents and five methods of communication.

Rate yourself from 1 (not confident) to 5 (very confident).

Which things would you like to learn more about?
Which things would you like to practise again?

Share your thoughts with a partner.

› Grammar practice

Infinitives (with and without to)

GRAMMAR FOCUS

Base form with **to**

When we follow one verb (or a verb phrase) with another verb in a sentence, we can use the base form <u>with</u> to. Look at these examples from Unit 9:

- I help customers **to find** their platforms.
- It's quite difficult **to drive** in London.
- Yesterday, I wanted **to buy** some trousers…
- I use my phone **to listen** to music…

When we use more than two verbs in a sentence, it is not necessary to add **to** each time:

- it's my job **to meet** guests and **welcome** them to the hotel.
- I use computers **to copy, save** and **email** my photographs.

The base form with to can also be used after about (and the verb, to be). For example:

- They are about **to build** a new school. (They haven't started building the school, but they are planning or preparing to build it.)
- Aliya is about **to buy** a new phone.
- Conor is about **to change** his laptop for a better model.

Base form without **to**

Some verbs are followed by the base form <u>without</u> to, especially modal verbs such as can, could, must, might, should. Look at these examples from Unit 9:

- …sometimes you can **hear** traffic noise.
- Some days, when I arrive at work, I can't **park** my car.
- It might **be** quicker than driving!
- I wish I lived in the city centre, then I could **walk** to work.

Verb patterns with base form (without to)

The verbs, let, make, see, hear, feel, watch and notice are followed by object + base form (without to) + (in) direct object. For example:

- Jay made Tariq **drop his books** on the floor.
- Did you see **her take the money**?
- I heard **Mr Moss shout at the children**.

1 Reading 📖

Copy and complete the sentences with the correct form of the infinitive in brackets (with or without *to*). The first one has been done for you.

a   We wanted <u>to drive</u> (drive) into the city, but it was too busy.

b   My friends and I might _____ (meet) at the new café this weekend.

c   You should _____ (try) that new restaurant – it's really nice.

d   I use my laptop _____ (do) my homework.

e   Lana visited the gym _____ (find out) about yoga classes.

f   Meg and her friends went to the park _____ (play) basketball.

2 Reading 📖

Find suitable sentences in i–vi to follow sentences, a-f.
The first one has been done for you.

a   Sam is wearing a smart suit.
   ii   He's about to go for a job interview.

b   Talia is feeling nervous.

c   Kris and Marek are feeling excited.

d   You need to take your umbrella.

e   Please could you finish your coffee?

f   That's a nice dress. Are you going to buy it?

   i   Their dad is about to buy them a new video game.

   ii   ~~He's about to go for a job interview.~~

   iii   I'm not sure. I was about to try it on.

   iv   She's about to do an exam.

   v   It is about to rain.

   vi   The café is about to close.

3 Writing 📝

Sort the words to make sentences using the verb pattern, **verb + object + infinitive (without to) + (in) direct object**. The first one has been done for you.

a   us /made / Mrs Sharma / the classroom /tidy up.

   Mrs Sharma made us tidy up the classroom.

b   the class early/ leave/ the students / let /Mr Murrey

c   leave / The boys / the train / the station/ didn't hear

d   watched / We / the old house / the builders / pull down

e   a third goal / The football fans / their team / watched / score

f   Milo / did you / When / see / into the sports centre / go

Adjectives with prepositions

GRAMMAR FOCUS

Some adjectives are followed by a specific preposition in a sentence. The preposition often comes before the <u>object</u> of the verb, for example, a noun (or pronoun). Look at this example from Unit 9:

- My favourite building is the sports centre. It's behind Main Street and is very **popular** with <u>my friends</u>.

There are no fixed rules, so it helps to learn the adjectives + prepositions together. Here are some examples to help you (but remember that there are exceptions).

We use **adjective** + at, for skills and abilities:

- Jared is **good** at <u>design technology and art</u>. He is working **hard** at <u>these subjects</u> at school this year.

We use about and of to talk about feelings:

- Abeed was **upset** about <u>losing his wallet</u>.
- Maryam is **proud** of her <u>computer science project</u>.

We can also use adjectives with in, with (see first example above) and by.

- Do you want to be **involved** in <u>this project</u>?
- We were **impressed** by <u>the new building</u>. It's amazing!

1 Reading 📖

Copy and choose the correct preposition to complete the sentences.

a   Jess is fascinated at/by all kinds of new technology.

b   Mike gets annoyed in/about using computers to fill in forms.

c   Ishani is worried about/in how much she uses her phone.

d   Bilal is interested of/in the design of buildings.

e   Tia is afraid of/at failing her exams this year.

f   Jude is better at/by science subjects than art and design.

2 Writing 📝 ᴬᴮᶜ

In your notebooks, use any of these adjectives to write five sentences about your skills, interests and achievements. Remember to use the correct preposition. Then compare your sentences with a partner. How are you similar?

interested	fascinated	great	proud
good	impressed	experienced	

> # Chapter 10
> # Cultures and celebrations

IN THIS UNIT YOU WILL:

- read and talk about texts about different cultures
- practise using phrasal verbs to talk about cultural celebrations
- practise using relative pronouns to give information about festivals
- talk about the benefits of learning a language
- think about your own language skills
- talk and write about your own country.

> 10.1 Special occasions

Use these activities to learn about different types of celebration.

1 Reading 📖 ABC XYZ

People often celebrate personal events and occasions. Here are four people talking about a recent celebration they attended. In pairs, read their descriptions and match each one to a summary.

Dom

'I had my 14th birthday last month, so I invited my friends to a party and they all said 'yes', except one who was on holiday. I love sports, especially football, so we had the party at the local sports centre. We played football then afterwards we went upstairs to a room where we had some great food.'

birthday
wedding anniversary

Antonia

'I got married last year. It was the best day of my life. To celebrate, we had a big party with family and friends. It was the best way to make the occasion really special. There was lots of food, lots of people and lots of dancing. There were flowers and balloons everywhere. It was a very colourful event.'

Bako

'I married my lovely wife 25 years ago, so we recently celebrated our wedding anniversary. We planned to have a small celebration, but our son and daughter organised a surprise for us – they invited most of our friends who were at the original ceremony to visit us. That was a lot of people! Unfortunately, my friend Marius couldn't accept the invitation because he lives abroad.'

Chayya

'My son was born recently, so we have just had the ceremony where we named him. It is a special family occasion. My husband wrote our son's name and said it quietly into his ear. We named our son 'Aadesh'.'

a A celebration of the beginning of a marriage.
b A celebration that happens after the birth of a child.
c A celebration of the day that someone was born.
d A yearly celebration of the day a couple got married.

2 Reading 📖

Look again at the descriptions in Activity 1. Decide if the sentences are true or false.
Can you correct the false sentences?

a   All of Dom's friends accepted his birthday invitation.

b   Dom had his birthday party at home.

c   Antonia's guests were a very important part of her wedding.

d   Antonia had a small quiet wedding.

e   The guests at Bako's anniversary party were new friends.

f   Not all Bako's friends could attend his anniversary party.

g   During the ceremony, Chayya's husband only spoke his baby son's name.

3 Speaking 💬

In pairs, make a list of the different things that people choose to celebrate. It might
be big family events or things such as getting a new job. Discuss your list with your
partner. Ask each other:

- What do people usually do to celebrate each event?
- Why do people feel it is important to celebrate these events?

4 Speaking 💬

In pairs, talk about a recent celebration you have had. Ask your partner:

- What was the celebration?
- What did you do?
- Who was there?
- What did you enjoy about it?

5 Listening (track 10.1) 🎧

Listen to Drew talk about wedding celebrations in the USA.
Answer the questions below.

a   What is an engagement?

   i   When the couple say they will get married.

   ii   When the couple give each other a present.

   iii   When the couple meet each other's families.

b   At the wedding ceremony:

   i   the couple give each other some flowers

   ii   the couple give each other some jewellery

   iii   the couple give each other some cake.

c   Which of these things happen at the wedding ceremony? Choose two correct answers:

   i   The guests have a party.

   ii   The couple say special words to each other.

   iii   The couple dance together.

   iv   The bride carries something natural.

   v   The couple wear casual clothes.

SPEAKING TIP

Remember that frequency adverbs such as 'often', 'usually', 'always' and 'every year' can be used to describe traditions and cultural habits that always happen. For example:

When people have a wedding, they usually have a meal.

d Which of these things usually happen after the wedding ceremony?
Select two correct answers:

i There is a large meal of special food.

ii The bride keeps her wedding flowers.

iii The bride and groom dance together.

iv The guests cut the wedding cake.

v The guests dance before the bride and groom.

6 Reading 📖

Read Talia's email. What is the purpose of the email?
What are Talia and her friends going to do?

Hi Santok

How are you? We're going to have a surprise party for Ross at my house. He's had a difficult year, with his dad's illness, so we want to make him feel happy. We aren't going to tell him anything before! If you are free next Saturday, you should come - we'd love to see you.

If you can make it, could you bring some food? Maz is going to make the birthday cake. Leo is going to prepare some party food. I think he's going to do a pasta dish and some spring rolls. I am going to cook a rice dish. Also, we are all going to give $5 towards a birthday present for Ross. We're going to invite his friends from university too, so there will be about twenty people.

Hope to see you there!
Talia

GRAMMAR FOCUS

We use **going to** + <u>verb,</u> to describe plans for the future. These are plans that we have decided before. We form this future tense with the verb, to be (am / is / are) + **going to** + <u>base verb</u>. For example:

- Maz is **going to** <u>make</u> the birthday cake.
- I am **going to** <u>cook</u> a risotto with rice.
- …we are all **going to** <u>give</u> $5 towards a birthday present…
- What are you **going to** <u>buy</u> Ross for his birthday?

We often contract the forms of the verb, to be, especially when we are talking. For example:

- We're **going to** <u>have</u> a surprise party for Ross
- I think he's **going to** <u>do</u> a pasta dish…
- We aren't **going to** <u>tell</u> him anything before!

7 Reading and Writing 📝 📖 ᴬᴮᶜ

Complete these sentences about future plans. Use **going to** and the correct verb from the word box. Then write sentences to answer the last question (f) about yourself.

meet   move   watch
have   do   play

a   Our family <u>are going to move</u> house soon.

b   Our class _____ a test next week.

c   I _____ my friends next weekend.

d   Tonight Thao _____ a film at home.

e   They _____ an important football match tomorrow.

f   What _____ you _____ next week?

8 Writing 📝

You are going to write an email to a friend. Read the activity below.
Use Activities 6 and 7 to help you

Celebration

You are organising a surprise celebration for a friend. Write an email to your other friends inviting them to the surprise celebration. You should write 100–120 words and:

- say who you are organising the surprise celebration for
- say why you are organising it
- explain what will happen at the celebration
- explain where and when it will take place
- say why your friends should come.

WRITING TIP

When you write to friends, you can write more informally. You can start by saying Hi everyone, but remember that you must still use correct English.

Make a plan of what you will say for each item in the list.

Next, think about the people you are writing to and how that will change the way you write. When you have finished your first draft, check that you have covered all of the bullet points.

You could start like this:

Hi everyone,
I am organising a surprise celebration for…

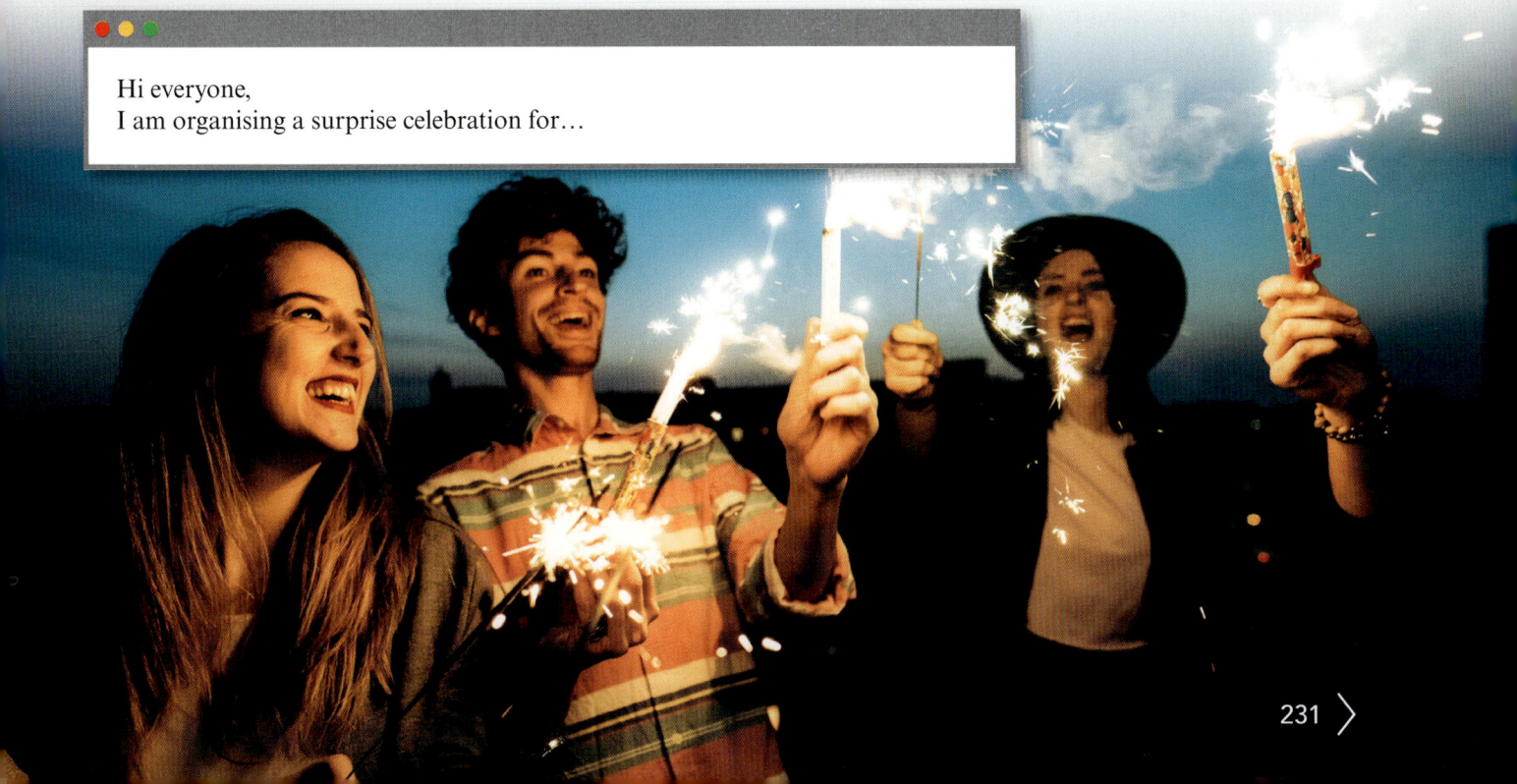

> 10.2 Festivals

These activities will help you learn about different events and how to describe them.

1 Reading 📖

In Singapore, the Night Festival is a summer celebration. Read Dai's description of the festival and then answer the questions below.

Singapore Night Festival

Last year, my friend Fang and I were visiting Singapore. We decided to visit the Night Festival. It takes place every August in the Bras Basah area of Singapore.

We waited for the sun to go down, then took a bus and got off near the area where the museums are. We got there at about 8 pm. All the buildings had lights on. It looked amazing against the night sky. The colours were so bright and beautiful.

There was so much to see and do at the festival! The museums were free to enter and there were people playing music everywhere. We watched dance shows, theatre performances and tried some delicious food. When it was time to go, we picked up more tasty snacks to take back to the hotel.

I would really like to go back next year. I would like to go with Fang again because we get on so well. He is good fun, and we share the same interests. When you go on holiday with a friend, that is so important!

a   When does the Night Festival happen?

b   In which part of Singapore does the festival happen?

c   When did Dai and his friend arrive at the festival?

d   Where did Dai see the wonderful colours?

e   What kind of entertainment was there at the festival?

f   Why would Dai like to go to the festival again with Fang?

g   Would you like to go to the Singapore Night Festival? Why or why not?

2 Speaking 💬

Have you ever been to a festival in your country? It could be a large
event or something small that took place in your town. In a group,
ask each other:

- What was the name of the event you went to?
- Who did you go with?
- What did you see and do at the event?
- What did you enjoy most about the event?

GRAMMAR FOCUS

Phrasal verbs are common in English. They are used frequently in informal
English. Phrasal verbs contain a verb with a **particle** – a word used together
with the verb. For example (phrasal verbs are in blue).

- We waited for the sun to go down…
- … we picked up more tasty snacks …

The meaning of these phrasal verbs can be easily understood from the verbs
and particles:

Phrasal verb	Meaning
go down	become lower and disappear – the writer is waiting for the sun to set.
pick up	To collect something.

Some phrasal verbs have meanings that cannot be easily understood from
the individual parts. For example:

- We get on so well.

In this example, the phrasal verb, get on, means, to have a good relationship.

KEY TERMS

phrasal verbs:
phrases with a verb
and particle which
has a different
meaning from the
meaning of its
separate parts

particle: a word that
works with a verb in
a phrasal verb, such
as go *down*, pick *up*,
get *on*

STUDY SKILLS

There are some aspects of English, such as irregular verbs and phrasal verbs,
that don't follow usual rules or meanings. Always learn both parts of phrasal
verbs together, in a 'chunk'. This will make it much easier to remember. As you
study, keep notes of unusual words and phrases that don't follow regular rules.

3 Speaking 💬

In pairs, say these sentences aloud and try to work out the meanings of the underlined
phrasal verbs. Compare your answers with another pair.

a I have everyone's ticket here. I will give out the tickets when we arrive at the event.

b I will send back the reply tomorrow.

c I must get up early tomorrow – the festival starts at 8am!

d I will help you to pick out a nice shirt for the wedding.

4 Listening (track 10.2) 🎧

Listen to Liu Yang talk about Chinese New Year. Choose the correct answer in the questions below.

a How many days does the new year celebration last for?

   i 12   **ii** 15   **iii** 25

b Who celebrates with fireworks?

   i children   **ii** families   **iii** companies

c Which festival shows it is the end of the celebrations?

   i a festival with food   **ii** a festival with lights   **iii** a festival with fireworks

d What is inside the red envelopes given to children and young adults?

   i invitations   **ii** money   **iii** pictures

e What does the colour red mean?

   i success   **ii** money   **iii** love

5 Speaking 💬 🗣

a Read the words below from Activity 4 aloud with a partner.
Copy the table and put the words in the correct group.

> communities   families   ~~weeks~~   ~~things~~   celebrations   businesses
> fireworks   lamps   streets   envelopes   adults

Words ending in /s/ sound	Words ending in /z/ or /lz/ sounds
weeks	things

b Can you add two more words to each group?

6 Writing 📝 ABC XYZ

Imagine you are telling someone from another country about an important festival in your country. Write your description. Use Dai and Liu Yang's descriptions to help you.

- When is the festival?
- How long does the festival last?
- What happens during the festival?
- Who do you celebrate with?

On the day of the festival we get up at…

As soon as the sun goes down, we…

PRONOUNCING ENGLISH

Pronouncing 's' at the end of words

We pronounce 's' as /s/ when it comes at the end of words ending in /f/, /k/, /p/, /t/ and /th/ sounds (for example, weeks). We pronounce 's' as /z/ at the end of words ending in /b/, /d/, /g/, /l/, /m/, /n/, /r/ and /s/ (for example, things).

> 10.3 National days

These activities will help you learn about ways to describe national days around the world.

1   Reading 📖

Read the following descriptions of Guy and Fulori talking about national days in their country. Decide if sentences a–e are true or false. Can you correct the false sentences? Then talk about questions f and g with your partner.

Guy: Thanksgiving in America

In America, Thanksgiving is an important day that takes place on the fourth Thursday in November. It is a day where we remember the good things that have happened during the year. At Thanksgiving, we celebrate all of the food that we are lucky to have. Lots of other things happen at Thanksgiving, such as special sports matches. Thanksgiving is the start of the exciting holiday season which lasts until the end of December.

Fulori: Fiji Day

I live in Suva which is the capital city of Fiji. It's a great place to spend Fiji Day, which is a celebration that takes place on the 10th October each year. On Fiji Day we celebrate all the good things about our country. There are lots of different events including dances and special meals. On Fiji Day, we celebrate with all of our friends from all different cultures. My friend, who is from India, says it is the most important day of the year.

a   In the USA, Thanksgiving happens during the summer.

b   During Thanksgiving people give thanks for positive things that took place during the last 12 months.

c   At Thanksgiving, the only celebration is a family dinner.

d   Fiji Day celebrates positive things about the capital city.

e   Fiji Day is celebrated in many ways, including with good food.

f   Fulori says, 'We celebrate with all our friends from all different cultures'. What does this tell you about Fiji Day?

g   Do you have any similar celebrations to Thanksgiving and Fuji Day in your country? What happens?

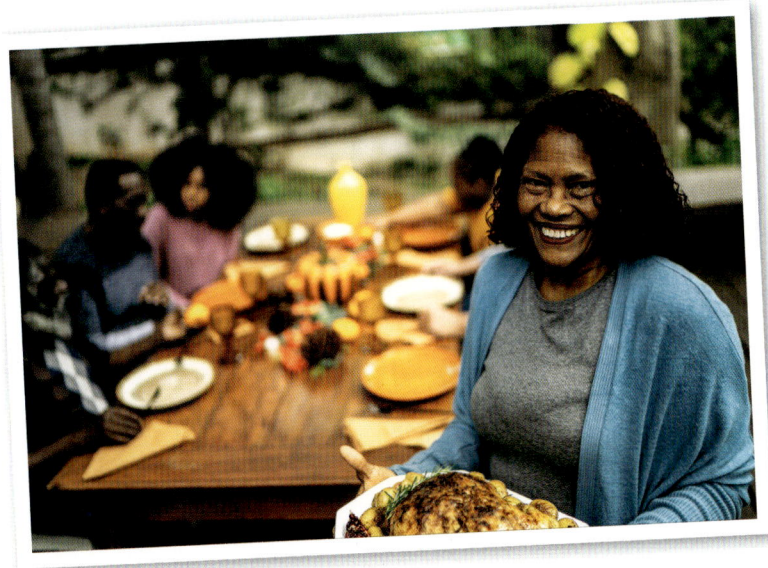

GRAMMAR FOCUS

Relative pronouns are linking words that connect two parts of a sentence. Relative pronouns introduce **relative clauses** – a part of a sentence that gives more information about a noun.

The relative pronouns, **who**, **which** and **that**, are used in the descriptions in Activity 1:

-**who** introduces a clause about people. For example:

- My friend, **who** is from India, says it is the most important day of the year.

-**which** introduces a clause about objects and places. For example:

- Thanksgiving is the start of the exciting holiday season **which** lasts through December.

-**that** is also used to introduce objects, things, and sometimes people. For example:

- In America, Thanksgiving is an important day **that** takes place on the fourth Thursday in November.

Some sentences with relative clauses include a comma to separate the relative clause from the main clause. When the relative clause is used to show that the person or thing in the clause, is equally important in the information in the sentence, then a comma is not used (see last two examples). However, a comma is needed when the relative clause gives additional information about the person or thing. See in the first example above, and also this one:

My dad bought tickets for a Thanksgiving sports match, **which** was a lovely surprise.

KEY TERMS

relative clause: adds information to the main clause of a sentence

relative pronoun: joining words which introduce a relative clause and connect information from one part of a sentence to another

2 Reading 📖

Match the sentence halves to make sentences about festivals.
Look carefully at the relative clauses and pronouns.

a All over the word, people celebrate days

b In some festivals, there are people

c In the UK, children like celebrating Pancake Day,

d Diwali is an important festival for Anisa's mother,

e The Trinidad and Tobago Carnival is a huge festival,

i <u>which</u> is a festival about food.

ii <u>which</u> is famous for its music and costumes.

iii <u>that</u> are special in their culture.

iv <u>who</u> dress up in traditional costumes.

v <u>who</u> is from India.

3 Reading 📖

Choose a country and find information about an important celebration or national day of that country. Find out:

- the name and date of the national day
- three things that happen on the day.

4 Speaking 💬

Work in small groups. You are each going to do a short presentation about the national day that you have learned about. Tell your group:

- which country's national day you learned about
- the date or the time of year that the national day happens
- three things that happen on the national day.

You can use the descriptions in Activity 1 and your notes from Activity 3 to help you. Use relative pronouns and clauses where possible:

In..., they celebrate a public holiday called..., which is on...

It is a day that...

5 Speaking 💬

In pairs, talk about how well you performed the speaking activity in Activity 4. Ask each other:

- How challenging was it to explain national day events and traditions? Was there any vocabulary or language structures that you needed but didn't know?
- Did you use relative pronouns in your description?

> 10.4 Countries and languages

These activities will help you read about and discuss countries and their languages.

1 Speaking 💬

What do you know about other countries apart from your own? In pairs, write a list of four English-speaking countries around the world and some brief notes about them. You could include:

*   the capital city
*   well-known places
*   information about food, landscape, sport or culture.

2 Speaking 💬

Join with another pair and share your notes from Activity 1. In your group, ask each other:

*   Have you ever visited any of these countries? What did you enjoy about them?
*   Which countries would you like to visit in the future and why?

Use this activity to practise talking about past and future events. Here are some ways you could start:

When I was younger, I went to Nigeria with my parents.

Last year, I spent some time in Canada.

In the future, I would like to visit Jamaica.

When I am older, I might study in the UK.

Notice how each of these sentences begins with words showing *time*.

3 Speaking 💬

In your group, give each other feedback on Activity 2.

*   How clearly did your partners explain their ideas?
*   Did they use a range of vocabulary?
*   Did they use the correct tenses?
*   Did they use time phrases correctly?

4 Listening (track 10.3) 🎧

Gamba was born in Zimbabwe but now lives in London. Listen to him describe his experiences of living in England and learning English. Answer the following questions.

a   Why did Gamba and his family move to London?

b   What does Gamba say was the most difficult thing about leaving Zimbabwe?

c   What are two things Gamba likes about living in London?

d   What does Gamba not enjoy about living in London?

e   What two things did Gamba find difficult when he started to learn English?

f   What helped Gamba improve his English skills?

g   What does Gamba say is the main benefit of speaking another language?

5 Speaking 💬

In pairs, talk about the difficulties and benefits of learning another language. Ask your partner:

•   What did you find hard when you first started learning English?

•   What helped you improve your English skills?

•   Why is learning another language a good thing to do?

•   How do you think you will use your English skills in the future?

> **STUDY SKILLS**
>
> It is important at different stages of your learning to think about your progress. This is good for making you feel more confident, and also shows you ways that you can improve. One way to do this is to look back at your work from the start of your course and compare it to your most recent work.

6 Writing 📝

Think about your progress during this course. Write down a list of:

•   three things you have improved this year

•   three things that you would like to improve

•   ways that will help you to improve – what could you do to get better at English?

You could include comments on topics, vocabulary, grammar or individual skills. Find time to discuss your thoughts with your teacher.

One thing I have improved this year is...

7 Writing

You are going to write an email to a friend. Read the activity below.

Learning English

Your friend is thinking about learning English. They have sent you an email asking for your advice. Write a reply to your friend giving your views and advice. You should write 100-120 words and:

- say why learning a new language is a good thing
- explain what you enjoy about learning English
- explain what you find challenging about learning English
- give three tips that will help them to learn English.

Make a plan of what you would say for each item in the list. Make sure you think of three useful tips for the last item. When you begin to write your letter, think about the opening line. Here is one way you could start:

Hi,

It's lovely to hear from you. I'm glad you are going to learn English. Learning a language is a good thing to do because...

> **WRITING TIP**
>
> Always make sure that you know the main purpose of any piece of writing before you start. For example, when you write to give advice, you must give clear tips and ideas to help. Include this in your plan at the start. Always check your plan before you write – make sure it answers the question!

ENGLISH AROUND THE WORLD

Many people in India enjoy watching films in their leisure time. Films from around the world are shown, but India's own Bollywood films are very popular. The Bollywood film industry is the biggest one in the world. Bollywood films often use Hindi and Urdu languages, but recently, a lot of films have used English for songs and speech too.

> 10.5 Travelling the world

These activities will help you read and write about countries and places around the world.

1 Reading 📖

In pairs, read the four paragraphs about interesting and unusual places around the world. Match the four paragraphs to photos a, b, c and d.

Mario: 'My favourite place is Moscow in Russia. In winter it is extremely cold, but it is so exciting. There are lots of interesting buildings and, because it's a capital city, it gets very busy. I like visiting cities – there's always so much to see and do.'

Janek: 'The most interesting place I have ever visited was the rainforest in Peru. At first, I found it hard to get used to the high temperatures and heavy rain, but it was so beautiful. There were so many different types of plants and animals that I'd never seen before.'

Thea: 'The most beautiful place I have visited is Iceland. I lived there for six months and enjoyed the interesting landscapes very much. There were amazing views of waterfalls and lakes. I saw the wonderful 'Northern lights'. These are green and purple lights in the sky, which were fantastic and the people were very friendly.'

Francesca: 'Last year, I went to Botswana. It was fantastic. I spent most of my time travelling in the back of a vehicle watching the animals. I'd never been so close to lions. I am a keen photographer, and I took hundreds of pictures.'

2 Speaking 💬

Look again at the pictures and paragraphs from Activity 1. Work in pairs. Describe one of the pictures for your partner. Don't say the country name – your partner should guess! Then ask each other which of these places would you like to visit? Why?

I'd love to visit Iceland because I am interested in volcanoes.

3 Reading 📖

Read Li Hua's description of visiting Scotland. In it, she explains why she thinks people should visit this country. Answer the questions below.

Scotland – a place you must visit

I've visited a few countries including India, America and Brazil, but the prettiest and most interesting place I have visited is Scotland. I went there last year and I can't wait to go back.

Scotland is in the northern part of the UK. There are lots of different places in Scotland from busy cities to beautiful countryside. I started my visit in Edinburgh, the capital city. There's so much to see and do. As well as exploring the shops and trying different restaurants, I enjoyed visiting the castle and the zoo.

On the last part of my visit, we travelled to a much quieter area – the Highlands. There are lots of hills, mountains and lakes there. One day, I went on a boat and visited one of the many islands off the coast. It was a calm, sunny day and we saw some beautiful sea birds. The landscapes were amazing! I took lots of photographs and spent time walking around the island.

Next time you are thinking about travelling abroad, go to Scotland. It's an amazing country with lots to do and friendly people, who made my visit really special.

a   Which places does Li Hua compare Scotland to?
b   Why do you think Li Hua says, 'I can't wait to go back'?
c   What did Li Hua do in Edinburgh?
d   What photos do you think Li Hua took on the islands?
e   What else did Li Hua like about Scotland?

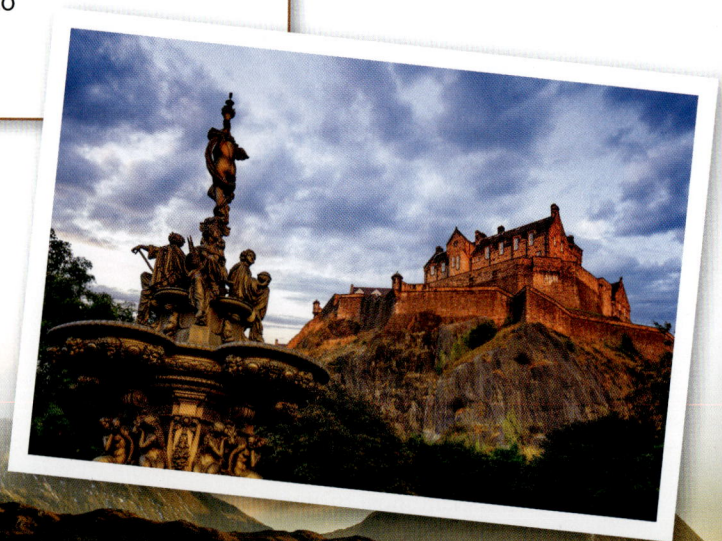

4 Speaking 💬

In groups, talk about the most interesting parts of your own country. How would you describe it to somebody who has never visited your country? Ask group members:

- What can you tell me about the different parts of your country?
- What interesting places are there to visit?
- What are the most popular foods in your country?

After your discussion, make a list of reasons why people would enjoy visiting your country.

5 Writing 📝

You are going to write an email to an English friend. Read the activity below.

Visiting your country

Will, a friend who lives in England, has emailed you. He might visit your country next year and has asked you for information. Write a reply to Will giving him information about your country. You should write 100-120 words and:

- describe two interesting places
- explain why he would like those places
- explain the types of food that are popular in your country
- explain why you think he should visit.

Start by looking at your notes from Activity 4, then plan what you would include for each item in the list. Write the last line. Here is one way you could end your letter:

If you want to know more information, just ask me. I'll be happy to help.

PROJECT

As a class you are going to produce a spoken book about different cultures around the world for the younger students in your school.

Each class member should select a different country or nationality. Find out unusual information about the country you select, such as interesting customs, foods or history. When you have found your information, write some notes and practise speaking about the country for 2 minutes.

When you have practised, each person in the class should record their talk. You can use a phone to record your talk. You could even add some music or sound effects. Have fun listening to them. Which country sounded the most interesting to you?

EXAM-STYLE QUESTION

Speaking practice

Use this activity to test your speaking skills.

Topic conversation: countries

Choose a country.

Ask your partner the following questions.

a   Tell me three facts about the weather and climate of your country?

b   What are your favourite places to visit in your country?

c   What kind of food is typical of your country?

d   Who would you take with you and why?

e   What is the benefit of visiting or learning about other countries?

[Total: 15]

CHECK YOUR PROGRESS

How confident do you feel about what you have learned and practised in this unit? How many of the things below could you do?

1   Name three different types of celebrations.

2   Give three examples of phrasal verbs.

3   Write three sentences containing relative pronouns.

4   Write a short paragraph about the benefits of learning a new language.

5   Write a short paragraph about your own country.

Rate yourself from 1 (not confident) to 5 (very confident).

Which things would you like to learn more about?
Which things would you like to practise again?

Share your thoughts with a partner.

› Grammar practice

Present simple passive

GRAMMAR FOCUS

We use the present simple passive to talk about actions happening now. We use it when we want to focus more on the action and not who does it.

We make the present simple passive with the present form of the verb **be** (**is / are**) + past participle. Look at these examples of affirmative sentences:

- Thanksgiving **is** celebrated every year in November in the USA.

- In Fiji, all communities **are** invited to Fiji Day celebrations.

We make the <u>negative</u> form with **isn't (is not) / aren't (are not)** + past participle.

- At a traditional American Thanksgiving dinner, the family usually eats turkey. Other types of meat **aren't** usually served.

We use a <u>question word</u> + **is/are** + past participle to make questions.

- <u>What</u> kind of meals **are** prepared for Fiji Day celebrations?

We use **is/are** + past participle to make yes / no questions.

- **Are** desserts served during Diwali celebrations?

In passive sentences, we sometimes use prepositions, <u>by</u>, <u>with</u> and <u>of</u>, to give more information.

- During festival time in Mexico, the streets **are** often decorated <u>with</u> flags <u>by</u> the people of the city.

- The coloured flags **are** made <u>of</u> paper.

---

1 Reading and Writing 📖 📝

Change the verbs in brackets into the present simple passive to complete the facts about Thanksgiving Day. Write the passive forms in your notebook. The first one has been done for you.

Each year, Thanksgiving Day ᵃ<u>is celebrated</u> (celebrate) on the fourth Thursday of November. At a traditional dinner, turkey ᵇ_____ (serve) and the rest of the dinner ᶜ_____ (prepare) with fruit and vegetables, such as potatoes, yams, pumpkins and cranberries. Traditionally, these ingredients ᵈ_____(produce) in North America. Then, usually dinner ᵉ_____ (follow) by a pie for dessert. Often, the pie ᶠ_____ (make) of ingredients such as pumpkin, apple or pecan nuts.

In many homes, the whole family ᵍ_____ (expect) to help prepare the special meal. Often, other family members ʰ_____(invite) to take part in the celebration and people often travel great distances to be with loved ones at this time.

Modal passives: Present tense

GRAMMAR FOCUS

We can also create passive sentences using modal verbs (for example, **can, might, must, should, need to**). We make present tense modal passives with the **modal verb** + <u>be</u> + past participle.

- Mum's birthday present **should** <u>be</u> delivered on Thursday.
- The birthday food **must** <u>be</u> prepared on time!
- Ollie's hair **needs to** <u>be</u> cut before the wedding.
- The wedding cake **can** <u>be</u> ordered tomorrow.

1 Reading and Writing 📖 📝

Maisie and Archie want to make a cake for the birthday party of their three-year-old brother, Ben. In your notebooks, complete their mum's instructions with the correct verb and form. The first one has been done for you.

> bake ~~make~~ write
> decorate serve cut

a The cake mustn't be <u>made</u> with nuts – Ben has a nut allergy.

b The cake should be _____ at an oven temperature of 180C.

c It can be _____ with some sweets and chocolates on the top.

d It should be _____ on a big plate.

e Please make a big cake! At Ben's party, the cake needs to be _____ into ten pieces.

f 'Happy Birthday Ben' must be _____ in big letters on the top!

Past simple passive

GRAMMAR FOCUS

We use the past simple passive to talk about past actions and events.

We make the past simple passive with the past form of the verb **be (was / wasn't / were / weren't)** + past participle. For example:

- The Thanksgiving festival **was** started in the USA in the 17th century.
- Last year, all our family and friends **were** invited to our Diwali celebrations.
- Unfortunately, the cards **weren't** delivered in time for Jenny's birthday.

For the past simple passive, we make questions in a similar way to the present simple passive:

- How **was** Diwali celebrated at your school last year?
- **Were** fireworks lit during the Diwali celebrations?

1 Reading 📖

Cara and Jaya are looking at photos of a friend's wedding. In your notebooks, complete their conversation with the correct verbs below in the past simple passive. The first one has been done for you.

design   ~~invite~~   not deliver   make   give   decorate

Cara: Look, here are some photos of Sabine's wedding. All her family and friends ^a <u>were invited</u>.

Jaya: Let's see. Sabine's dress looks beautiful, what ^b _____ it _____ of?

Cara: Silk, I think. It ^c_____ by her friend who works for a famous clothes brand. And this is the reception in the garden at her parent's house. The garden ^d_____ by some of her friends with all these lovely lights.

Jaya: It looks amazing! And what are these things on the tables?

Cara: Oh, they are gifts for the guests. All the guests ^e_____ a little photo frame as a present.

Jaya: What a nice idea. Was there a wedding cake?

Cara: Yes, eventually! It ^f_____ until later in the day because the cake company made a mistake with the date!

2 Speaking 💬

Find a photo of a celebration with some of your family and friends.
Describe it to a partner. Try to use some passive sentences.

Here's a photo of…

Let's see. All the food looks amazing!

Yes, most of it was made by my aunt. She…

> The English-speaking world

English is one of the most important languages in the world. It is spoken in over 100 countries as a first or second language. It is the first language in the United Kingdom, Australia, Canada, New Zealand, the United States of America and some Caribbean islands (Jamaica, St Lucia and the Bahamas). It is one of the main languages in many other countries and states across Africa, Asia, the Americas and Oceania. It is also the most popular second language for students to study!

1 Work in pairs. Answer the questions in your notebook.

  a How many people speak English as a *first* language?

   i over 300 million

   ii over 400 million

   iii over 500 million

  b These languages have the highest number of speakers in the world. English is third. Which languages are first and second?

   i Arabic

   ii Hindi-Urdu

   iii Chinese

   iv Spanish

   v Russian

  c There are different varieties of English all over the world. Where does Singlish come from?

   i Sierra Leone   **ii** Sri Lanka   **iii** Singapore

  d Here are four countries where English is one of the main languages. Which country has the largest number of people?

   i Kenya

   ii Jamaica

   iii Pakistan

   iv The Philippines

  e Which two subjects below are taught in English at some international universities?

   i history   **ii** science   **iii** mathematics

f   English dictionaries are always changing! How many new words are added each year?

   i   over 100

   ii   over 1000

   iii   over 10 000

g   In international football, who needs to speak good English?

   i   the referee

   ii   the players

   iii   the coach

h   Other languages often borrow words from the English language. In Spanish, what does 'footing' mean?

   i   football

   ii   dancing

   iii   jogging

i   Which country makes Bollywood films, often in the English language?

   i   India

   ii   USA

   iii   Botswana

j   English is one of the main languages in these important international organisations. Choose a word to complete their titles.

> Olympic   Space   Nations

   •   The United _____

   •   International _____ Committee

   •   International _____ Station

2   In the countries below, English is the native language or one of its main languages. Your teacher will show you a world map. Can you find the countries?

> Australia   Belize   Botswana   Canada   Fiji   Ghana   Guyana
> India   Ireland   Jamaica   Kenya   New Zealand   Nigeria   Pakistan
> The Philippines   Singapore   South Africa   Tanzania   Uganda
> United Kingdom   United States of America   Zambia   Zimbabwe

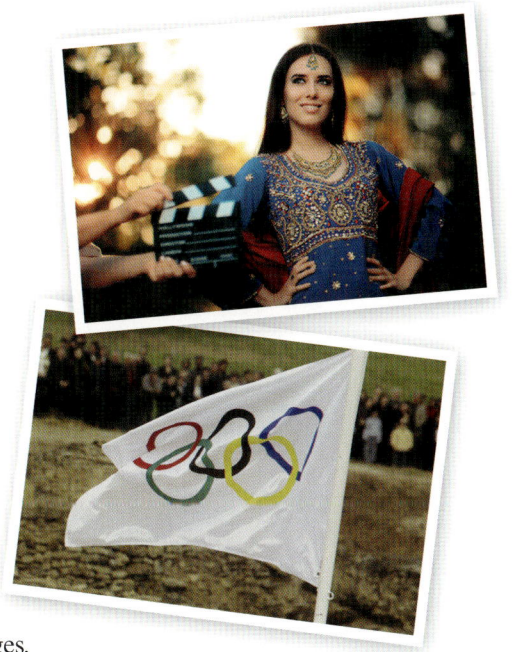

3 **a** Now can you match these ten capital cities to ten of the countries in Activity 2?

> Canberra   Ottawa   Suva   Georgetown   New Delhi
> Dublin   Wellington   Kampala   Lusaka   Harare

b Which cities can you see in the photos?

4 Work in pairs. Match the English-speaking countries with their flags.

> Australia   Belize   Canada   Guyana   Ireland   Jamaica
> Kenya   New Zealand   The Philippines   United Kingdom
> United States of America   Zimbabwe

5 Work in pairs. Are these sentences about the English language true or false?

a There are about 1.5 billion learners of English in the world.

b There are no English-speaking countries in South America.

c One of the oldest words in the English language is 'I'.

d There are 25 letters in the English alphabet.

e You can spell the sound, 'ee' in seven different ways.

f India has less English speakers than the United Kingdom.

6 Work in pairs. Think about your own language. Which words from English are often used? Share your ideas with another pair. How many words can you think of?

〉Glossary

obligation	something that you must do or have a duty to do	98
ordinal number	a number that shows the order of something, such as first, second, third	134
particle	a word that works with a verb in a phrasal verb, such as go *down*, light *up*, get *on*	233
past participle	the base form of the verb + -ed. It can be used to form a verb tense or an adjective.	126
past perfect simple	used to show events in the past	212
phrasal verbs	phrases with a verb and particle which has a different meaning from the meaning of its separate parts	233
possessive pronoun	words that show who the object belongs to, such as 'his', ''her', 'their'	7
preposition	words that show where things are	21
present perfect simple	used to describe present events that are connected to the past, e.g. I have always taken the bus to school	207
prepositional phrase	a group of words that begin with a word such as 'in', 'before' or 'at'	59
prepositional verb	a verb that is followed by a dependent preposition in a sentence	151
quantitative adjectives	adjectives that describe the amount of something	186
quantitative pronouns	pronouns that describe amounts of something	186
regular plural nouns	nouns that become plural when adding -s, -es, or -ies	84
regular verb	a verb that -ed is added to when writing in past tense	39
reflexive pronoun	these are used to draw attention to the person or people in the sentence	28
relative clause	adds information to the main clause of a sentence	236
relative pronoun	joining words which introduce a relative clause and connect information from one part of a sentence to another	236
reported command	a description of something someone has been told to do	158
reported speech	a description of something someone says	158
second conditional	talks about things that are not real or less likely to happen	163
subject pronoun	words such as 'he', 'she' and 'they' that talk about who or what is doing the action in a sentence	7
subordinating conjunction	a word that joins a main clause and a subordinate clause, such as 'although', 'because', 'if'	5
suffix	an addition to the end of a word, such as -er or -ion	106
superlative	a type of adjective that shows that the thing or person has more of something than any others that are similar (for example, 'funniest' or 'smallest')	13
synonym	a word that means nearly the same as another word	103
time adverb	a word that shows when something happens (for example, 'first', 'today', 'weekly', 'last year', 'since 2010')	145
tone	the way that someone speaks or writes that suggests mood and feelings	138
uncountable nouns	nouns that cannot be counted or divided	83
visual aids	pictures and other images to help with a presentation	148
zero conditional	talks about things that are true	161

> Syllabus vocabulary list

Common adjectives

afraid
amazing
attractive
bad
big
boring/dull
brilliant
broken
busy
calm
careful
clear
clever
close
cold
comfortable
correct
cosy
crowded
dangerous
dead
deep
different
difficult/hard
dirty
dry
early
easy
electric
empty
enormous
exact
excellent
exciting
extra
fantastic
fast
final
fine
free (free of charge)
free (available)
friendly
fun
general
glad

good
great
hard
heavy
high
horrible
hot
kind
light
lively
lonely
loud
lovely
low
lucky
mobile
modern
narrow
necessary
negative
new
noisy
normal
old
old fashioned
perfect
pleased
polite
popular
positive
possible
previous
quick
ready
real
recent
rich
safe
(the) same (as)
shy
silent
silly
similar
simple
slim
slow
small

soft
strange
strict
strong
stupid
sure
surprised
terrible
tidy
true
typical
unhappy
upset
useful
useless
warm
well-known
wet
wide
wonderful
worse, worst
wrong

Common adverbs and prepositions

Place

above
across
after
around
behind
below
beside / next to
between
down
everywhere
from
here
in
inside
nowhere
off
on
out
outside

over
over there
somewhere
there
to
under
up
upstairs
with

Possibility

definitely
maybe
possibly/perhaps
probably

Frequency

always
daily / every day
never
normally
often
rarely
too much
usually

Manner

badly
carefully
clearly
easily
especially
quickly
slowly
very
well

Emphasis

certainly
even
really
so

Degree

all
exactly
instead
just
not enough
only
quite
without

Numbers

Cardinal numbers
zero, one, two, three, four, five, up to a million

Ordinal numbers

first, second, third, fourth, etc.

Fractions

half, a third, a quarter

Other numerical vocabulary

a lot (of)
all / every one
almost
approximately
around
both
double
each
enough
everything
half
how much / how many
little
many
more
more or less
most
nearly
nothing
number
once, twice, three times, etc.
plenty
several
some
the only one
total
various

Common verbs

to achieve / manage to
to agree
to approach
to arrange
to arrive
to ask for
to be
to be able to
to be interested in
to believe

to belong
to bite
to book
to borrow
to break
to break up
to bring
to build
to carry
to catch
to change
to chat
to check
to climb
to collect
to come
to complete
to contact
to continue / carry on
to cover
to copy
to decide
to decrease
to delay
to describe
to discuss
to do/make
to dream
to drink
to drop
to dry
to eat
to encourage
to end
to enjoy
to enter / go in
to feel
to fill
to find
to finish
to fix/repair
to follow
to forget
to get ready
to give (a present)
to go
to greet
to guess
to happen / take place
to hate
to have
to have to

to help
to hold
to hurry
to increase
to invite
to jump
to keep
to kick
to lend
to let
to lie / tell lies
to like
to listen to / hear
to look after
to look for
to look like / seem
to lose
to love
to meet
to miss
to mix
to move
to need
to order
to paint
to pick up
to prefer
to pull
to push
to put
to receive
to remember/remind
to repeat
to return
to scream/shout
to see/watch
to share
to show
to shut
to sing
to sit
to smoke
to speak/talk
to spend time
to stand
to start/begin
to stay
to steal
to stop
to swim
to take

to teach
to tear
to tell/say
to thank
to think
to throw
to try
to turn on/off
to use
to visit
to want
to worry

A Everyday activities

Time expressions

afterwards/later/then
again
at last
before
date
day/week/month
during/while
finally
firstly
future
immediately
it's my/your turn
last
late
meanwhile
moment
monthly
next
past
season
since
sometimes
soon
still/yet
suddenly
the day before yesterday
the following (week)
till/until
today
week / last week / next week
weekend
when
year / annual / yearly
yesterday

Time

(It's) half past seven / (a) quarter to
    seven /
(a) quarter past seven.
(At) one/two o'clock.
afternoon
clock/watch
evening
half/quarter of an hour
hour
midday
midnight
minute
morning
second

Days of the week

Monday
Tuesday
Wednesday
Thursday
Friday
Saturday
Sunday

Months

January
February
March
April
May
June
July
August
September
October
November
December

Seasons

spring
summer
autumn
winter

Eating and drinking – Meals

breakfast
dessert
dinner
lunch
main course

meal
picnic
starter

Eating and drinking – Fruit and vegetables

apple
apricot
aubergine
banana
beans
cabbage
carrot
cauliflower
cherry
coconut
cucumber
fruit
garlic
grape
lemon
lettuce
mango
melon
mushroom
onion
orange
peach
pear
pepper
pineapple
plum
potato
raspberry
strawberry
tomato
vegetables
vegetarian/vegan food
watermelon

Eating and drinking – Other food

biscuit
bread
butter
cake
cereal
cheese
chilli
cream
curry
egg

flour
honey
jam
jelly
oil
omelette
pasta
pepper
rice
salad
salt
sandwich
soup
sugar
toast
yoghurt

Eating and drinking – Meat, fish and seafood

chicken
fish
lamb
meat
sausage
seafood
steak

Eating and drinking – Snacks

burger
chips
chocolate
crisps
ice cream
pizza
snack
sweets

Eating and drinking – Drinks

coffee
cola
drink
juice
lemonade
milk
mineral water
soft drink
sparkling water
still water
tea

Eating and drinking – Tableware

bowl
chopsticks
cup
fork
glass
knife
mug
pan
plate
pot
saucer
spoon

Eating and drinking – Verbs and expressions

to be full
to be hungry
to be thirsty
to drink / have a drink
to go on a diet
to have a barbecue
to have breakfast/lunch/dinner
to prepare food
to serve

Eating and drinking – Adjectives

cooked
fresh
raw
spicy
sweet

Body and health – Body parts

ankle
arm
back
beard
body
bone
chest
ear
eye
face
finger
(left/right) foot
head
heart

knee
leg
moustache
mouth
neck
nose
shoulder
skin
stomach
throat
toe
tooth
voice

Body parts – Verbs and expressions

to breathe
to have a bald head
to see
to smell
to touch
to wear glasses

Body and health – Health and illness

appointment
dentists
doctor
medicine
nurse
pharmacy
plaster

Health and illness – Verbs and expressions

to be (un)healthy / in good
    health
to be ill / have an illness
to be tired
to break (a leg / an arm)
to cut your finger / cut yourself /
    have a cut
to do exercise
to fall down
to feel better/worse
to feel ill/sick
to get better/worse
to go to the gym
to have a cold
to have a fever
to have a headache/stomachache/
    toothache

to have an allergy
to have the flu
to hurt
to lie down

Travel and transport

adventure
ambulance
baggage/suitcase
bicycle
boat
bus
bus stop
car
delay/delayed
direction
driver
ferry
flight
journey
map
motorcycle
passenger
plane
platform
railway
(return / one way) ticket
tourist
tourist information office
train
tram
trip
visit

Travel and transport – Verbs and expressions

to arrive
to be/get lost
to cross (the road/street)
to depart/leave
to drive
to fly
to get in / out of
to get on / get off
to go hiking
to go straight ahead
to go travelling
to park
to take the bus
to travel by bus/train
to turn
to walk

B Personal and social life

Greetings

Good morning / good afternoon /
    good evening!
Goodbye
Hello/Hi!
How are you? I'm (not) well.
How's it going?
I have to go.
Nice to meet you.
Pardon?
See you later/tomorrow.
Sorry / excuse me
Thank you, but I can't. Let's do it
    another day.
Thank you
Welcome!
Why don't we…? / Shall we…?

Exclamations/interjections

How annoying!
How interesting!
How nice!
What a shame! / What a pity!

Invitations

to accept an invitation
to invite
to turn down/refuse an invitation
Would you like to (go to the
    cinema)?

Family members and relationships

adult
aunt
baby
boy
child
childhood
cousin
daughter
elderly
family
father/dad
first name
friend
girl
granddaughter
grandfather/granddad/grandpa

grandmother/grandma/granny
grandson grandparent
guy
husband
man
marriage
married
mother/mum
neighbour
nephew
niece
older/younger brother
older/younger sister
parent
relative
single
son
surname
teenager
twin
uncle
wedding
wife
woman

Family members and relationships – Verbs and expressions

to be born
to be pregnant
to call / be called
to die
to grow
to grow up
to live
to marry
to spell (your name)

Physical appearance

beautiful
blonde
curly
dark
fair
fat
good-looking
handsome
long
old
poor
pretty
short

slim
straight
tall
thin
ugly
young

Character and mood

active
angry
bored
crazy
curious
excited
exhausted
famous
funny
greedy
happy
important
intelligent
interesting
lazy
nice
pleasant
polite
quiet
rude
sad
satisfied
sensible
serious
tired
unhappy
unpleasant
worried

Character and mood – Verbs and expressions

to be in a good/bad mood
to cry
to get annoyed/angry
to hug
to kiss
to laugh
to like/love
to smile

At home – Rooms and furniture

balcony
bathroom

ceiling
dining room
door
floor
furniture
garage
hall
study
stairs
wall
window

At home – Bathroom

bath
comb
hairbrush
mirror
shampoo
shower
soap
tap
toilet
toothbrush
towel

Bathroom – Verbs and expressions

to brush teeth
to brush/comb hair
to have a bath
to have a shower
to wash your face

At home – Living room

armchair
carpet
chair
chest of drawers
living room / lounge
picture
rug
shelf (s) / shelves (pl)
sofa
table

At home – Kitchen

bottle
box
kitchen
sink
tin

Kitchen – Verbs and expressions

to boil
to chop
to cook
to cut
to freeze
to fry
to get lunch/dinner ready
to grill/barbecue
to roast

At home – Bedroom

bed
bedroom
blanket
closet/wardrobe
cupboard
duvet
lamp
pillow
sheet

Bedroom – Verbs and expressions

to be sleepy/tired
to go to bed
to get up
to lie down
to rest
to sleep
to wake up

At home – Household tasks

to clean
to cook
to do the laundry
to do the washing
to do the washing up
to iron
to lay/clear the table
to sew
to take the rubbish out
to tidy up / clean the house

At home – Garden

flower
(back/front) garden
gate
path
plant

tree
wall

Garden – Verbs and expressions

to do some gardening
to grow vegetables
to plant

At home – Household appliances

air conditioning
barbecue
battery
charger
cooker
dishwasher
electricity
freezer
fridge
gas
heating
iron
microwave
oven
plug
radio
speaker
telephone
television/TV
washing machine
watch/alarm clock

Household appliances – Verbs and expressions

to break
to open/close
to phone/call/ring / to make a phone call
to push/pull

Colours

black
blue
brown
dark
gold
green
grey
light
orange
pink

purple
red
silver
white
yellow

Clothing and accessories

backpack
bag
belt
boots
button
cap
clothes
coat
dress
earring
fashion
glasses
(a pair of) gloves
hat
jacket
jeans
jewellery
jumper/sweater
kit
necklace
pocket
purse
raincoat
ring
sandals
scarf
shirt
(a pair of) shoes
shorts
skirt
(a pair of) socks
suit
sunglasses
swimming costume/trunks
tie
tights
trainers
trousers
T-shirt
umbrella
uniform
watch

Clothing and accessories – Verbs and expressions

It fits / doesn't fit.
It is casual.
It is smart.
It is too loose/tight.
The trousers are comfortable.
to get dressed/undressed
to put on
to take off
to try on
to wear
What size?

Leisure – Leisure activities

to go fishing
to go to a concert
to go to a music festival
to go to the theatre
to listen to (pop/classical/rock) music
to listen to music on headphones
to watch TV / a thriller / a romantic film / a comedy

Leisure – Hobbies

climbing
drawing
painting
singing
to play the drums
to play the flute
to play the guitar
to play the piano
to play the trumpet
to play the violin
to play the clarinet
to write a poem / short story

Leisure – Sport

ball
bat
bicycle
champion
equipment
fan/supporter
football pitch
game/match
goal
golf course
medal

prize
(badminton/tennis) racket
(hockey) stick
team
tennis court
trainer/coach

Sport – Verbs and expressions

to do athletics
to do gymnastics
to do yoga
to go cycling
to go jogging
to go running
to go sailing
to go skateboarding
to go skating
to go skiing
to go snowboarding
to go surfing
to go swimming
to play badminton
to play baseball
to play basketball
to play cricket
to play football
to play golf
to play hockey
to play rugby
to play table tennis
to play tennis
to play volleyball
to ride a bicycle/horse
to score a goal
to take photos
to win a competition/race
to win a medal

C The world around us

People and places - Continents

Africa
America, (North/South/Central) America
Antarctica
Asia
Australasia
Europe
The Arctic

People and places – Countries and nationalities

Student's own nationality + country of residence
Student's own language + any other language(s) studied

People and places – Cardinal points

north
south
east
west

Nature and environment

air
beach
branch
climate
coast
desert
dust
earth
environment
farming
forest
grass
hill
island
lake
landscape
moon
mountain
nature
pollution
recycle/recycling
region
river
sand
sea
sea shore
shade
shadow
sky
star
stick
stone
sun
top
underground
view

volcano
waterfall
wave
wood
world

Nature and environment – Climate and weather

climate change
cloud
cold
degree
fog
heat
humid
ice
lightning
night
rain
snow
storm
sunshine
thunder
weather
weather conditions
weather forecast
wind

Nature and environment – Animals

animal
bear
bird
cat
chicken
cow
dinosaur
dog
duck
elephant
fish
fly
horse
insect
lion
monkey
mouse
pet
rabbit
rat

sheep
snake
spider
tiger

Communication and technology – The digital world

advert/advertisement
app/application
blog (post)
blogger
(group) chat
computer
digital camera
document
DVD
file
folder
game
information
internet
keyboard
laptop
list
mail
memory (stick)
menu
(text) message
mobile phone
mouse
news
online
online safety
page
password
PC
photograph
printer
program
screen
selfie
social media
software
speaker
tablet
touch-screen
video
website
wi-fi

The digital world – Verbs and expressions

to make a call
to click
to copy
to download
to email
to fill in
to find
go online
to post online
to save
to send
to upload

Communication and technology – Documents and texts

article
bill
book
brochure
certificate
comic
form
guidebook
letter
magazine
newspaper
note
notebook
passport
postcard
ticket

The built environment – Buildings and services

apartment/flat
building
bus station
café
cathedral
castle
cinema
clinic
coffee shop
college
entrance
exit
factory
farm

garage
ground floor
gym
hospital
hotel
house/home
library
lift/elevator
museum
office
petrol station
police station
post office
restaurant
school
service station
sports centre
stadium
swimming pool
theatre
train station
university
zoo

The built environment – Urban areas

airport
bridge
bus stop
car park
corner
metro/underground
motorway
neighbourhood
pedestrian crossing
place
playground
roundabout
square
street/road
town/city
traffic
traffic lights
village

The built environment – Shops and shopping

bakery
bank
bill

bookshop
butcher
cash
change
changing room
cheap
closed
coin
credit card
customer
expensive
kiosk
market
on sale
open
price
receipt
sales
shop/store
supermarket
waiter/waitress

Shops and shopping – Verbs and expressions

How much does it cost?
to buy
to complain
to get a refund
to go shopping
to pay
to rent (a bike)
to sell
to spend money

Shops and shopping – Mass and units

centimetre
gram
kilogram
kilometre
litre
metre

Shops and shopping – Size

big
enormous
large
long
medium size
short

small
tall
tiny

Shops and shopping – Shapes

circle (n.), round (adj.)
square (n.), square (adj.)
triangle (n.), triangular (adj.)

Shops and shopping – Materials

cotton
glass
gold
leather
metal
paper
plastic
silver
stone
wood
wool

D The world of work

Education – Educational institutions

nursery
primary school
private school
secondary school
university

Education – Places and people

canteen
course
department
director
education
school year
schoolyard/playground
student
subject
teacher

Education – In the classroom

(black/white/interactive) board
bell
book
desk
dictionary
eraser
notebook
notice
(sheet of) paper
pen
pencil
pencil case
poster
ruler

Education – School subjects

art
biology
chemistry
computer science / IT
drama
geography
history
languages
maths
music
physical education / PE
physics
religious education / RE
science
sport

Education – Studies

break
class (group of students)
classmate
exam/test
example
exercise
homework
lesson
mark
project
question
result
school report
term
timetable

Studies – Verbs and expressions

to answer
to ask (questions)
to experiment
to explain
to fail
to know
to pass
to practise
to read
to revise
to study
to take notes
to understand
to write

Work – Professions and careers

actor
architect
artist
baker
boss
builder
businessman/businesswoman
chef
cleaner
cook
(bus/taxi) driver
engineer
farmer
firefighter
flight attendant
guide
hairdresser
lawyer
manager
mechanic
nurse
photographer
pilot
police officer
postman/woman
receptionist
salesperson
secretary
shop assistant
singer
soldier
teacher
vet
waiter/waitress

Work – Place of work

business
company
employee
employer
job
office
salary
work

Place of work – Verbs and expressions

to be unemployed
to earn
to find/search for a job
to get a job
to get promoted
to go on holiday
to retire

E The international world

Culture and celebrations

birthday
to celebrate
festival
fireworks
New Year
public holiday
special occasion
wedding anniversary

> Classroom language

Language to use with your classmates

- Can you check my work?
- Can I borrow a pen?
- What page are we on?
- Does my work make sense?
- Your work looks good!
- Can you show me how to do that?
- Have I spelled this correctly?
- Here's what I wrote.
- I think this is the right answer.
- I really enjoyed that. Did you?

Language to use with your teacher

- What time does the lesson start/end?
- Sorry I'm late.
- Can I do anything to help?
- Please can I have a … ?
- Can I have some paper, please?
- Do we work in pairs for this?
- Can I swap seats?
- How do you say … in English?
- I've finished my work.
- Here's my homework.
- Have you marked my work?
- Can I finish this for homework?
- What should I do now?
- Are there any more practice tasks I can do?
- I really enjoyed the lesson.
- Could I use the bathroom, please?
- I need to go to the nurse.
- My friend isn't feeling well.

Language to help you understand your work

- What does … mean?
- How do you spell …?
- I have a question.
- I do not understand this.
- Is this correct?
- Can you help me with this, please?
- Could you explain that again, please?
- Can you check that I've got this right, please?
- Will you show me how to do that, please?

› Acknowledgements

The authors and publishers acknowledge the following sources of copyright material and are grateful for the permissions granted. While every effort has been made, it has not always been possible to identify the sources of all the material used, or to trace all copyright holders. If any omissions are brought to our notice, we will be happy to include the appropriate acknowledgements on reprinting.

Thanks to the following for permission to reproduce images:

Cover kaisphoto/GI; *Inside* **Unit 1** Roc Canals/GI; Alexander Spatari/GI; Taiyou Nomachi/GI; Imgorthand/GI; Maskot/GI; Piyaset/GI; Jose Luis Pelaez Inc/GI; Linda Raymond/GI; Siri Stafford/GI; Jasmin Merdan/GI Chepko Danil Vitalevich/Shutterstock; Suzanne Tucker/Shutterstock; ProStockStudio/Shutterstock; pathdoc/Shutterstock (x2); Creatista/Shutterstock; Morsa Images/GI; Vishal Jain/GI; ProfessionalStudioImages/GI; Urbazon/GI; Mayur Kakade/GI; JGI/GI; SolStock/GI; OktalStudio/GI; By Ah_fotobox - Andreas*H/GI; Andrewmedina/GI; Image Source/GI; Richard Ross/GI; Morsa Images/GI; Dimitri Otis/GI; Morsa Images/GI; Peter Dazeley/GI; Alain Shroder/GI; Rosmarie Wirz/GI; PM Images/GI; Mascot/GI; Sutipond Somnam/GI; Catherine Falls Commercial/GI; Kathrin Ziegler/GI; David Papazian/GI; RapidEye/GI; **Unit 2** NadiaCruzova/GI; Jacobs Stock Photography/GI; Peter Cade/GI; Arundhati Sathe/GI; Monkeybusinessimages/GI; ozgurdonmaz/GI; Andreas Kindler/GI; MoMo Productions/GI; Photodisc/GI; PeopleImages/GI; Xavierarnau/GI; Andresr/GI; Tetra Images/GI; Justin Lewis/GI; Plume Creative/GI; PeopleImages/GI; Sami Sarkis/GI; VictorDigitalVision/GI; Chris Whitehead/GI; Dmytro Aksonov/GI; Prostock-Studio/GI; JGI/GI; South_agency/GI; NoSystem Images/GI; **Unit 3** Katrin Sauerwein/GI; Alexander Spatari/GI; Nortonrsx/GI; D3sign/GI; LauriPatterson/GI; GMVozd/GI; 10'000 Hours/GI; Mikolette/GI; Bankkgraphy/GI; Eskay Lim/GI; Inna Klim/GI; Lena Ivanova/GI; Monkeybusinessimages/GI; Kathleen Finlay/GI; Zoonar RF/GI; GoodLifeStudio/GI; Lyndon Stratford/GI; Juliannafunk/GI; Filadendron/GI; Grafoto/GI; © Manogna Reddy/GI; Electravk/GI; Oscar Wong/GI; Siriporn Kaenseeya/GI; VioletaStoimenova/GI; Peter Cade/GI; Delihayat/GI; SolStock/GI; SDI Productions/GI; Halfpoint Images/GI; David Sacks/GI; AlexanderFord/GI; Image Source/GI; PeopleImages/GI; SolStock/GI; **Unit 4** Dolgachov/GI; SDI Productions/GI; SolStock/GI; Skynesher/GI; Westend61/GI; FangXiaNuo/GI; Moodboard/GI; FatCamera/GI; Catherine Falls Commercial/GI; Image Source/GI; Andrea Chu/GI; Track5/GI; SDI Productions/GI; Klaus Vedfelt/GI; Xavierarnau/GI; SolStock/GI; Skynesher/GI (x2); Kali9/GI; SFI Productions/GI; UmbertoPantalone/GI; Monkeybusinessimages/GI; SDI Productions/GI; **Unit 5** Westend61/GI; Reza Estakhrian/GI; Westend61/GI; Hermione Granger/GI; Hinterhaus Productions/GI; Martin Barraud/GI; Ezra Bailey/GI; Jon Feingersh Photography Inc/GI; Onzeg/GI; Sturti/GI; JackF/GI; Ryan McVay/GI; Johan Mård/GI; Extreme-Photographer/GI; Betsie Van Der Meer/GI; Marc Romanelli/GI; andresr/GI; Mike Harrington/GI; Simon D. Warren/GI; AaronAmat/GI; Vitalii Petrushenko/GI; Monty Rakusen/GI; Martin Barraud/GI; Â© Rana Faure/GI; Luis Alvarez/GI; Extreme-Photographer/GI; Lane Oatey/GI; Simonkr/GI; Dean Mitchell/GI; Yagi Studio/GI; NASA/GI; Klaus Vedfelt/GI; Seksan Mongkhonkhamsao/GI; **Unit 6** Songphol Thesakit/GI; Andrew Holt/GI; Westend61/GI; HasanHaider/GI; Copyright By Siripong Kaewla-Iad/GI; Rrocio/GI; Wundervisuals/GI; Kyryl Gorlov/GI; Patrick Bennett/GI; Maremagnum/GI; Photo_Concepts/GI; Kyoshino/GI; MStudioImages/GI; Felix Cesare/GI; Miodrag Ignjatovic/GI; Sciepro/GI; Primeimages/GI; **Unit 7** Oleh_Slobodeniuk/GI; Abstractdesignlabs/GI; espiegle/GI; Jackyenjoyphotography/GI; Ajay Panigrahi/GI; Gary John Norman/GI; Daisuke Kishi/GI; Kypros/GI (x3); Blackred/GI; Gian Lorenzo Ferretti Photography/GI; Edward Armstrong/GI; Yahiya Tuleshov/GI; Westend61/GI; Omersukrugoksu/GI; Bet_Noire/GI; Virojt Changyencham/GI; Mikroman6/GI; Janiecbros/GI; Andrew Bret Wallis/GI; Michael Blann/GI; Dougal Waters/GI; Nuno Condeça/GI; Alexkich/GI; Enrique Díaz/GI; Mayur Kakade/GI; Phynart Studio/GI; Miodrag Ignjatovic/GI; Ayzenstayn/GI; Hugh Sitton/GI; TommL/GI; TanawatPontchour/GI; David C Tomlinson/GI; **Unit 8** Focqus, LLC/GI; Gallo Images/GI; Hagens World Photography/GI; Paul Burrows/GI; José Gieskes Fotografie/GI; Mint Images/GI; Buena Vista Images/GI; Jeff Dai/GI; Little Dinosaur/GI; Matt Anderson Photography/GI; Alys Tomlinson/GI; Paul McCready/GI; Emil Von Maltitz/GI; Da-Kuk/GI; @ Didier Marti/GI; Westend61/GI; Photos By R A Kearton/GI; Juan Maria Coy Vergara/GI; John Lamb/GI; Kelly Cheng/GI; Anouchka/GI; Monty Rakusen/GI; Peter Cade/GI; Monty Rakusen/GI; The Good Brigade/GI; LeoPatrizi/GI; Anne Gabrielle/GI; Andriy Onufriyenko/GI; Deniss Kantorovics/GI; Martin Ruegner/GI; **Unit 9** Mbbirdy/GI; BJI/GI; Tom Werner/GI; Image Source/GI; Rana Faure/GI; Klaus Vedfelt/GI; Allan